Child by Child

The Comer Process for Change in Education

Child by Child

The Comer Process
for Change in Education

Edited by
James P. Comer
Michael Ben-Avie
Norris M. Haynes
Edward T. Joyner

Foreword by Lois Jean White

**TEACHERS
COLLEGE
PRESS**

Teachers College, Columbia University
New York and London

Published by Teachers College Press, 1234 Amsterdam Avenue, New York, NY 10027

Library of Congress Cataloging-in-Publication Data
Child by child : the Comer process for change in education / edited by James P. Comer . . . [et al.] ; foreword by Lois Jean White
    p. cm.
   Includes bibliographical references and index.
   ISBN 0-8077-3869-7 (cloth : alk. paper). — ISBN 0-8077-3868-9 (pbk. : alk. paper)
    1. School improvement programs—United States. 2. Educational change—United States. 3. Child development—United States. 4. Community and school—United States. 5. Education—Parent participation—United States. 6. Student participation in administration—United States. 7. Comer, James P. I. Comer, James P.
LB2822.82.C45 1999
371.2'00973—dc21   99-21584
                                                                            CIP

Printed on acid-free paper
Manufactured in the United States of America
07 06 05 04 03 02 01 00   8 7 6 5 4 3 2 1

CONTENTS

No-fault does not mean no accountability. The adults involved in schools today can become truly accountable for fulfilling responsibilities to all our children. Senior educators discuss this urgent need at a round-table discussion at the Rockefeller Foundation in New York and in one-on-one follow-up conversations with Michael Ben-Avie of the Yale Child Study Center.

A sixteen-year-old student at Benjamin Banneker High School in Brooklyn, New York, discusses why school communities need in-depth knowledge about students' lives outside the classroom.

Comer schools in the most difficult area of Chicago have set a new standard for self-improvement, according to the education community's most respected independent researchers. In vivid stories from individual schools, the teachers, administrators, and parents of the Chicago Comer Team recount how they turned around their schools and their school communities.

The principal of a pre-K through sixth-grade Micro-Society school in Yonkers, New York, explains how the school functions as a real-life community, with students running a bank, legislature, courthouse, IRS, post office, newspaper, and more. The school community used the Comer Process to prepare its students for success by aligning its organization, governance, instruction, and accountability. More than 60% of the students come from homes in which languages other than English are spoken, but their standardized test scores for reading in English have increased.

Students at Helene Grant Elementary School in New Haven, Connecticut, achieve scores on statewide tests that tower over those of other schools, not only in their impoverished neighborhood but in most middle-class neighborhoods as well. Their principal attributes the children's success to their parents' involvement in every aspect of school life, and details how other principals can create the same relationships in their schools.

Children's healthy development is the starting point, focus, and goal of all SDP endeavors not only in the classroom but also throughout the school and the wider school community. Here SDP's director of operations describes how to keep child development central to administrative matters, relationships, budgeting, staff development, and curriculum planning.

Guilford County, North Carolina, is one of the most successful school systems in the nation and uses the guiding principle of collaboration as the focal point of all school business. The members of the Comer Action Team detail the collaborative experiences that have reinvigorated their school communities and led to remarkable increases in school performance.

FOREWORD

This comprehensive and compelling book documents exactly what it takes to initiate meaningful and lasting reform in America's public schools. *Child by Child: The Comer Process for Change in Education* is a single volume that administrators, educators, parents, and community leaders can turn to as a valued resource for improving schools.

First-person accounts and case studies graphically illustrate what academic research has suggested: that schools are dynamic organisms dependent on the participation of the entire community for vitality and success. The voices of teachers and students alike resonate throughout its pages. Their stories speak to each of us because our children's future is also our destiny.

For more than a century, the National PTA has worked to build coalitions of support for our nation's children at home, at school, and in the community. At the same time, we've offered training for parents to enable them to serve as full partners with educators to offer the best possible learning environment for their children.

This is extremely important because parents are the link between the home and the school. In many instances, parents feel they have nothing to offer or they feel intimidated by having to go into school buildings. To develop rapport with parents in my Parent Involvement workshop, I often tell the following personal story:

I must have been between the third and fifth grades when this incident occurred. I know because a second grader would never have had enough courage in those days and a sixth grader would have had more sense than to engage in such folly. I was always a talker in class, a very good student, but a talker nevertheless. This particular morning, after many warnings, my teacher announced in a clear and crisp voice, "Lois Jean, go to Mr. Tipton's office."

There was dead silence in the classroom because Mr. Tipton was "the formidable, well-dressed, and feared-by-all" principal. He walked the halls and, at the slightest hint of disturbance or disorder, produced a metal-tipped wooden paddle from his well-cut sleeve and administered the appropriate discipline to the deserving offender.

I remember walking down the hall toward Mr. Tipton's office when the sight of the main entrance of the school seemed more appealing than the entrance to the principal's office. Walking out that door when no ringing bell had signaled the time to exit was exhilarating, but the exhilaration was short lived.

After I arrived home, my grandmother listened to my story and hurriedly sent me on my way back to school. She assisted my travels with a phone call to Mr. Tipton, explaining my exit and return to school. Needless to say, Mr. Tipton was waiting for me at the main entrance of the school. He proceeded to walk me to his office and explained that he would punish me only because I had left school and gone home. He magically produced the paddle and administered several quick hits to the palms of my hands. I remember that experience to this day and, although it was a negative one, that was the experience that compelled me to become involved in my own children's education.

Many parents have had bad experiences in school, which cause them to fear even the idea of going into the school building. The National PTA has successfully addressed this and other barriers that prevent parents and families from becoming involved in their children's education. Recently, we've developed national standards for school and community leaders on how to create, implement, and evaluate successful parent involvement programs. Our goal is to promote collaboration that cuts across cultural, economic, and social barriers. Clearly, the standards support the work that is being done in the schools and classrooms described in this volume.

In each of the accounts you will read here, parents and professionals have been asked to rethink their approach to student learning. Some have reacted with outright resistance, others with cautious enthusiasm and eventual acceptance. Without exception, child or adult, the authors speak of the value of building strong relationships with one another, with students, with parents, and with the community at large.

While cohesion of community is essential to any reform effort, of equal importance is the individual relationship between teacher and student, parent and child. This book emphasizes the need to recognize children's social and physical capabilities alongside their cognitive development. A classroom of children is a congregation of individuals.

It is the responsibility of the teacher to acknowledge and respect the unique characteristics of each child, as well as to educate the entire class. It is the responsibility of the parent to assist the teacher actively in that effort, to communicate consistently, clearly, and frequently with the teacher and school administrators, so the best possible environment for learning is created and sustained.

Teachers and administrators also need access to training and resources to help them improve their own skills. Examples here abound, from in-service experiences to retreats and continuing education. An environment that fosters continuous learning keeps faculty filled with fresh ideas and inspired to try new things in the classroom.

Life-long learning by itself is not enough however. Collaboration and teamwork also contribute to school success. Outstanding examples of effective coalition-building are highlighted in the chapters devoted to that topic. Mistakes made and lessons learned will serve as blueprints for other schools striving to make needed changes. Consideration is also given to innovative curriculum practices as well as to achievement standards and assessment. Keys to evaluating a child's conceptual and analytical understanding are discussed in detail. The importance of designing curriculum that will reflect state and national standards is emphasized.

Much space is given to the need for developing strong community ties among schools, businesses, and social service providers. The National PTA has long understood that only when these groups work together can significant changes be made. Our organization has served as a natural forum for discussion of all factors that affect our children. It is hardly coincidental, then, that many of the chapters here cite PTA leaders as serving as the catalyst for reform.

Finally, *Child by Child: The Comer Process for Change in Education* serves as a discourse on the value of determination and persistence. It champions hope over despair and success over adversity. It is an important book because it addresses one of our most basic needs: preparing our children for lifelong success.

Lois Jean White, President
The National PTA

ACKNOWLEDGMENTS

We extend our sincere thanks to the district facilitators, superintendents, principals, school staff, parents, and students within the SDP network. Every national SDP staff member, regardless of position or unit, contributed to the development of this book and deserves our appreciation.

We are grateful for the interest expressed by First Lady Hillary Rodham Clinton in the School Development Program.

We would like to acknowledge the kind and generous support of various philanthropic organizations that have supported our work over the years, including the Carnegie Corporation of New York, Charles E. Culpeper Foundation, DeWitt Wallace-Reader's Digest Fund, Exxon Foundation, Ford Foundation, W.T. Grant Foundation, John D. and Catherine T. MacArthur Foundation, Melville Corporation, New American Schools Development Corporation, The Rockefeller Foundation, The Skillman Foundation, and the Spencer Foundation. We are particularly thankful to The Rockefeller Foundation. Without their support we could not have achieved as much as we have in recent years. Specifically, we appreciate the confidence in our work expressed by Marla Ucelli.

We are also grateful for the inspiration that we have received from our colleagues at the Yale Child Study Center. In particular, the SDP has been privileged to benefit from the leadership and guidance of Dr. Albert Solnit and Dr. Donald Cohen.

We extend special thanks to Carole Saltz and Carol Chambers Collins of Teachers College Press, Columbia University. Thanks to the insightful editorial guidance of Carol Collins, this book is more readable and more helpful to parents and teachers.

Faye Zucker has been inspiring us with her enthusiasm since 1995, when she asked us to write *Child by Child* and *Rallying the Whole Village*. Now she wants a book on math and science literacy and we hope you will be seeing that one next year.

We are grateful that Dreama Plybon Love, Education Program Manager, The National PTA, agreed to be a "critical friend" during the writing of the book. Thank you.

The engaging photographs that appear in the book are by Michael Jacobson-Hardy and Laura Brooks.

We would like to acknowledge the artistry of Russell Shaddox, graphic designer, who produced the schoolhouse diagram found in this book and the Six Developmental Pathways poster.

A special thanks to Thedra McCrae, Pupil Personnel Services, Benjamin Banneker Academy for Community Development, for her help in organizing the Banneker student writing group.

We appreciate the diligence and wit of our proof editing team of research associate Beverly Crowther and consultant Linda Brouard.

Trudy Raschkind Steinfeld, our consulting editor, has become a cherished member of the Yale School Development Program's (SDP) "village." Through her insightful queries and ability to make a text sing, Trudy has enriched every page. All the authors have benefited from her clarity of voice and thought, her empathy with the reader, appreciation of a story well told, and her ear for words.

The Editors

PROLOGUE

Child by Child

The Comer Process for Change in Education

James P. Comer, M.D.

Dr. James P. Comer meets with students at the first Comer Kids' Academy at Yale.
Photograph © 1999 by Michael Jacobson-Hardy.

When children are developing well, they learn well.

Children are born growing and learning. If they are able to interact well with helpful adults they will learn, first about themselves and their environment, and eventually, demanding, high-level academic material in school. The responsibility of every society is to provide children with adults and with institutions that can help them develop and learn at that high level. With such help they will have a reasonable chance to meet their adult tasks—family membership, perhaps child rearing, work, and citizenship. And when this is the case for most people in a society, that society has a reasonable chance to survive and thrive for a sustained period of time.

In the past most people could meet adult tasks without a high level of education. In our modern, fast-changing society, however, most people must receive a high level of education. From early childhood, people require experiences that foster physical, social, psychological, ethical, linguistic, and cognitive growth and development before school and in school.

To me, what I have just said is a truism too obvious to need elaboration, a "no brainer" in contemporary parlance. Nonetheless, many in the modern school reform movement are concerned about issues of power (matters of choice, charters, vouchers, privatization); test scores; and what parents, teachers, administrators, politicians want—not what children need to grow, develop, and meet their adult tasks and responsibilities. I understand the angst and "do something . . . anything . . . quick" climate, given the importance of education. But unless reform is child centered, children and the society alike are going to be hurt—are being hurt.

To Reform Schools, We Must Understand the Complex Dynamics That Affect Them

Improving public education is tough work. Although our School Development Program team is convinced about the nature of the problem and what needs to be done, there is no national consensus. This makes it difficult to build the infrastructure and large pool of professionals needed to improve and sustain the quality of schooling.

Most people assess and understand issues from the dominant cultural perspective that learning is primarily a function of intelligence and will, rather than development. We can't measure the impact of development or life conditions directly. Our research tools are too crude to help a great deal. Thus, we use the test performance of individuals—knowledge acquisition and sometimes utilization—because it appears that we can quantify it. We know that such findings are limited predictors of ability, but we need something to help make placements and policy decisions.

Outcomes are usually reported without an understanding of the dynamics that produced them. Much education research is like measuring the impact of waving a hand-held fan on a feather and comparing it to a control, when both feathers are in a powerful wind tunnel. Taken together, the following constitute the powerful social wind tunnel that has an impact on education: parents, families, teachers, communities, income, attitudes, beliefs, and institutional policies on human growth and functioning. Understanding these dynamics can guide intervention, whereas outcome findings often lead to labeling and blame of all involved—students, parents, schools, groups.

In the absence of knowledge about these dynamics, and particularly about how schools really work, policymakers respond to power blocks and their own beliefs and interests. And well-meaning people too far removed from schools often think and operate from huge misconceptions, making them vulnerable to the best policy and program "sellers." Discussions of theory and research often provide bits and pieces of information that can be confusing, misused, or simply useless. If only the people in the education trenches could speak for themselves!

To Reform Schools, We Must Start Where the Children Are

In *Child by Child: The Comer Process for Change in Education* the people in the trenches get to tell their story. Students, parents, teachers, principals, superintendents, school board members, business partners, and others give you nuggets of their lives and work in school that capture not only the moment but also the changed context they have helped to create. You will hear real people express doubt, certainty, distrust, curiosity, fear, pride, anger, joy, danger, safety, disappointment, hope, loneliness, friendship, confusion, learning, failure, and success—a gamut of emotions and experiences. Most importantly, you will hear people in very difficult situations *doing* it, making schools work when almost nothing else around them is working. You will see and hear the power of caring, individual efforts and the power of group and leadership efforts. The authors will tell you how they overcame many different kinds of obstacles and got good outcomes.

To Reform Schools, We Must Keep Pace with Our Changing Society

The stories in this book are mostly from low-income, predominantly minority schools. But some are from districts that include middle- and upper-income students from families that are well educated and well employed. The issues are the same for all—child development, learning, and the abil-

ity or inability of adults at home, in school, and in the community to promote children's learning and development at the needed level. The differences and obstacles are largely matters of degree and frequency.

An assistant principal in a highly acclaimed high school serving high-
income families told me, with a mixture of sadness and relief, that he was
looking forward to his year-end retirement. He felt that the emotional problems of the students had increased steadily over the years, and that these
problems were not receiving adequate attention in school. Nonetheless, the
students he served were from environments in which there was a definable
path to life success. Models and guides were available in and outside their
family networks. Although many students were not faring well in adolescence, most had had early childhood experiences that would give them a
good chance to be successful at meeting life tasks once they got through the
difficult period. And, while the school challenge was overwhelming for
many, the school provided some support staff. When young people have
adequate social skills, attitudes, and family network connections, professional help outside the school is more available, the legal system is less punitive, and future employers are more forgiving of the past.

Even well-developed, well-functioning young people make mistakes
simply because they have limited experience and poor judgment. Poor kids,
more often from minority groups, can't afford to be underdeveloped or
make mistakes; but this is more likely to be the case. The path many poor
kids must tread through adolescence to successful adulthood is far, far more
dangerous. And their parents, through no fault of their own, are often not
able to instruct and protect them. The school and institutions beyond the
school must help. But the school staff and community organizations promoting youth development, also through no fault of their own, are not prepared to help.

Even when they try, it is difficult. Let me illustrate by reviewing the admirable effort made by John Lauritzen, the AT&T executive, and his
African-American third grade lunch buddy—in a school and district making a very impressive effort to help children who too often are written off
(see Chapter 22). Mr. Lauritzen was shocked when his lunch buddy told
him that he wanted to be a drug dealer when he grew up. (Kids work with
what they know about and can identify with to achieve understanding and
direction. The only people with money and cars in the youngster's neighborhood were drug dealers.) Perceptive and deeply concerned, Lauritzen
took his lunch buddy to work and exposed him to a range of colleagues,
Black and White. Several months later a grateful note from the youngster's
mother indicated that the youngster now wanted to be an AT&T manager
when he grew up.

It is a heart-warming story and it shows the kind of work that must be done. But the challenge facing that young lunch buddy is much greater than when I was growing up in a working class family sixty years ago. At any point I could have thrown in the education towel and earned a living in the steel mills that puffed smoke all around me. Most of my African-American friends had fathers who were working in those mills. I attended the same schools as the students whose parents my mother had worked for as a domestic. The church culture—reinforcing the beliefs, attitudes, and values of the mainstream culture—was at the core of my family network. And "a better tomorrow for the children" was the creed of my parents, and of many other parents who were migrants from the South.

Motivation, models, and support were within my reach, and still it wasn't easy. While my parents provided me with the necessary development, my three best neighborhood friends of similar ability succumbed to alcoholism, crime, and mental illness. My family network and church culture gave me the necessary sense of belonging and the belief in my right to be here and to be somebody, to achieve. They picked me up, soothed my wounds, and sent me back into the fight when the silent but intimidating buildings at the predominantly White university told me I didn't belong, and when a White professor's approving attitude about my "A" paper turned to "F" when he discovered the paper was mine.

To Reform Schools, We Must Focus on Relationships and Child Development

These conditions do not exist for too many young people like Mr. Lauritzen's lunch buddy. The only institution that can help him, and many young people like him, move from wishing for to actually having a successful career is the public school. And most schools cannot help children achieve life success unless the staff grow—grow in the way you can almost feel the growth of parents, teachers, teacher aides, and administrators described in this book. Staffs can't grow unless they receive the instruction, time, and support to understand the need to change and how to manage the risk involved in thinking and working differently. And too many policy makers and practitioners do not understand the need to create a supportive social context because they took their own social context for granted and because the culture says that success is a simple matter of intelligence and will.

I acknowledge that some youngsters like the young lunch buddy will succeed in school and in life without changes in our system of education. These are our heroes and legends. But a modern society can't survive and thrive on a glorious few while losing the able many.

Why, then, doesn't everybody just *do* it—observe, listen, read, and *do* it? Unfortunately and fortunately, human beings and human systems don't work like machines or like computers. *Children's*—and also teachers', administrators', parents', outside lay and professional helpers', curriculum's, instruction's, assessment's, technology utilization's, in short everyone's and everything's—*development* depends on *relationships*. I have often said that relationships are to development what location is to real estate: We need relationship, relationship, relationship. The best instructional methods, curricula, and equipment are not going to produce good outcomes in bad relationship environments, which are found most often where students, parents, and staff are all underdeveloped or unable to express their abilities and potential.

The education enterprise did not evolve from a child development base. Training, preparation, and practice in education focus instead on curriculum, instruction, assessment, and now on technology enhancement. The interest in behavior that began about a generation ago is largely abstract and college based; it is not applied, and it is not adequately relevant to the classroom. And education practitioners, like all of us, think and act from the dominant cultural belief that success is due to intelligence and will; as a result they carry a deficit, rather than a developmental orientation.

To Reform Schools, We Must Develop Group Goals, Trust, and Accountability to Standards

Nonetheless, we should not be discouraged. Some schools *are* doing it: growing and helping children develop and learn against the odds. And as truly concerned people like John Lauritzen get a close-up view of the talent we are wasting and what is possible, the push will grow for schools that provide young people from non-mainstream backgrounds with the developmental and learning experiences they need. Because our economy can't afford to carry people who can carry themselves and help others, we will eventually create a system of schooling in which all adults involved help young people develop and learn at an adequate level. How this can take place is shown in this book.

Professional development activities described in this book, including the Developmental Pathways Study Group (Chapter 16) and the balanced curriculum process (Chapter 18) in which the staff make promises to each other, reflect exemplary professional development, growth, and practice. (Many educators in communities that work, largely because parents are well educated and well employed, take such activities for granted.) But posting your teaching units on the door of the teachers' lounge to observe your own and your colleagues' omissions and duplications requires trust and mutual respect. This kind of careful assessment and self-imposed accountability to each other and to students is far more important where students are more dependent on schools for academic learning. Students like the lunch buddy absolutely need it. But in difficult communities with difficult schools, trust, accountability, and mutual respect don't exist, and can't be mandated. These conditions must be created. Without them, school staff can't just observe good practice and replicate it.

There are many narratives in this book about how our School Development Program helps school people move to a child development and learning orientation; how the structures and processes serve as organizing, planning, assessment, and community-building mechanisms. Nothing more needs to be said here. But our critics claim that a child development focus without a standards-based curriculum with research-based evidence of test score gains is of limited value; that we pay too little attention to raising test scores. Not true. In schools where the School Development Program mechanisms and processes are adequately applied, our approach has helped to produce such good to unbelievable gains that one system retested the students. They did slightly better the second time than the first!

Our research shows that our efforts increase the capacity of the local staff to work from an appropriate conceptual framework, in a collaborative way so they can carry out diagnostic, preventive, and growth promoting interventions as good professionals should. They are not slaves to a "canned" curriculum. But we are not opposed to prescribed curriculum approaches when the staff and school have the capacity to adjust them to the needs of their students: We are working in schools in which our model complements a variety of curriculum approaches.

Incidentally, some observers have lumped our program among the "canned" approaches. The descriptions in this book show otherwise. Ours is a set of mechanisms and processes based on a child development conceptual framework that simultaneously provides structure, flexibility, and creativity. It is exciting to visit schools using the same principles in different ways as their own needs and creativity dictate.

And if you find a school using our process that is not paying attention to curriculum, instruction, and assessment, it means that it is not fully and faithfully replicating our approach. Nothing helps the self-esteem of a child more than learning to read or to meet other academic challenges. But in schools serving underdeveloped children, the adults must know how to create the conditions to make high-level academic learning possible for all. And even that is not enough.

You will read the interesting discussion of the Micro-Society school (see Chapter 4). We had a similar program during our early years that we are now renewing; then it was called The Social Skills Curriculum for Inner-City Children. It grew out of our realization that children from main-

stream, better-educated, better-employed parents are motivated and learn
things relevant to school expectations simply by growing up in their families. Our curriculum simulated real world activities—government, business, health care, leisure time, and so on.

Much of what we ask non-mainstream children to do is as intimidating to them as those silent university buildings were to me in the 1950s. In
the 1980s a mother brought her petrified son to me on the first day of enrollment at Yale. Exposure to friendly faces in foreign places—and all foreign programs and activities—makes everything less daunting. That
student is now a successful professional. I call it "connecting to the mainstream." When schools simulate the real world and develop curriculum activities in the real world they reduce the possibility that students will later
feel this threatened. Yet even this is not enough.

Most people are fair, but at some point somebody is going to tell or
imply to minority kids that they are not competent no matter how well
they perform. But because being a student is a state of becoming, many are
vulnerable to the opinion of naysayers. And the further one aims across
the socioeconomic spectrum, the more vulnerable one is. Again, the ex-
ceptional few won't be bothered. But most, particularly where family support is lacking, will need community support—organizations, people,
supplementary education programs—that help them understand and manage the antagonism.

To Reform Schools, We Must Make Financial Commitments and Policy Changes

Finally, if we really want to make it possible for large numbers of underdeveloped young people to succeed, we will need some financial and programmatic policy changes. But a consensus is needed among the key policy
makers about how children learn, what the people who help them need to
know and to be able to do, and what the organization and management of
the system they work in needs to be like. Significant discussion and discovery are needed before this can occur. Also, schools of education must be
organized and operated to prepare pre-service teachers and administrators
to do the kind of collaborative diagnostic and problem-solving work you
will read about here. There will be less resistance and fear when they are
prepared or expect to work in this way.

Our School Development Program team has worked to help people
change in a way somewhat analogous to the way the county agricultural
agent worked to help farmers be more productive at the turn of the twen-
tieth century. The Agricultural Extension Service helped to make America
the breadbasket of the world. Today's economy needs to have educated

workers, but our schools can't change even when they want to. Rather than turning to radical new and unproven formats of schooling, we should create an Education Extension Service that helps all involved in the education enterprise to put child development front and center, and move toward a system of education that will keep the nation in the economic and democratic forefront in the twenty-first century.

Even the most difficult question of all—fair funding—can be considered reasonably from this perspective. The question will no longer be about equal or even compensatory funding. It will be about the cost of a program that promotes functional rather than dysfunctional community, family, and school performance, and in turn, good child development and good performance as adults. Of course, the cost to society will be far less than the cost of poor adult performance. The stories in this book demonstrate that attending to the developmental and the academic at the same time is not only possible but mutually beneficial. They demonstrate that the community can become a valuable extension, resource, and supporter of schools.

PART I

Improving Children's Lives

Michael Ben-Avie

We begin in Part I with the voices of adults across the country who are working daily to improve the lifepaths of children: community members, business leaders, school board members, superintendents, principals, teachers, students, and parents.

Their work is grounded in the principles of the Comer Process, the school-wide intervention formulated by Dr. James P. Comer, associate dean of the Yale University School of Medicine. In 1968, Dr. Albert Solnit, then director of the Yale University School of Medicine's Child Study Center, recruited Comer to lead a new initiative bridging child psychiatry and education. The School Development Program (SDP) is the organization charged with implementing the Comer Process in school communities. The history of the School Development Program (SDP) has been detailed in *Rallying the Whole Village* (Comer et al., 1996). In this book, we turn from the theoretical foundation to accounts of individuals who are immersed in the work. Nevertheless, a brief overview of the Comer Process will be helpful, as it is referred to repeatedly by chapter authors.

The Comer Process: A Team Approach and a Developmental Focus

The SDP brings together people who have experience in working with youth at different stages of their development and in different environments. Parents, school staff, community members, the school psychologist, guidance counselor, school nurse, special education teacher, attendance officer, and pupil personnel workers all join together and use a common language for talking about children. Participating school communities organize themselves into three teams that are the hallmark of the Comer Process: the School Planning and Management Team, the Parent Team, and the Student and Staff Support Team. The three teams make critical decisions about how to most effectively promote student learning and development, and operate according to three basic principles: consensus, collaboration and no-fault. Every year, the School Planning and Management Team (SPMT)

1

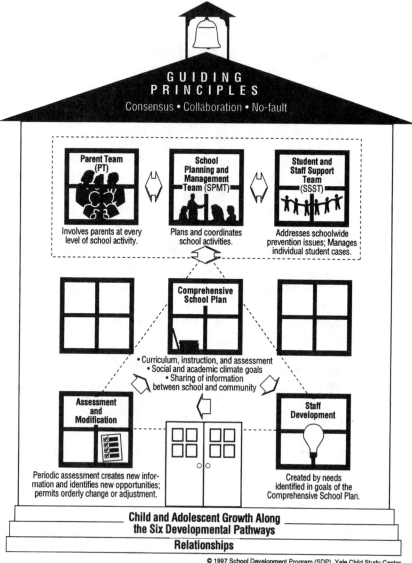

Figure I.1: Model of the Comer Process.

develops a Comprehensive School Plan, which serves as a common road map that gives direction to the year's activities at the school, and includes measurable goals and objectives. The document identifies instructional priorities; increasingly, provides the school with a balanced curriculum for student achievement and development; sets milestones for assessing the accomplishments of the school and the students; indicates specific goals for improving the social and academic climate of the school; and outlines a plan for the sharing of information between school and community.

Of all the prominent educational reformers, only James Comer talks about healthy child development as the keystone to academic achievement and life success. Comer uses a metaphor of six developmental pathways to characterize the lines along which children mature—physical, cognitive, psychological, language, social, and ethical.

The SDP school community uses the six developmental pathways as a framework for making decisions that will benefit children. In schools using the Comer Process, far more is expected from the students than just cognitive development.

Assessing Change: Do Test Scores Tell the Story?

The purpose of this book is to draw attention to the broader aspects of promoting children's learning and development, and to portray the daily reality of those who implement the Comer Process. However, student performance on standardized tests is a common yardstick for measuring the success of a change initiative; a significant shift in the test scores of a group on the scale of a school does indicate that real change has occurred. Therefore, it is important to note that the structural changes detailed in these chapters have been accompanied by some important changes in student achievement levels.

The following samplings of data are all from school districts and schools that you will read about in this book:

In November 1998, Northwestern University issued a press release announcing the results of the well-respected researcher Thomas D. Cook's four-year evaluation of ten elementary schools in Chicago's inner city that implemented the Comer Process under the direction of Youth Guidance. Schools were randomly assigned as Comer or control schools. Cook's report notes that "Comer schools are now improving at faster rates in both math and reading than control schools, particularly in the last two years. The Comer schools started behind the control schools in both math and reading, but caught up to them four years later."

Not only did students' academic achievement and school climate improve, but also the students said that "they experienced less anger and were more in control of negative emotions. Their reports of mischievous and delinquent behaviors showed steadily declining trends relative to the controls on a measure that other researchers have shown is related to criminal conduct in adulthood." According to Cook, professor of sociology at Northwestern University's Institute for Policy Research and primary author of the report, "The Comer experiment is one of only a few school reform projects that targets both academic performance and behavior modification. *It is rare to see both effects come about at the same time*" [italics added] (*Comer school reform project improves both academics and behavior*, 1998).

The district ranking of the Bowling Park Elementary School in Norfolk, Virginia—based on the fourth graders' performance on the Iowa Test of Basic Skills (ITBS)—went from 25th (out of 35 elementary schools) to number one, in just one year. On the ITBS, the national percentile rank of the average composite score for fourth graders went from 43 to 90 between 1995 and 1996. Bowling Park was the first CoZi School, a collaboration between Comer's School Development Program and Zigler's School of the 21st Century (see Chapter 6).

Students in Guilford County, North Carolina, have improved steadily in the core subjects of reading, writing, and math in the four years since three smaller school districts were merged into a single county system in 1994. Early in the merger process, Superintendent Jerry Weast and Deputy Superintendent Lillie Jones introduced the SDP at the district level as well as in over forty schools. In Chapter 22, the Comer Action Team cites particular examples of progress in their schools. In 1996, Guilford County students scored two points above the nation, five points above the state, and seven points above the average for southern states on the National Assessment of Educational Progress (NAEP). On the Iowa Test of Basic Skills, the Guilford County schools had higher performance scores than the state as a whole. The dropout rate in Guilford County has fallen to the lowest level among large districts in the state.

For schools and districts that successfully implemented the balanced curriculum process (see Chapter 18), positive results followed. In New York City, gains in reading were made by three elementary schools (P.S. 27, P.S. 43, and the Eugenio María de Hostos Micro-Society School), all under a state "watch" in 1994 to improve the performance of students scoring below state-defined minimum standards. Over a three-year period, the improvement rates ranged from +7% to +45%. In Guilford County, North Carolina, the balanced curriculum process was implemented at Hampton Elementary, Welborn Middle, and Western Guilford High Schools. At Hampton Elementary, the "class cohort" (the same students over time) improved 24% over a three-year period on the state reading test, which measures percentage of students scoring above 2.5 on a 4.0 scale. At Welborn

Middle, improvements for class cohorts ranged from an increase of +7% to +15%. At Western Guilford High School, there was an improvement for different class cohorts of +16% and +7% of students scoring at the higher levels on the state tests in English I and English II respectively. In Brooklyn's Community School District 13, seven schools that did *not* implement the balanced curriculum process saw a decrease of -6% from 1996 to 1997 of students scoring above grade level. In contrast, seven comparable schools that did implement the process saw an increase of +7% (Squires, 1998).

The SDP's Essentials of Literacy Process uses an eclectic approach to promote literacy among students who have slipped through the cracks and have been tagged as problem readers. In 1996–1997, at its pilot site in New Haven, Connecticut, of the eighteen third grade students who were reading at a first grade level at the beginning of the school year, all of them improved at least one grade level; over 50% were reading at or above the third grade level by the end of the school year. As a result of the success of the program at its pilot site, in 1998 New Haven Public Schools expanded the SDP's Essentials of Literacy Process to ten of its elementary schools. Over the next three years, the district plans to implement the process at the third grade level in all of its elementary schools.

But these data are only a small part of the story. Although they are an important indicator of the magnitude of the changes brought about by SDP school districts and school communities, they cannot convey the commitment of the many individuals who work to bring about the changes, or help others to understand how to translate the principles of the Comer Process into action that proceeds from day to day, week to week, year to year. For that part of the story, we needed to write this book.

In this book, we relate powerful experiences of change that we have encountered in school communities. Instead of presenting statistics and theory, the authors introduce you to the day in/day out processes through which change occurs. They show that the SDP provides the foundation for change, the overarching structure and process. The SDP creates a culture of collaboration that increases the *capacity* of school districts and schools. Thus, superintendents, central office staff, school boards, principals, school staff, parents, and schools of education not only react to change, but anticipate and manage change. On a wider scale, our authors also describe how the SDP has had an impact on national and local policy; on child and adolescent development; on student performance; on school organization and community development; on preservice preparation of educators; on training and professional development; and on theory development.

We invite you into the rich experience of the SDP's culture of collaboration in which positive ongoing change is not only imaginable but inevitable.

References

Comer, J.P., Haynes, N.M., Joyner, E., and Ben-Avie, M. (1996). *Rallying the whole village: The Comer process for reforming education.* New York: Teachers College Press.

Comer school reform project improves both academics and behavior. (1998). Evanston: Northwestern News on the World Wide Web (http://www.nwu.edu/univ-relations/media/).

Squires, D. (1998). *A balanced curriculum process: Results so far.* New Haven: Yale Child Study Center.

CHAPTER 1

No-Fault and Accountability

*Michael Ben-Avie, Adelaide Sanford, Lester Young, Jr.,
Shelia Evans-Tranumn, Cassandra Grant, Edna Vega,
Edward T. Joyner, and Trudy Raschkind Steinfeld*

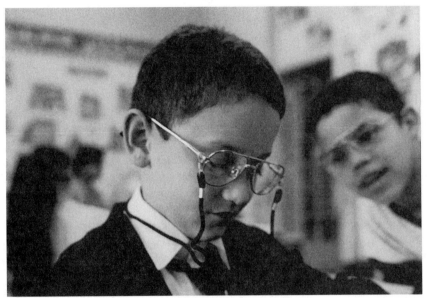

Photograph © 1999 by Michael Jacobson-Hardy.

*In education, as in society as a whole, there are many who blame others rather than
recognize how they themselves contribute to poor outcomes. A roundtable discussion
about the need for awareness began at the Rockefeller Foundation on April 9, 1996, and
continued thereafter at the Yale School Development Program. Questions on the agenda:
How can school people and public policy makers become truly accountable for fulfilling
their responsibilities to all our children? And how can we help them to be better able and
more willing to accept that accountability?*

These Are the Issues in Your Building: Defining Accountability
by Edna Vega

I grew up in the Bronx school district where I am presently working. My mother still lives down the block from my district office. When I was a child, I went to two of the schools in this district, P.S. 43 and I.S. 139. I thought these two schools were the very best in the world. Imagine how I felt on becoming superintendent to discover that these schools were in redesign because they were designated as failing (Schools Under Registration Review).

District Seven is part of the congressional district with the highest level of poverty in the United States. It also has the highest poverty index rating in the New York City school system. Forty-two percent of the families are dependent on public assistance, 56% of the adults 20 years old and over have not completed high school, and 61% do not speak English at home. For the majority of our families, the hospital emergency room is the source of primary care. There is a paucity of recreational programs, which leaves many children with little to do after school and sometimes results in a period of time where children lack adult supervision. There are only two libraries, open only part-time, and no bookstores within the district. Police in the 40th Precinct monitor at least seven gangs with significant membership. Daily, our students are exposed to drug abuse, violence, crime, unemployment, teenage pregnancy, homelessness, illness, and domestic abuse. We have the highest incidence of asthma in the City of New York. Students are still struggling with trying to read because they can't read when they don't have glasses or when they have asthma and they can't come to school. And out of 1,200 teachers in our district last year, 300 were uncertified. The Board of Regents always says that the majority of the uncertified teachers are in the Bronx, in the lowest performing schools. We had to provide a program of professional development to help the uncertified teachers.

However, in addition to the large housing projects, there are many unique brownstones and prefabricated one- and two-family houses under construction throughout the community. Under the long-term planning of the Federal Empowerment Zone, a revitalization of the area will take place. Throughout the community, there are numerous senior citizens centers that offer a variety of services for families. Hunts Point Multi Service Center provides direct medical care to the students in six of the district's schools. The community continues to maintain a large number of houses of worship and parks where families can gather to celebrate their beliefs and traditions.

The school system holds people accountable, but it does not tell them what they are accountable for. In reality, you can hold people accountable only if you've spent time with them and told them, "These are the expectations, this is what you need to do." For example, in our system, data are very important. Principals, administrators, teachers, generally do not know what to do with the data that they get because no one has ever worked with them on the interpretation of the data. So we're holding them accountable for student achievement, but no one has sat down with them to say, "Look, these are your children, and these are the quartiles in which your children fall, these are the types of strategies that you need to use in order to move children, these are the types of things that you need to know in order to be able to move them." I've said it very clearly: I think everyone works very hard, but they don't work wisely because they don't know what to do.

When I became superintendent, I met with each and every principal for a reflective conversation. I showed them a graphic picture of their students' achievement data. I said, "This is where your school is right now. These are the issues in your building." I've even had them use markers to color-code lists of teachers so that we could clearly see who needs help: Green is for the teacher that's ready to go and teach well, yellow is for the teacher that you have to reflect and work with, and red is for the teacher that's in danger, probably a new teacher or someone that has been teaching for a long time without adequate supervision. I'm helping them look at how to identify the teachers and how to look at the data in their building. I am helping them to put in place a "test sophistication program" in their schools. Test sophistication is a process of analyzing data, identifying in what areas, specifically, the students are having problems, and determining strategies to address those areas.

A no-fault mindset is important when supporting principals and teachers. I tell them, "Let's look at this situation we find ourselves in and figure out how can we move this building." It's not about blaming anybody else. It's typical for teachers to blame the parents. I've had people go as far as saying, "Well, what did you expect from my scores? Look at the kinds of kids I'm getting from the elementary school." But so what? Our job is to educate any child that walks in through those doors. Parents send us the best they have at home. We can't start off with blaming the parents because of the home situation or blaming the previous teacher or the previous elementary school that didn't do what needed to be done.

I can't tell a principal, "You have to improve your reading scores. I'm going to hold you accountable for them." No, I need to be very specific. For example, we have eight low-performing schools in the district. I'll meet with a school and show the principal, say, that only 30% of the students are reading at the state minimum standards. This means that there is a 70%

difference between their current achievement in reading and the goal to have 100% of students meeting the state minimum standard. This year we'll agree to decrease the deficit by 15%, a realistic and manageable goal. The school, therefore, would have to go up to 45%. I'll then say, "There has to be an increase in reading and math by this amount by the end of the school year, this is how you go about doing it, this is how you identify your students—and I'm going to give you money for an extended-day program to support those children in the bottom quartile." I'm also going to say, "If you do not have textbooks, let's make sure new, up-to-date textbooks are ordered. You need classroom libraries. How can we support and fund classroom libraries?" The point is: You hold them accountable, but you give them all the support you can in order to meet that particular goal.

After supporting people, then it is possible to hold them accountable. I ask principals, "How are you as a principal organizing your building? If I see that you've hired all new teachers and you put them all in third grade, I, as your immediate supervisor, have to have a conversation with you because this is not in the best interests of those children." So the issue of accountability is needed—but only after first providing support with a no-fault mindset. Also, accountability has been traditionally used as a form of punishment in the school system and not as a form of reward. However, if you hold people accountable and they achieve, then their accomplishments can be celebrated.

Providing Developmental Experiences for School-Dependent Children *by Regent Adelaide Sanford*

We expect results. Yet the school system has no consequences except for the children. I say to policy makers: How can you have successful teachers, principals, school board members, regents—and only the children are unsuccessful?

Children in underserved, poor neighborhoods are "school dependent." That's an Adelaide Sanford term. It means that in most instances the town library is not open or, if it's open, nobody's there reading fairy stories that relate to the child's life. It means that there's no museum. It means that there's no Y with programs of swimming and all of that. It means that the child is dependent upon the school for everything that is educationally centered. It means that if you want this child to have piano lessons or violin lessons, the school is going to have to be there because there's no music school in the community. There's no 92nd Street Y there. There's no Brooklyn Museum. There's no Pratt that has a free Saturday program for artists.

The school is the only place where that child can get the social structures that he or she needs to succeed.

When I started my work as a school supervisor, I had to work with teachers who felt that if a child had never gone to the circus, had never seen a cow, had never been to the zoo, then the child had no "concepts" and therefore the teachers couldn't teach him or her. That's what they thought. "He has no concepts. He comes without them." I said, "You make the concepts. You've got the blocks. You've got the doll corner. You've got the paper. If you feel the child needs to see a circus, let's create a circus. If you feel that he needs to know what a farm is, let's create it in this room because there is no other place for him or her at this time."

That's what I mean by school dependent: The school has to do that until society decides to support all people in all neighborhoods. After all, the Y is not self-funded. It receives money from foundations. Foundations could put a Boys' Welcome Hall there. There's no reason why there couldn't be a museum there. We need to bring everything into schools that children need to be able to compete, and cooperate with each other. In my school, we developed a group that used to go out and sing. We'd go all over to make money so that the children could move from the circus in the kindergarten classroom to the Big Apple Circus, so the children could go from not ever having been to a museum that related to their lives to exploring a museum where there would be things that told the story of the struggle of their people. We raised money to do this because we knew that the school had to give the children enough confidence, based on meaningful and relevant experiences, for them to be able to compete and cooperate in the world. We raised money for them to have carfare to go where they could take swimming lessons. We even had to raise money for the school to be open after 3:00 p.m.

Some children are "experience deprived." That's not the same thing as being "culturally deprived." Experience deprived means not having had the experiences on which the textbooks, curriculum, and tests are based. Therefore, the school must accept the responsibility for providing these kinds of experiences. Schools must also accept their responsibility for providing teachers who have the attitude that if they give the children these experiences, the children will be able to master them.

Go into early childhood classrooms in communities that are economically deprived. You won't see any clay. Forget about finger painting. Forget about all of those manipulatives that children need. The word for this kind of room is "devoid." And yet the teachers will tell you that the children can't read! As if the children could be stimulated merely by words. Words! Then go into a school where children are doing well. You'll find just the opposite—every possible kind of material; every kind of costume; every kind of paper—cut outs, colors, shapes, textures; living things—gerbils, plants—all providing enriching experiences. That's a developmental approach, knowing to put things in this room for children to see, touch, taste, smell, and manipulate. They don't worry about whether the children's clothes get dirty—they're going to have finger painting, they're going to work with clay. They're going to build something, and it can stay here because they're coming back tomorrow to finish it. They don't have to take it all down because they're only there for half a day and the other class is coming in. And there's enough of everything. They don't have to share the scissors. I remember when one little boy was told to share the scissors so he tried to take the screw out so he could give another child half of the scissors. What are you going to do? These children are absolutely experience deprived. They are material deprived. They are resources deprived.

It's not a question of family or culture. It's a question of educators accepting the responsibility to develop a program that meets the needs of these children. Most schools of education don't ask teachers to approach this classroom and say, "Here's a child, and I am to take this child as he comes to me and make this child whole." Compare that with doctors. They try to do something. They don't say, "Well, you smoked. Too bad, go home and die." But that's what we say to the children. They come into kindergarten and first grade, and we put them in special education. We're determined that they're not going to make it because their mother didn't do this or their father didn't do that. No one is saying to the teacher, "You must say, 'Either I can teach or I can't.'" I said to the parents in my school, "Look: If your child fails, I fail. Because if your kid fails there's no reason for me to be here and accept this check. Even though the world may say it's not enough money, I'm here and I'm being paid. I'm supposed to make a difference. If I can't make a difference, then I shouldn't be here." There's no point in my coming here every day and saying, "Well, I can't teach this child to read because he doesn't have a book at home or because his mother doesn't come to school or because his father isn't there." That's outrageous, but we accept that in education.

You can't mandate a caring, nurturing teacher. But think: If you take a child out on his roller blades, you don't take him to a lot full of pits and rocks and broken glass. You take him to a smooth surface to learn. You don't take him to a dangerous area and say, "Now you've got to learn here on your own." Yet that's what we're doing to our children. Responsibility begins with adults—and the system, policies, and structures they develop. One of our ultimate goals is to create and develop a sense of personal and group responsibility for children. Children must see responsibility modeled by the adults and society around them.

Identifying Educational Malpractice: No-Fault Does NOT Equal No-Accountability

Trudy Raschkind Steinfeld: I am very struck by what you say about failure and consequences of failure. When my son was having trouble with eighth grade math and we were trying to find out how to help him, his teacher tried to be reassuring by saying, "Well, twenty percent of kids don't do well in Sequential Math I. They're not mature enough. Next year they'll take it over in high school, and they'll do much better."

Edward T. Joyner: That's educational malpractice. Where would she get that information?

Trudy Raschkind Steinfeld: Every year twenty percent of her children don't work well. And, of course, because their failure feels toxic to her, she can't take a rational look at it. She's not alone. Every day, teachers walk into class and they are scared of their students' failure to learn. They are fighting against their fear, and they are pushing it away and trying not to see it. That wastes so much of their energy. It wastes so much of their creativity.

It seems to me that when the Comer Process comes into a school, it teaches people how to repair their relationships not only with each other but also within themselves. Then they can have the courage to receive and the clarity to ask for the help they need to teach better. I think the Comer Process actually helps save teachers who might otherwise be asked to leave.

Edward T. Joyner: It is a question of will. The Comer Process saves people who want to be helped and who become engaged in the process of self-improvement once they are given nonjudgmental feedback about their performance. I think that what Regent Sanford was talking about was the whole notion that failure is limited to children.

If every teacher permitted himself or herself a twenty percent failure rate—just use that as an example: In a school of a thousand students, you're talking about two hundred kids. If you have two schools like that, you're talking about four hundred kids and so forth. The whole mentality is that some students will learn and some won't and that there's nothing that can be done about it.

I would like to distinguish for the record the difference between a problem-solving orientation based on the principle of no-fault and the change strategy of encouragement and consequences ("pressure and support"). Our program uses no-fault problem solving because you can't solve a problem and blame somebody at the same time. But it does not mean that after consistent educational malpractice, you don't hold people accountable and make appropriate placement—

whether it is placing a person on probation or actually placing them out of the system.

One of the most powerful ethical principles in medicine is *first do no harm*. As policy makers, administrators, teachers, custodians, we have a collective responsibility to guard against putting children in harm's way. In fact, that ought to be an iron-clad rule: There are dire consequences for anybody working with children who places them in harm's way either wittingly or unwittingly. And certainly educational negligence and malpractice harm our children.

Rising to a Standard of Excellence
by Shelia Evans-Tranumn

Part of my responsibility is the oversight of New York City Public Schools. The New York City Public School system has more than one million children located in more than twelve hundred buildings. I also am the Department's senior manager responsible to the Commissioner and the New York State Board of Regents for recommending and implementing policies on school improvement. When I left the New York City Board of Education after twenty years of service and started working for the State Education Department, I had to begin to look at the whole issue of failing schools, raising standards, and school improvement efforts within the context of the goals established by the New York State Board of Regents' philosophy, "It Takes a Whole Village to Raise a Child." I then had to take a realistic look at the fact that the state had identified schools in 1989 as low-performing schools—Schools Under Registration Review—and in 1993 the majority of those schools still had not made significant progress despite good intentions and a comprehensive view of the responsibility of the village in creating positive student outcomes.

I operate out of a cultural milieu that says, "We must strive for excellence." As an African American, excellence in family and community relations as well as excellence in job preparation and performance were mandatory for success. But I discovered that in discussing the broad concept of urban education, there was little or no discussion of academic and cultural excellence for children who needed it the most. There was a discussion, however, of how we could help these students struggle up the ladder of remediation to reach minimum standards.

The following sample test passage gives an indication of the minimum standard for reading comprehension that we expect children to reach by the spring of their third grade year:

Bears are big. They need a lot of food. Bears eat meat. They eat bugs. They eat berries. They eat honey. They eat fish, too. Bears feed in the spring. They feed in the summer. They feed in the fall. Bears look for food then. They fish.

We identify schools in the State of New York as low performing or as Schools Under Registration Review because as few as nineteen percent of the third grade students in some schools can read and comprehend a passage of this nature on a state examination. As educators and policy makers we have to ask ourselves a critical question, "Is this the standard that we accept for our own children by the end of the third grade?" I am sure that my colleagues will agree, we do not accept less than excellence and mastery for our own children; therefore, our moral commitment to public service should demand that we not accept less for anyone else's child. What we have found is that in one out of ten public schools, fewer than 53% of third graders scored above the state reference point, and in New York City, in one out of ten public schools, fewer than one-third of third graders could read this passage. There is something drastically wrong with this picture, something drastically wrong.

The challenge for me was clear. How could we get people within school buildings and school systems to understand that change must happen? I mean, we had tried to motivate change. We had tried to encourage change. Now, we had to legislate change. We had to regulate change. The perceptions of some people about the abilities of some children are so low that they are willing to accept this poor showing as the minimum standard for which to strive. And yet, at the very same time in our state, we have schools that set the standard for excellence and they produce Westinghouse and National Merit Scholars. But by and large, the majority of the children, particularly in large urban sectors and particularly children of color, are expected to reach only minimum standards.

Fortunately, what we found was that this process, the School Development Program, could be used, in fact, to "rally the whole village" to think about change in a different way. Under Regent Sanford's leadership, the Board of Regents formed the Regents Advisory Committee on Low-Performing Schools. The Committee visited schools in different locations throughout the state. And what did we find? We found teachers and principals who would get to school at six o'clock in the morning and leave at seven o'clock at night. They were working very hard. They had convinced the parents that they were working very hard. Parents would say, "My principal is there. He's caring, he's understanding. The teachers love our children. They care and they understand them. They are always busy, busy, busy." But we found that they were working hard doing the wrong things.

And so a lot of time was spent chasing their tails—working hard, photocopying one page after another, writing work on the board for students to copy, lecturing, and sending letters home. To make sure that the school was a safe environment, children were in their seats, they were quiet with their hands folded, and they were copying from the board (never mind that they didn't understand what they were copying from the board). When you walked into a classroom, children would happily open up their notebooks and say, "Look at what a wonderful student I am: Look at how much work I have copied into my notebook."

And then we would begin to question them. For example, in a junior high school biology classroom in New York City, I spoke to a student who was busy copying vocabulary words into her notebook. "I see you have a beaker as your vocabulary word. Have you ever seen a beaker?" "No," was the reply. "What about a microscope?" The student responded, "Oh, yeah, we saw that one day when the teacher took it out of the closet and brought it to lab class." There was a façade of education taking place—that the teaching and learning process was actually going on within the building. It was just teacher-dominated work, and the worker-bees did not understand that the tasks they so diligently performed were out of sync with the reality of what they needed. The children were left there as empty vessels, not receiving the knowledge that was supposed to be theirs by Constitutional right.

We also found teachers who were willing and very able, and there was also excellent teaching and learning going on. In fact, children in a Long Island school said, "If you want to see someone who knows how to teach, we'll take you, we'll show you." We also found teachers who were willing but unable. They had been trained in antiquated teacher education institutions. When teacher training programs were developed approximately fifty years ago, programs focused on developing strong academic programs that would enable those who attended to be able to function effectively in society. Preparing teachers to teach children to function in a global society, where information access is universal and immediate, is a challenge that teacher training institutions have not mastered. Just as the world has changed, schools have changed and students have changed, so teacher-training institutions must also change. It would be extremely helpful to the national, state, and local reform movements if teacher-training institutions could help prospective teachers to work with the entire village to bring all children to levels of mastery rather than to minimum competency.

Teachers do not come into the school system with the knowledge and skills that they need in order to effectively educate an increasingly culturally and academically diverse student body. Because of diminishing re-

NO-FAULT AND ACCOUNTABILITY

sources allocated for in-service staff development, these teachers are not receiving the on-the-job training that they so desperately need. In Australia, four percent of the budget for a school must go into staff development. Here in America, we have poor preservice training and limited in-house staff development. Then we expect willing but unable teachers and principals to function at an excellent level. The superintendent's role, the principal's role, and the teacher's role should have a built-in staff development process.

Once we train teachers, principals, and superintendents, then part of the work must include bringing parents in as real partners. Many of the initiatives that are being implemented nationally simply talk peripherally about parent involvement. New York State felt that parent involvement was so important that the Board of Regents regulated it. We didn't leave it up to schools to say, "We'll make the decision whether or not we want to have parents at the table." Commissioner's Regulation 100.11 says that parents must be at the table because we understand that some of those unwilling, unable people that are leading schools are not going to be confident enough to invite parents to sit down with them. We have opened the dialogue to give parents the language of power (which is the language that is spoken around the table). Now, we must monitor the process to ensure that it happens.

When I looked at all this and looked at what we must do with almost one hundred schools in the State of New York that were not meeting minimum standards, I knew that the State Education Department had to engage the support of partners within the learning village. We had to be clear about what we were going to do to change negative results. For the first time the department is developing plans to deregister schools that fail to meet higher academic standards. The state reference point that establishes "Bears Are Big" as an indicator of the level of performance that is minimally expected must be raised. We are also seeking to establish, once the standards have been raised, performance goals at 90% for children and schools. Finally, we know that as we raise the standards, the number of schools that will need the kind of support and guidance that a program like the School Development Program can offer will increase. It is a tremendous job to rally the whole village. It is more than a notion. It is more than a paper plan. It is more than a meeting or a staff development session. You can plan, meet, and then go back into a school and find that absolutely nothing has changed. What we are really talking about and advocating for, on a national, state, and local level, is a systemic reform process that is research based and child oriented. The Comer Process is an effective instrument for reaching that goal.

No-Fault Is a Special Way of Engaging in a Relationship

Michael Ben-Avie: School communities that implement the Comer Process reach common agreements among home, school, and community about how to reach educational goals. Parents and teachers share accountability for the students' success. Parents become strong partners in education when they have a clear understanding of standards and assessments as well as the role they may have in educational change.

Cassandra Grant: What I think is so effective about the Comer Process is that it provides parents and schools with the needed tools to successfully identify problems and negotiate solutions for the betterment of all children.

No-fault is a special way of working through a problem by engaging people in a collaborative process that emphasizes openness and honesty. When fault is no longer looked for or assigned, people are able to disagree with each other without becoming disrespectful or angry. When there is no-fault, people are able to accept and even become curious about the differences they perceive in each other. No-fault is the structure that supports people even from different cultures and with different levels of understanding while they open up to each other and listen and really hear each other. No-fault is also a process. When you use it to work through a problem, you know that at some point you'll be able to draw a conclusion, or establish a time frame for the discussion to continue, or provide additional information for an issue to be examined. When this happens, you know that throughout the process all participants will feel they are being treated fairly. Finally, no-fault is a new way of establishing accountability. The bottom line that each participant envisioned at the outset changes. Instead of one person being held accountable for the problem, no-fault allows all people to become accountable for the solution. Once you are able to establish no-fault, blaming no longer takes over as the main agenda. The team is then able to focus on the real role of collaboration and consensus in moving the school's agenda forward. In our experiences with school restructuring, we have found that school communities have a difficult time applying these principles.

Low-performing schools often approach the problem of school improvement using nonproductive methods rather than incorporating the principles of consensus, collaboration, and no-fault. Two very common mistakes are blaming and adopting new programs. Schools will often see these methods as the only prescription for change. Almost everyone wants to figure out who's to blame rather than working with the principle of no-fault. Trying to figure out who's to blame just diverts precious time and money. The real challenge for schools has to be in listening to each other, examining the data, respecting differences, and working together as a team on goals which can be mutually agreed on.

New programs in reading and math are often eagerly embraced in a school's attempt to expeditiously bring itself up to standards. This generally occurs while ignoring other critical areas that require attention. What is needed is to comprehensively address the multitude of contributing factors that will help to assess the overall condition of the school.

Initially, when a school has been identified by the New York State Education Department as failing, the situation becomes very tense. The list of Schools Under Registration Review (SURR) is made public. Parents know that the state has declared their children's school as so low-performing that it might be closed. Teachers know that they are working but not succeeding. The New York State Education Department first establishes a team to assess the status of the school. The team generally consists of a state liaison such as myself, a superintendent of a school district outside of New York City, a teacher, an administrator, a New York City Board of Education member, and a parent. The school is visited by the team to evaluate its status. Conducting a sober, open-eyed review of all aspects of the school provides the district, school, and community with a first-step approach towards school improvement. Recommendations are offered for addressing problems in the areas of instruction, curriculum and development, staffing, school discipline, school resources, and the physical plant. The school district is encouraged to take an active and supportive role in assisting the school to improve. We also emphasize the need for parent and community involvement. We can't look at schools or families in isolation. It is important that schools see themselves as extensions of the family and of the community in which they exist. Schools play a major role in communities in trouble. Where you see children placed at risk, you see communities at risk.

The real challenge for schools has to be in how school boards, administrators, teachers, parents, and community members collaborate in identifying the problems and solutions as a team. The Comer Process provides a formalized structure that promotes a cooperative environment to address these issues. Consensus, collaboration, and no-fault serve as a foundation for all stakeholders. These principles allow everyone the opportunity to become fully engaged in a process that is *revealing and non-confrontational*—one that respects the differences and opinions of all participants. In the case of these schools, this process is a group examination of the facts.

We tell school communities up-front that there is a cut-off point. Schools have only three years to demonstrate improved educational results for *all* students. We don't want to cut schools off. We don't want to revoke their registration. We don't want to leave neighborhoods without successful educational institutions. We know that ultimately that would affect communities and families. However, we cannot tolerate schools that consistently fail to educate children. Schools are the foundation of our society. As a society, we have to hold ourselves accountable if we allow our schools and communities to fail.

Seeing All the Children, All the Time

Lester Young: We talk about "equity of outcome" in Community School District Thirteen. There are some youngsters who are doing well, and there are some schools that are working. The critical question in my mind is that the measure should be how well are all the children doing—not how well are some of the children doing. The consequence has to be levied based on how well all the children are doing.

My experience tells me that the reason why schools do not succeed is because they don't know how. When it comes to engaging schools in a process that gives them some autonomy to make decisions, you have to be very careful. Autonomy to make decisions in behalf of children is a right that has to be earned. I say to schools, "Until you demonstrate that you can make good decisions in behalf of children, you shouldn't be allowed that opportunity." It is critical that policy makers and the leadership levy consequences for school systems that allow large portions of the population to fail year after year.

I am in complete agreement with the issue of consequences, but I think the heart of it has to be centered around the issue of equity of outcome—we have to have a system that looks at all the kids, not just some.

There is always resistance to any change, but what you also find is that once people are successful, then they are more likely to want to change and engage in behaviors that result in their success. While I am a firm believer in this as a strategy, I also know that you have to bring schools to a particular point where they realize, "We are the adults in that building and in that community," and realize that they can make a difference. In our district, after we have discussions about what we want our youngsters to be like, the next discussion focuses on what our teachers need to be like, what our administrators need to be like, and what our schools need to be like.

Michael Ben-Avie: What would you say to a teacher who cannot possibly imagine what you see? There are teachers who are struggling and trying but are reaching a point where they feel like they have to give up. What would you say to a teacher like that?

Edna Vega: I see teachers that have been in the same room for twenty-five years and keep books in cellophane wrap so they don't ruin them. In their minds, they are doing the right thing. We need to look at people as individuals. We have some people who need to leave and some who need to be ignited. The system has not treated the teachers too well, either.

I have found in the Comer schools that the focus is not the adults—it's the children. The guiding principles become a way of life in the school building. I find that in schools where the Comer Process works, it works well because everyone buys into it and truly believes in the guiding principles.

Cassandra Grant: When we look at school reform, we often look at education just in terms of the achievement of students. What we really are discussing when we look at the Comer Process are those issues that affect the family and the child in a larger context. And that points to the ethics on which our society stands. The Comer Process is not just a program or project, but rather it is a way of life that begins with the heart-to-heart connection we must make with every child.

Resources for Parents

Joyner, E. (1996). *Ebony National PTA guide to student excellence* [videotape and guidebook program]. Chicago: Johnson Publishing Company, Inc., and Conrad and Associates, Inc.

National PTA (1997). *National standards for parent/family involvement programs.* Web site: http://www.pta.org.

CHAPTER 2

My Grandma and Me

Michelle Tyson

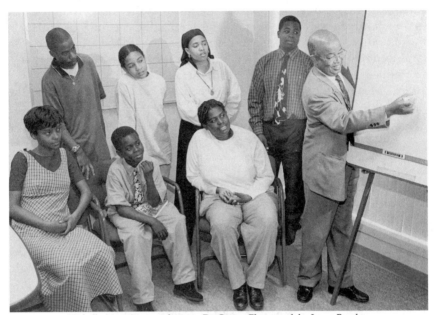

Michelle (center) is seated next to Dr. Comer. Photograph by Laura Brooks.

When a student suddenly starts to do poorly in school, one might suspect that she is being irresponsible. But Michelle skipped school because she was being super-responsible to her ailing grandmother. A long-range goal of all SDP school communities is to develop collaborations that can support families so that students can continue to attend school, no matter what is going on at home.

When my grandma was 45, she adopted my mother because my mother's mother had died. My mother was only a couple of weeks old at the time. My mother loves my grandma with all her heart. She would do anything for her.

In the spring of 1996, at the age of 86, my grandma had her leg amputated below the knee because of poor circulation. She's 87 and she's an independent woman, and it's so hard for an independent woman to become dependent on her daughter after 87 years of working for herself. My mother is caring for my grandma now because of the way my grandma took care of her.

My grandma was in the hospital for about three weeks, and then she came home. I don't even know how to describe it. Every night, she used to cry out because her leg hurt her.

I Had to Stay Home, and My Grades Fell

My mother stayed with her for a couple of weeks, until my grandma was doing great. My mother didn't have enough money at the time to hire a nurse, so I had to stay home from school for three days out of every week. During this time, I dropped drastically in all my grades. My grades had been 85s and 90s, and now they were 65s and 70s. And I was like, "Oh, Lord!" I had never seen a 70 before. I told my mother I wasn't doing really well in school; I kept thinking about my second mother being at home and having a hard time.

My mother and I took turns staying in the house. My mother has four kids, but I'm the oldest daughter. Every day I came from school and changed her dressings. Sometimes I had to pick her up and put her in the wheelchair. After a couple of months, she began to wheel the chair for herself. And that's the time when my happy face came back on, because that meant that my grandmother was back to being herself. I had to stay home two or three days a week for a couple of months.

This Ordeal Has Brought My Mother and Me Closer Together

I am one person in twenty directions every day. My mother is my backbone. Without my mother, there wouldn't be any Michelle right now, just a crazy Michelle, because I would be going crazy.

One thing my mother told me is, "That's life." There are a million explanations for those two words. My mother is a very hard-working woman who has supported me for all my life. It was so hard to see her working so hard to do things for my grandmother. My mother put everything into my grandmother and everything into us. She wants us to be somebody. She believes in God, and God is the Savior. And to hear my mother say those two words made me feel, "Is that all? 'That's life'?" I was not mad, but I was confused and angry at the same time. But my mother was telling me that God put us on this world for a purpose.

I pray to God every night so that I can understand how my grandmother feels. My mother explained to me that God is good, and without God there would be no purpose. I know that if you believe in God, you have all the strength in the world. Nobody can knock you down. By talking to God and telling this Soul your problems, this Entity is actually listening to you. And I can ask God to hug me and help me.

My mom really loves me. She always told me that she loved me, but before the ordeal, it was hard for me to say it to her. Now, I'm saying it forever. "I love you, mama. And I know that you're doing this for me and for the whole family." She's like the sunshine in my life.

I've Had to Give Up Many Special Opportunities

Before my grandmother became ill, I used to be a very active student. I used to be in all the programs in the school. My favorite program was debate. I was on the debate team for four to five months. After the spring term in 1997, eight of us on the debate team spent one week in Atlanta, Georgia of hard, intense work. It was like the army to me. Every morning I got up at 6 o'clock. I had to be ready at 9 o'clock. And from 9 to 9, debate was my whole day. It was hell for the first three days. Then I got used to it. I won my first plaque there because of the work I put in. I was so proud of myself because for me to go through this ordeal and thinking about what's going on at home and being with a stranger in my room was very hard.

A couple of months later, my grandmother had her first heart attack. It happened at home, and we had to rush her to the hospital, and I was so sad because I thought my grandmother was going to die on me.

This term I had to drop out of debate.

Editors' Postscript

During the summer of 1998, Michelle spent two weeks as an intern in SDP's national office at Yale.

CHAPTER 3

Chicago Scenes

*Vivian V. Loseth, Thomas A. Barclay, Juan I. Alegría,
Della A. Alfred, Rodney L. Brown, Joan Dameron Crisler,
Phyllis Shalewa Crowe, Carol Edwards, Christine Hides,
SuAnn Lawrence, Lisa A. Marth, Lany Miller, Barbara Monsor,
Michelle Adler Morrison, and Savannah Browning Smith*

Photograph © 1999 by Michael Jacobson-Hardy.

In the twenty SDP schools in Chicago, implementation of the Comer Process is directed by Youth Guidance, a long-established social service agency. The facilitators' orientation toward intervention, action, and community involvement has produced outstanding results.

Child by Child: The Comer Process for Change in Education. Copyright © 1999 by Teachers College, Columbia University. All rights reserved. ISBN 0-8077-3868-9 (pbk.), ISBN 0-8077-3869-7 (cloth). Prior to photocopying items for classroom use, please contact the Copyright Clearance Center, Customer Service, 222 Rosewood Dr., Danvers, MA 01923, USA, telephone 508-750-8400.

Welcome to Chicago *by Thomas A. Barclay*

I would like to take you to Brown Elementary School. I think it is important for you to see where we do what we do. Dr. Comer asked us why we
decided to start the Comer Process in the most difficult areas of the city of
Chicago. We realized that if we moved into those areas and showed success,
then we could do whatever is required anywhere else. We selected areas
that exhibited the level of poverty and hopelessness that we had seen and
worked with every day in the past, believing that the Comer Process can
bring a sense of hope to the schools and families.

The School and the Stadium

Brown Elementary School is in a deprived neighborhood even though it's
next to the stadium where the Chicago Bulls and the Chicago Black Hawks
play. That multimillion-dollar stadium is surrounded by poverty. At Brown,
what you see is a nice facade. For the Democratic National Convention in
1996, the city did a wonderful job of manicuring some of the facilities and
buildings on the Near West Side. If you had come here in 1994, you would
have seen an abandoned-looking, graffiti-marked building. Now you'll see
a nice-looking outside and a playground freshly built. But you'll also see
that some kids are still struggling with behavioral and other problems that
come with living in hopelessness and poverty.

We wanted to sensitize the teachers to where our kids come from. Two
years ago, we arranged a tour for the entire faculty inside the Henry Horner
Housing Projects. As a result, some teachers said, "I didn't know this was
happening." Most of them never had crossed the street to see where the
children live. They would get in their cars and go home. Most were not involved with this community. They would call parents over, but never
crossed the street to go over there and talk with parents. When I asked,
"When was the last time you were over there?" and they answered, "Fifteen years ago, eighteen years ago," I said, "Well, things have been changing since then."

There are children in the school who cannot sit in their seats. We understand that because there are drugs in this community. You might see
some children misbehaving because of something they experienced over
the weekend. There could have been shootings in the housing development, but often we don't pick up on it unless we say, "Let's talk about this."
In 1997, a woman was beaten to death by her boyfriend. Her kids, who
were students at Brown School, saw this happening and, afterwards, saw
their mother lying in a pool of blood. We are talking about a type of event
that happens almost on a weekly basis in this particular environment.

We Give Our Best, and the Students Succeed

What is positive about Brown now is the full-time social worker and the Student and Staff Support Team (SSST), which addresses some of these events and lets children know that there are people inside the building who are available to talk with them. Teachers are able to refer children to the SSST when they are not sure what is going on, so they can continue to teach the other children. When we understand why a child is so out of control, we can say, "Oh, there's a reason why this child is acting this way."

I think I see beyond the hurt of these kids. I look within them and I see a lot of potential, and I know that what we need to do is help heal the hurt to reach the potential underneath the scabs. I was the commencement speaker at Brown last year and I realized again, as I looked at the graduating class, that a lot of these children have not had the leadership and support that most children have had. Through being in Brown over the last five years, I sense that when we give ourselves to students, they do very well. We saw some test scores jump up in 1996. I believe the improvement in test scores can be attributed to the way the Comer Team, based at the Youth Guidance social service agency, and the school's Student and Staff Support Team have addressed some of hurts the students have. Underneath the hurt, underneath the scab, is very often a bright child.

The Gardens *by Savannah Browning Smith*

For about twenty-three years, I have been a teacher at William H. Brown Elementary School in Chicago on the Near West Side. We're very close to where the Chicago Bulls play at the United Center. As a matter of fact, Michael Jordan "helps" me when I teach math and science. On a classroom wall is a poster of Michael Jordan reading books. We do Bulls math. After every game, I bring the newspaper in and we discuss the scores. I'll write on the board the scores of the Bulls and their opponents. Find the sum. What's the difference? Compare the two. I was having a hard time teaching five-digit place value, but when Michael Jordan scored 25,000 points, they knew that. So I started off with 25,000. I went from 250 to 2,500 to 25,000. So now we're keeping up with Michael Jordan's total career points. We made a prediction as to when we thought he would hit 26,000.

I emphasize science in this classroom, perhaps because I was not surrounded by science as I grew up. It's just been in the last ten years that I have been exposed to hands-on science and the math it leads to. I like exposing the kids to hands-on science because I think it can eliminate the kinds of anxieties I had about math and science. The students gain confidence from hands-on projects when, for instance, they use litmus strips to test the soil at Garfield Park Conservatory.

I was looking out of my classroom window one day at Henry Horner Homes and I said, "Sure does look dismal over there. I think some flowers would look very pretty." I went across the street on my own and talked to the supervisor of the maintenance department. I said, "You think we could plant some seeds to grow a garden out here?" He said, "Yes, that sounds pretty good. Why don't you come back and see me next year, and we'll see what we can do." The following spring, when I went back, he said, "I've got some good news for you." I said, "I have some good news for you, too. We started growing things in the classroom." He said, "Well, I have even better news. We have some money left over in one of our budgets, and I ordered some plants." He showed me what he had ordered, and I was just overwhelmed. He said, "There is one catch. Instead of having two sites, we'd like for you to do about nine or ten gardens." I said, "Oh, but the children are just second graders. How are we going to plant all those gardens?" He said, "Well, we have an earth digger. We will turn the earth for you and prepare it, and that way they won't have all that heavy labor to do." And I said, "Yes, I think we can do that." And we did.

We went out almost every day when we had our science and our math. The wind would be blowing the dirt in our faces and it would get in our eyes, but the children just loved it. It would rain on us, and we'd just say, "Oh, we're going to grow, too. The rain is going to grow us just like it's going to grow the flowers."

It didn't even dawn on me until about two or three years ago that I was just really attached to this community, and flowers and plants were my way of giving back to the community for my being here these twenty-three years. I've seen children grow up in this community. As a matter of fact, the father of the young man who sits at the first desk on the left-hand side in my class this year was my student.

The South and North Gardens

Our fine arts teacher and our parent chairman wrote a proposal two years ago for a $25,000 school beautification grant. We made the first cut, but we were not one of the finalists. Yet a few months later, we received a grant that was twice as big from Lever Brothers Company and Jewel Food Stores. There is a big copy of the check in our main office that says, "$60,000 to Brown School." An architectural firm designed the playground. They said, "Well, what do you want this to be?" We had input from the neighborhood, school, and community. Every child in the school had an opportunity to say what he or she wanted in the playground. We established a committee, and we put all the ideas together. This activity was on only one side of the school, on the south side, the side that faces the stadium. Anything will grow there because it gets sun all day long. I never asked whether there were any plans to do anything at the same time on the other side of the school, the side that faces the housing projects. The Democratic National Convention was coming up, and they wanted this school to be an attractive place to the outside world. Nobody except the residents would see the north side.

The north side of the school is a real challenge because it is shaded. With the other gardens, I mostly learned by doing. For this north garden, I myself had to go to "school" to learn how to plant on the north side. The funding for the garden came from the Community Greening Program of the City of Chicago's Department of Environment, and the University of Illinois Cooperative Extension Services. One of the requirements of the program is participation in their classes. As part of the class, I was taught how to make a blueprint for the garden, which is a native woodland garden.

The children learned what their teacher had to go through to plan a garden—how there was reading involved in it as well as science. They were just thrilled by it all. The garden tools are regular sized tools, they're not children's tools, and yet they learned how to use them safely and well. The plants arrived in May 1996. Well, it rained for about two weeks, and the plants were here in the classroom, and we were watering them and trying to nourish them along. By that time a lot of the teachers saw that this room looked like a greenhouse, and they started stopping by. I said, "I'm very glad you came to our classroom because we'd like to use you. We need to have you help us put these in the ground." We asked teachers who could commit to giving us a half hour or forty minutes of help, and seven or eight classes did. Even the little kindergarten children came out. They picked up the trash for us because every day things were blowing through the big spokes in the fences. We appreciated their help.

We finally got the plants in the ground after a lot of rain, and then we had a drought. It didn't rain for almost a month. I was glad the garden wasn't on the south side of the building because that side gets most of the sun. Still, I was fearful that the plants would not make it during the drought because they were so young, but fortunately most of them did.

In August, the garden was looking nice. Around Labor Day, preparations started for the Democratic National Convention. People came with the big scaffolds to place equipment on the roof. The school housed police command headquarters for the Convention at the United Center. The Convention itself was over a couple of days before school started.

We Keep on Going

What happened to the garden? The garden was up and going then. It was in its fall bloom. Those plants that had bloomed the first year were still blooming. Minor damage had been done to the garden when stuff was put on the roof for the convention. When they started taking things off, they didn't get anything to hoist it down; they just threw it over. Our roof needed extensive repairs. I didn't know when I put the garden in that the order had been in for more than ten years to have these repairs done. Next they came to tuck-point the building. We were long overdue for it. This, too, caused damage to the garden. The garden, at the end, was ruined.

People asked me, "Savannah, Savannah—are you going to give up on planting a garden?" You know what I said? I said, "Oh, no! We keep on going!" And as a matter of fact, we've already started. On the floor in the middle of my classroom is my worm composting bin. Worms have been busy at work making this dirt into top-notch soil.

You know, I feel about the children in my class the way I feel about that garden: I didn't give up on the garden, and I've never given up on a child, even when a child had me puzzled. When I first started working here, I had a young man who just reduced me to tears. He was just seven, but he had a police record. His parole officers came to school once a month to see him. I went over to Major Adams from the Henry Horner Boys' and Girls' Club for help. He came over to the school to observe the boy in my classroom to see what he was doing here. He said that we should form an alliance to provide him with continuity of support among the adults in his life, and find an area in which he will succeed. And we did.

I have a picture of Dr. Comer on the wall. Every student learns about Dr. Comer and the guiding principles that we have here at Brown School. I play his tapes for them, the two tapes on which he talks about his childhood and what his mother did for her children. The children say they just can't believe that someone could come from his circumstances and become *Dr.* James Comer. I say, "Well, you can, too! Who says because you were born in Henry Horner that has anything to do with your brains?"

A Principal's Perspective on Parent Involvement
by Carol Edwards

If you ask teachers, "How many of you want parents in your room?" twenty-five percent of hands might go up. If you say, "Your evaluation will include the degree to which you have included parents," more teachers will come up with some superficial things for parents to do, like bringing in cookies or

Kleenex. But when you say, "There is value in having parents here," and when you model that in your own behavior, then you get another level of participation. I believe in that value, and I demonstrate it, and my staff sees parents as helpers in facilitating and promoting a quality educational program.

As the principal of Lillian R. Nicholson School, I look at parent involvement in various ways. On one level, parents are engaged in school policy making and governance because they are involved in open discussions about how we will use Chapter I money. On another level, Chicago legislation requires parents to be members of the Local School Council. At yet another level, we informally involve parents in the process of school improvement planning.

Would I like to have more parents involved? Yes, I would. How can we do that? I don't have all the answers. What I do know is that, just as parents have different interests, they also have different degrees of interest, and they choose how they want to be engaged in any process. How parents perceive the role of schools and perceive the history of parent involvement in schools can either impede or promote their involvement. Some parents say, "The school is your ballpark and mine is at home," so either they don't see involvement as their role or they don't feel comfortable coming in to the school and making that their role. We therefore involve new parents in areas that complement the work of the school—activities that do not require them to become engaged in the issues that have an impact on teaching and learning. We ask them: "Will you come to school and go with a class on a trip because we need a parent to go with the teacher?" "Will you come and work in the lunchroom because we need an extra pair of hands?" "Will you come and help my security guards because we need somebody else to help them at the door?" "Will you come and help with parent patrol because we're concerned about children getting back and forth?"

I think that parents ought to be truly invested in what happens to their children when they get to school. They should ask themselves, "How do I help the teachers teach my child?" Our school helps them answer that question with action. For example, my staff has been furthering their training in math and science instruction because we are in a three-year initiative that will make us a specialty school for math and science. Along with the teachers, ten parents have been trained (using Chapter I funds and additional funding obtained for us by the Teachers Academy for Mathematics and Science). They are ready to go into classrooms as volunteers and help teachers teach children because they now have the knowledge.

We have a parent room on the first floor in the middle of the corridor. In the parent room are tables, chairs, bulletin boards, and some clothes in the back. If we have clothing to give away, we do it in that room. Parent meetings and parent trainings are held in that room. Specific parent activities, such as distributing books to children as part of the Reading Is Fundamental initiative, are done in that room. Parents also visit other places around the school. They go in the lounge and have a seat. They eat with the teachers in the lunchroom. I remember a time when they would not have done that. I also remember a time when they would go into the lunchroom either before the staff or after. Now the parents just sit down next to teachers and eat.

Whenever parents and educators look at the educational process, each person will see some aspects and miss others. Dr. Comer emphasizes staying focused on the children and their six developmental pathways. The child development perspective gives us a neutral base for looking at issues. This focus has given us a common viewpoint as we develop our partnership even further to benefit all the children.

Investing in Children *by Joan Dameron Crisler*

The idea for establishing a bank within our school, Arthur Dixon Elementary School, came in 1993 from a program that was sponsored in Illinois by the state treasurer, Patrick Quinn. The program, "Bank-at-School" focuses on fifth and sixth grade students and is designed to teach them about the value of saving money. The original design of the program was for classroom teachers to work through a curriculum with the students. Each school would be paired with a community bank whose role would be to facilitate the opening of bank accounts by students. The bank would come to the school each month to receive deposits from the students. These monies would then be deposited in the sponsoring bank.

When we received the initial program information, I sat down as principal with my administrative assistant to discuss what our specific interest might be, given our school's focus on career development and entrepreneurship. We decided that we would like to get involved but in a much broader context. We agreed that we would request a bank sponsor and discuss with them the possibility of their not only facilitating the opening of bank accounts with our students, but also actually being willing to work with our students to teach them about the banking industry.

We selected Seaway National Bank, which is located in our school community and is one of the largest African-American-owned banks in the country. Our community, Chatham, located on the South Side of Chicago, is a middle- and working-class African-American community. I often describe it as being on par with Atlanta: Many prominent business owners and entrepreneurs still live in our community, and there are many historic and well-known African-American-owned and -operated businesses still located here. It is also what people refer to as a "graying" community. Some residents have owned homes in Chatham for thirty to forty years. Some people who were raised in this community and then moved away have now moved back to homes that had been owned by their parents or grandparents. But Chatham is not a one-dimensional community. We have many multifamily dwellings, and we have many families headed by single parents. We do have some unemployment and some families that are affected by many of the same social ills as communities all over this country—alcohol and substance abuse, gangs, child abuse and neglect. Overall, Chatham runs the gamut socially and economically, with some stark contrasts.

Seaway National Bank sent a vice-president to the school. We discussed our concept with her, and she was very enthusiastic about our ideas. In our first year, the bank's staff came out and discussed banking operations with all of our fifth and sixth grade students at an assembly. They presented an overview of all of the different jobs that existed in a bank and explained what was necessary to make a bank run efficiently and effectively. At that point, students were encouraged to apply for a variety of bank positions, which they did. They were required to submit a job application for each position they desired. Students were encouraged to solicit letters of recommendation as well as to prepare resumes. Managers as well as service staff from the Seaway National Bank came out and conducted job interviews with our students. After critiquing the interviews and reviewing the applications, they selected students to hold the various positions in the bank. Subsequent to that first year, the students who work in the bank (the executive staff) have conducted the annual interviews to select new bank staff.

There are eight executive positions at the bank—president, executive vice-president, and vice-presidents of marketing, customer service, teller operations, bookkeeping, auditing, and comptrolling. Each one of the bank vice-presidents supervises a staff of two to four other students. The students are trained by staff from the Seaway Bank whose job responsibilities mirror their own. Students hold their positions for a year. At the end of that year, they have to reapply for their banking position if they would like to remain employed in the bank.

We named the bank the Eagle-Dixon Bank. The eagle is the school's mascot, and the school's logo includes the eagle's attributes: "Proud, strong, and soaring to new heights."

The bank is open three days a week—Mondays, Wednesdays, and Fridays—from 10:00 a.m. until noon. Any student who is enrolled in our school, from pre-kindergarten to eighth grade, can open an account in our bank with a minimum $10.00 deposit and a parent's signature. We will open accounts for any student in our school or for any business. Businesses can open an account with a minimum $100.00 deposit. Today, there are about 300 passbook accounts. Seaway charges the school's account a minimal maintenance fee, as it does other accounts. Seaway invests the money and provides interest to the school's account the same as it does to all its other accounts. Once an individual account is opened, the child becomes the proprietor of the account and can make deposits and withdrawals on his or her own signature. We don't want the children to treat their bank account like a wallet so if a person makes more than three withdrawals of any size per quarter, their account is assessed a $1.00 withdrawal fee.

The Eagle-Dixon Community Bank looks and "feels" like a *real* bank. As a matter of fact, its ambiance is more luxurious than the average bank in most communities. We do not believe in selling fantasy to our kids. We believe very much in realistic life expectations. When we determined that we were going to have a bank, we set out to furnish the bank and to have the accoutrements that would be equal to any professional banking operation that these children might encounter. Our bank is very aesthetically pleasing. Each bank executive has a desk. Our bank receptionist sits at a large, beautiful desk and greets you as soon as you come in. The three-person teller station is glass-enclosed, and there are two customer service booths. We even have a walk-in vault. The teacher supervisor, Sandra R. Haynes, a retired teacher and full-time volunteer on this project, takes the money from the school and deposits it in the Seaway bank once a week. Seaway insures the money while it is in the school.

A University Partnership Helped Create Our First Business

After the first couple of years, when our fifth and sixth grade students were moving up into the seventh grade, we decided that the whole banking concept was too valuable just to cut those students off after the sixth grade. So, we developed an idea that could keep them involved as seventh graders. We were very fortunate to have a relationship with Chicago State University, whose College of Business had developed an Entrepreneurship Awareness Program (EAP) for adults. These adults, many of whom were public school staff, were then encouraged to return to their schools and to develop school-based businesses with their students.

Through Curtis James, the director of EAP at that time, an agreement was developed to allow a portion of the funding for their program (which comes from the Coleman Foundation) to be deposited in our students' bank. Then some of the adult students who were enrolled in EAP would be required to present their business plans to our seventh grade student Loan Board. The Loan Board would then determine whether or not those business plans had merit and were deserving of being funded. Small business "loans" (stipends) were granted in amounts ranging from $500.00 to $2,500.00.

Our first business venture, Eagles International Trading Corporation, an African imports company, was chartered and incorporated by our students. At that time, it was the only business in the state of Illinois that was actually owned and operated by children. It began as a joint venture with a gentleman in our community—a business owner who was associated with an African import business that operated out of New York. He came into our school as a mentor, working with some of our young people, particularly our African-American young men. Over time, he determined that it would be a great idea for him, in mentoring our young people, to teach them what he did as a businessman. And that's how it began—with discussions, with some modeling of behavior, with taking some young people out to trade shows and expositions. Soon, we all realized that these young people were, indeed, astute enough and bright enough and motivated enough to be able to operate a business successfully.

We began by selling fabric by the yard and by the bolt. This fabric is imported from five countries in Africa. The business has expanded to the point where we now also sell imported African artifacts (masks, sculptures, Ashanti stools, etc.), artwork, jewelry, greeting cards, clothing, caps, hats, umbrellas. We do some consignment business with various tailors and seamstresses, who create ethnic outfits and costumes and leave them in the store for sale. Any student in fourth through eighth grade is welcome to apply for a job and become involved in the business. We try to involve as many students as possible. The supervising teachers consider the relationships among the students and, may suggest, for example, that we open up one of the positions on the Board of Directors to a different student. Generally, the students accept one another's leadership.

The import business is open five days a week during regular school hours. In addition to parents and students within the school, we serve customers from the community at large. When a customer comes in, we usually call a pair of available students from their class. They take the customer up to the store and serve her. We have an implied agreement that if the students cannot maintain their class work—academically and behaviorally—we will suspend their bank and store work. We let our teachers know: We appreciate your support and cooperation, and we'll do everything we can to support you and cooperate with you. The primary job of the school is classroom teaching and learning.

Most of the proceeds from the business are reinvested into the business. However, at the end of the school year, employees usually receive a share-based stipend calculated upon the business's income for that year.

The amount of the share that a student receives is based upon the amount of time that the student has invested in the business. Once that is determined, he or she receives a check for either a full share, a half share, or a quarter share. And the check usually ends up being in the amount of several hundred dollars. Students often save this money in the school's bank, thus continuing the cycle of earning, then saving, and then investing. We're searching for an investment company that will take the time to open up accounts for the students as small investors.

Our Students Are Preparing to Excel in the Real World

The bank and the store are only two of the school's money-making enterprises because there are many people here who are willing to take risks, initiate their own projects, and follow through. There's also a desktop publishing company and a videodrama company that market their services within the school and also outside. These businesses have accounts in the Dixon-Eagle Bank. In addition, the school's dance company, led by a fourth grade teacher, is connected to the Joffrey Ballet—and winning awards.

We know that many of the employment opportunities that were available when we were children no longer exist. But students must have options if they are going to be able to be productive and to make a contribution to society upon completing their education. They need to have practical, real-world experiences to develop a reasonable understanding of just how our communities and economy operate. They have to develop a basic understanding of the value of money, how money is earned, how you benefit when money is saved and invested, how communities thrive or deteriorate based upon the amount and the types of economic investment in them. The students see these things occurring around them every day. They see stores boarded up. They see businesses that perhaps were once owned and operated by members of the community now being operated by individuals who do not live in, invest in, or value their community. They need to know and to have an understanding of what is going on around them. Whether they opt to become actively involved in controlling it is another issue. Our banking program succeeds in developing experienced young business people whose sophisticated skills and understanding of the work world will empower them as they grow up to shape the destiny of their community.

For My Grandson, Darius, with Love *by Lany Miller*

I live on the third floor of a nine-story high-rise. On each side is a three-story walkup. Our building is really the dividing line: Gangster Disciples on one side, the Vice Lords on the other end. I have seen people get shot. I have seen people die out my window. I've looked out and seen young guys that I knew from Pamper stage up until 15 or 16 years old lying out there in the parking lot with their brains blown out because they're in this gang thing. Brothers in the same house have shot each other because one was in one gang and one was in the other. This has been going on for maybe the last fifteen years. It's an everyday thing.

The children in our school see this. When it happens, the kids are nervous; they're upset. Sometimes for two or three weeks in a row we will come out early in the morning and make it up here to Chalmers School, and then our principal, Ms. Blackman, has to get the children because parents start coming in and saying, "They're shooting over there."

The kids are scared, you know. They say, "They're going to shoot me! They're going to shoot me!" You have to hug them, and when you hug these little babies, you find them trembling because they are really, really scared. They're up here, and word comes that their brother or sister or mother or somebody has been shot. Then there's no way to hold that child in here. They want to go. They're crying, they're all over the floor, and you're trying to comfort them, and it's just really hard. And while you stand there trying to help somebody else, tears roll down your face.

Ms. Blackman, our principal, has been wonderful about it. Sometimes she has called the police, and ten or twelve police come and stay around the school until the last child in this school is at home. That's the only way we can get home.

One nice, sunny day, Ms. Osborne and her two kids, my grandson Darius, and I were leaving school when a car rolled up. I'm very observant of people—teenage boys, especially. The driver parked right across from the school playground and two guys got out. I said to myself, "Why did they leave the car door open and the car running and one behind the steering wheel?" They walked to an alley past a vacant lot. All of a sudden we heard Pow! Pow! Pow! Bang! Bang! Bang!

I said, "Oh, my God!" We made it to the parking lot, and then the guys ran back our way. I grabbed my grandson because he's tall for his age, and I smashed him down behind a car. I pushed Ms. Osborne's kids down. She got down. One of the teachers hollered out the window, "Get those kids! Make them get down!" because there were some kids coming down the street from the park. I told myself, "I've got to get from behind this car to get these kids." So I ran across to another car hollering, "Get down! Get down!"

The two guys ran to their car and got in and took off. I got a good look at the car, and I gave the police a good description.

Usually I'm in the house and hear this, so I'm protected, but that time we were out in the open. I went in the house, took off my jacket, hung it up, and sat down in the chair. I was so shaky I had to call my daughter at work. She said, "Mommy, are you okay?" and I said, "Yeah, I'm doing pretty good. Once I calm down, I'm going to lay down and everything." And she said, "Okay. If you start feeling bad or something like that, just give me a call."

Darius was really scared. He went in his room and then he came back out and he said, "Grandma?" I said, "What?" He said, "I'm so scared." And I said, "Yeah, I know. So was I. But honey, they weren't going to get you. Believe me: Before I let them get you, they would've had to get me." He said, "But I didn't want them to get you, either." I said, "I don't want them to get either one of us. But if it came to that, you know, I'd have been all over you, you know."

This is what these kids go through, being in this area. They grow up with it, and that's all they talk about. You'd be surprised. You hear little kids say, "Yeah, he did so and so to me. I'm going to go home and get my brother's gun. I'm going to come back and blow his brains out!" There are no jobs here. Half the kids graduate and that's as far as they go. They come across the stage here and go over to the high school, and within a week or two all they've got in their heads is to get out there and make the quick money selling drugs. You see them out there, and their parents—I've never seen so many young parents—act like they don't even care. They don't care where the kids are coming from with this money and these new clothes. When I was a kid, I couldn't even bring something in the house that belonged to one of my friends. Believe me: Five minutes after it got in there, my mother knew it was there. So that was why we put the gang workshop and the drug workshop into the parent leadership training—to find out how to cope and how to help these children.

There's a history to the parent leadership training, of course. First you have to get the parents into the school and make them part of the school. Then you train them to be leaders.

Being a Parent in the School

I became involved with the school because Darius is here. I promised him. I worked for six years as an aide in the Lawndale Child Care Head Start Center in the building I live in, and I was there while he was there. When Darius came to the Chalmers School, I didn't want to get involved with the PTA. I remembered when my 36-year-old son was a student here. In those days, the minute the PTA had a decision to make, they had already made the decision before the parents even walked in the door and sat down. I didn't like that. It was like I was being dictated to. Why send me a flyer and invite me to the PTA meeting and then when I get here, everything is already decided by you? I really didn't want to be bothered with the PTA, but I was willing to volunteer.

Darius' teacher then was Ms. Donna Morris. She had been my daughter's teacher, too. It was amazing to see this teacher teach the way she did. I looked at her and I said, "This woman is outstanding," so I started volunteering in her room. Now Darius is in the fifth grade, and I've been volunteering all along.

I'm usually here at 7:00 in the morning to look after the basketball players. I make coffee and I go into the office, where I can monitor the front door and talk through an intercom. I let the teachers in early, and I answer the phone for teachers who are calling in saying they're not coming in that day. I take notes and give them to Ms. Crenshaw, the school secretary, when she comes in.

I'm also around to hug the kids. I have a policy that when the children have a nasty attitude or they're trying to fight, I hug them. I'm not going to let them fight because they could end up hurting each other. Once I get them apart, if one really wants to continue, I'll hold onto that one and I'll say, "I'm just going to stand here and hug you until you calm down." And it works. I say, "I'm not going to let you go. You're going to end up changing because I'm not going to move." I say this in the child's ear, "Are you okay? Now, since you're okay, tell me this: Were you really that mad? Was it really that bad? What did they say to you that triggered you off?" When they tell me, I say, "Why do you worry about what people say? Whatever they said about your mother, your father, whatever, you know your mother and father, right? Well, they don't. They're just saying something because they know it's going to trigger you off. Learn to hear and don't hear. When they say something about your mother, say to yourself, 'Yeah, okay,' and keep on walking."

I encourage parents to come up to their child's school and participate in whatever is going on. I talk and laugh and joke with them at the front desk. I invite them to parents' meetings. Some of the parents have heard that I'm bossy and pushy, but I show them the real Lany Miller. I love fun and games, but when it is time to be serious, I can be serious. When we have a project, I want it to be the best and I demand that everyone do their best.

How the Comer Process Changed the School

When the Comer Process came along, that was the best thing in the world because it made parents more aware of things. The Comer Process put everybody under the same umbrella. Now the parents are no different from anybody else. When Ms. Blackman walks in from the Board, whatever she knows, I know. What she tells her teachers, she tells to me. And I take it right back to my parents.

It's not like it was years ago when principals tried to keep everything away from parents. The parents never knew anything, and when a decision was made, if they didn't accept it, too bad. Now, you have an opinion. I sit on any council that they have here. I can say whatever I feel. I'm a human being. I have feelings. I have thoughts. And people respect me for the things that I say and I feel, as long as I say them with tact and as long as I am courteous and kind.

Della Alfred is our Comer facilitator. It's like someone sent her to me. She took me and the whole group under her wing. Thank God for Della Alfred. They asked me what I would like to end up doing, and I said, "I want to grow up to be just like Della Alfred! I want to be able to go anywhere, any time of day, and talk to anybody." And I have. I have been to United Way. I have talked to people connected to Youth Guidance. I went downtown and talked to bankers. When I asked Della, "What am I going to say to these people?" she said, "Just be yourself. Tell them how you got started and about the Comer Process and about rallying the parents." And I have.

The Comer Process also taught us how to relate to the teachers. For years, teachers thought that when parents came in, they wanted the teachers' jobs. But we don't want their jobs. We just want to help. So we have learned the best way to talk with each other. Ms. Blackman had a couple of staff members sit in on our meetings and give the teachers' point of view. So that way we had a chance to deal with a lot of little hostilities in one-on-one conversations, and the teachers got a chance to express their points of view.

The Parent Retreat

I had been to many different meetings and I was bringing a lot of information back to the parents, but I felt that I needed more training. I didn't want to say the same things over and over to the parents. I was afraid that I'd eventually lose them. So I asked Della, and she brought Thomas Barclay over. I said, "All the executive officers of the parent groups in all twelve Comer schools need to meet up where we can discuss different things. We can find out what we don't know and just hash it around, and everybody will end up knowing the same thing at the same time." He said, "That's a good idea," and he took it to Vivian Loseth, assistant director of Youth Guidance and director of the Chicago Comer Process, and she agreed.

To see if we could consent on the idea of having a longer meeting, all the officers from the twelve schools came to Chalmers School for a short meeting. When they got here, we had a little continental breakfast for them. We all took turns introducing ourselves, and I talked about the fact that we are sister schools and needed a chance to know each and everybody. Thomas said, "Well, Ms. Miller here, she has an idea and she wants to bring it to you and see whether you like the idea or not and want to consent on it." So I told them my idea about needing more training, and I was amazed. There were fifty people in that room, and everybody had the same thought, but nobody had brought it out. I said, "Anybody that wants to take the floor can," so everybody gave their opinion.

After they left, Thomas said, "I have never seen parents that thrilled to do something." We continued meeting every two weeks at Chalmers that first year. We had a flyer for each meeting, and we came up with an agenda of what we wanted to talk about. We broke the agenda down and ended up being in groups and committees.

We needed cheap transportation. We needed training about things going on in the schools because in some schools the people were saying that the teachers didn't want the parents in their classroom because they felt like the parents were in there trying to take over. We needed training in different legal things, in information from the Board, in how to be meaningfully involved and really help the teachers, in how to support the teachers in maintaining discipline, in how to really relate and help people in the office, in how to operate the ditto machines and other machines in the school, in how to have self-control over our own attitude, in stress management, in conflict resolution, in domestic violence.

When I brought the domestic violence information back to our parents, I was amazed. I had twenty-five people at the parent group meeting. I was amazed at the women who stood up and said, "I went through it. I had this." I had tears in my eyes because they were telling me stories. And you never knew it because you'd see this couple walking down the street and you'd think, "Oh, the perfect couple." But behind closed doors it was an entirely different thing.

The idea of a retreat for more than a day came up at one of the meetings. Thomas and Della said it would be more convenient if we did it overnight because that way we could get in two or three sessions on Friday and two or three on Saturday. Thomas checked on the budget. He arranged for me to talk with Nancy Johnstone at Youth Guidance, and the Annenburg Foundation came up with the money, and we went.

The parents planned the first retreat. Every two weeks from November all the way through June all the executive officers got together and planned how to set things up. During the summer we had the first retreat, and the parents led all the workshops.

I led the workshop on conflicts and resolutions. I gave everybody a page of conflicts, and I let them come up with the resolutions. And then we compared our resolutions and discussed them. I used my experience from the Head Start center.

Bringing the Workshops Home

We send out flyers, and we put on the flyer something to make parents come in, like lunch or cash door prizes. Then they show up. Once they get in here, the workshops really catch some of them, wake them up, and shake them up. And then we back them up. Thomas Barclay and Della Alfred and our guidance counselor, Dolores Sample, are there to follow through, and the Parent Connection Group helps them.

I feel that if you give a person something or let that person know that there's somebody there who can really help them—somebody who can get them off drugs, say — then they need someone who will stick by them through the whole thing. They don't need you to put them into a place and then they never see you. If you've talked them into going, stick by these people. Stay with them. This is what they're looking for. Their mothers and fathers have left them. They're on their own over there, you know, trying to raise their kids, and they want the attention of somebody to help them along. So, if that's what it takes, fine. I'm willing, you know.

CHAPTER 4

Success Speaks Many Languages

Fred Hernández

Photograph © 1999 by Michael Jacobson-Hardy.

The principal of a pre-K through sixth grade school in Yonkers—the second Micro-Society school in the country—explains how everything from the architecture to the curriculum to staff development reflects its organization as a functional real-life community. Among other programs, the children run a bank, legislature, courthouse, IRS, post office, and a newspaper. More than 60% of the students come from homes in which languages other than English are spoken. Using the Comer Process, the school community found a way to prepare the students for academic success by aligning its organization, governance, instruction, and accountability. The students have made tremendous gains on standardized tests for reading in English.

In the old days, America did not need everyone to learn English or algebra. My father did not learn English and still does not speak it fluently. However, he was successful in America because America needed a lot of hands and my father had two of those hands. But today in America everyone needs algebra and everyone needs to be proficient in English because of the information-rich, high-tech economy that's out there.

Eugenio María de Hostos Micro-Society School

Eugenio María de Hostos Micro-Society School, a pre-K through sixth grade school, is located in the southwest quadrant of Yonkers. Eugenio María de Hostos (born 1839 in Mayagüez, Puerto Rico; died 1903 in Santo Domingo) was a writer, philosopher, newspaper reporter, lecturer, and teacher. A tireless defender of the rights and liberties of America, he was also a proponent of education for Spanish-speaking peoples. The Yonkers Board of Education named its new magnet school after him to recognize the contribution of Latinos to the Yonkers city fabric.

The school's community is characterized by low socioeconomic status, a cycle of welfare dependency, unemployment, inadequate housing, and a high percentage of single-parent households. (Eighty percent of our students are eligible for free or reduced price lunch.) The area is experiencing an increase in the number of uninsured persons, in part because so many workers have recently lost their jobs. Four hundred and fifteen (91%) of the students reside in neighborhoods with inadequate access to primary care, as designated by the Ambulatory Care Sensitive Conditions indicators. Approximately 62% of the students come from homes in which languages other than English are spoken.

Using the Comer Process, Eugenio María de Hostos has found a way to prepare its students for this new world by aligning its organization, governance, instruction, and accountability. In 1992–1993, the year the school opened, only 37% of the third grade students met the New York state minimum standards in reading in *English*. By 1997, 87% of the third graders were scoring above the state reference point. Reading performance of sixth graders has similarly improved: 20% met the state standards in 1993, and 62% met the standards in 1997. Similar gains have been seen in math: In 1993, 57% of the sixth graders scored above the state reference point; in 1994, 64%; in 1997, 97% of the sixth graders scored above the state reference point.

In 1997, I was invited by Marion Buchbinder, assistant attorney general for the State of New York, to give a deposition. She had selected our school as a potential model of school improvement, and she wanted to learn more about us. Specifically, I was invited to explain why and how the school was improving.

The Macro Society

To understand why I was asked to testify, it is worth widening the frame for a moment. In 1986, the Yonkers chapter of the NAACP won a suit against the City of Yonkers. They showed that the Yonkers Public Schools had been segregated for forty years using the Saw Mill River Parkway as the east-west divider for the schools. All the minority students—African-American and Latino—attended schools on the west side and had fewer resources, and all the majority students attended schools on the east side and had more resources. The federal court decision was to issue a desegregation order and plan, Educational Improvement Plan Number One (EIP-1). The essence of EIP-1 was to desegregate the schools through magnet schools. I became the first principal of a new magnet school at the Eugenio María de Hostos Micro-Society School building.

The Micro-Society Program

Magnet schools are not new, but the Micro-Society idea is new. Eugenio María de Hostos, the second Micro-Society school in the country, was patterned after the first Micro-Society school, in Lowell, Massachusetts, which was developed by George Richmond. Richmond is also the founder of the Micro-Society, Inc., which is a consortium of schools throughout the nation. The architects of the school building, Anderson La Rocca Anderson, were able to capture the essence of the Micro-Society program: The school looks like the town square of a living community.

A Tour of the School

As you walk into the school, you find yourself in Freedom Square, a two-story atrium space. Market day is held in Freedom Square. Across from you is the governmental seat: the Legislature, the Courthouse, IRS, and Post Office. A bit to the right is the telecommunications center. Then there's the bank. Originally there were two banks, one run by the English-dominant students and the other run by the Spanish-dominant students. However, we realized that the competition between the banks was causing intergroup tensions. A meeting was held with staff members to discuss this concern. We decided by consensus that an integrated bank—a bank whose staff spoke many languages—would meet the needs of all of our students.

So now there's only one bank, First Micro-Society Bank, which is run by all the students. In the far right-hand corner, you see Global Publishing. Students write, edit, and publish newspapers and magazines as part of the language arts curriculum. Publications are in both English and Spanish and are distributed to the school community, including parents. The Family Interactive Center is next to Global Publishing. On the left-hand side of Freedom Square, you see the school office and the Office of Economic Development.

If you walk around the school, you'll see parents from the Family Interactive Center helping out throughout the school community. As you enter classrooms, it's going to be difficult for you to tell who's the teacher, who's the parent, and who's the teacher aide. You'll find children here who are limited in the English language interacting with English-dominant students. (English-dominant students use Spanish as a foreign language when engaging with other students because over 80% of the students are Hispanic and 65% of these students have limited English proficiency.) Students will tell you about their vision of a better world and how they see themselves as a stakeholder group that can make a difference because they already have made a difference in the school community.

School as Society Ought to Be

The Micro-Society program incorporates all aspects of the New York State and Yonkers Public Schools curricula into real-life learning. For instance, the students hold real City Councils at City Hall yearly to present issues that affect their lives in the Yonkers Public Schools. During one session that our children conducted, they presented the idea that bus shelters should be provided to students. Elected Yonkers City Council members realized that the students translated for one another. The City Council members said, "We have been making an assumption that everyone understands English, but if we want to engage the merchants in the city, we need to make sure we speak the languages that people understand." Soon afterward, our students invited government economic development officials and all the merchants of Yonkers' southwest quadrant to an economic summit that took place at our school. In the past, merchants in the quadrant felt excluded from community forums because the forums were always held only in English. It was the first time that the public officials participated in a community forum that was conducted in English, Spanish, and Arabic.

Today the government officials make sure translators are present during government and community forums. The merchants become aware of such government programs as revolving loans, low-interest loans, and commercial revitalization grants. Also, through monetary and human resources, the merchants support the school and community events. There can be no better lesson for students about their own potential for good citizenship and leadership than to make a significant difference for their whole community while they are still children.

The school has its own currency called Marras, in honor of Reginald F. Marra, superintendent of Yonkers Public Schools. There's no unemployment; everyone's employed in our society. Eugenio María de Hostos has its own court system through which conflicts are resolved by judges, lawyers, and witnesses so children understand the importance of using conflict resolution, documentation, gathering of data, presenting that data, and all the literacy skills that are needed for them to articulate their story. If a child comes up to me and says, "Someone didn't return some item," I ask, "What have you done so far to get it back? Have you tried negotiating with that person? Have you gone to the guidance counselor?" If the child has tried every strategy we taught and used every program we offer to no avail, I respond, "Take him to court!"

The school has a branch of the IRS because students need to understand the importance of taxes. The Micro-Society also has a government component. The classrooms are recognized as communities and everyone understands that they need to be represented, which is a very traditional value in America. The students are learning about the importance of voting and selecting classmates to represent them in the government. Our voter turnout is voluntarily 100% every year.

Through the newspaper, children learn the importance of writing and using that as a mechanism to document and communicate. So, too, with the telecommunication system, which is another mechanism to communicate to the school and our larger community of Yonkers. The Micro-Society program helps the students to understand that the world is bigger than just their block. They learn about the institutions that have an impact on the quality of their lives. However, the Micro-Society program by itself was not enough to raise the students' academic achievement. The school serves a predominately Spanish-speaking student population. An effective reading program was needed to help them also achieve fluency in English.

To Ensure Success for All, Rally the Whole Village

Success for All is the school's reading program. Elements of the program include a daily 90-minute time block dedicated to English and Spanish language arts throughout the school, student assessments every eight weeks, and small reading groups to which students are assigned according to performance. The bottom 30% of first-graders receive daily one-on-one instruction by certified reading teachers for a year. Eighty percent of the students receiving one-on-one instruction do not require this individual attention after one year. In 1992, when the school adopted the program, *Success for All* had only an English-as-a-Second-Language (ESL) design but not a bilingual model. We told the John Hopkins University facilitators that we would enter into a partnership only if they would allow us to pursue and develop a bilingual model, which we did by ourselves.

Prior to implementing the Comer Process, there was no consensus on an overall school strategy: In kindergarten, the students were taught in Spanish; in first grade, they were taught in English. Using the guiding principles of consensus, collaboration, and no-fault, the school community modified *Success for All* to suit the predominantly Spanish-speaking (ESL) student population. Bilingual students learn in Spanish from kindergarten all the way through sixth grade because the ability to speak Spanish is not a problem, a liability, in this building. It's an asset. Students who are Spanish-dominant are learning English as a second language, and students who are English-dominant are learning Spanish as a second language.

To accelerate the academic success of Spanish-dominant students, the school needs to focus on academics—and not only on English language acquisition. Otherwise, what America will have is people who can speak English but are academically unsuccessful. Our Spanish-dominant students are excelling in both learning the English language and in their academics. In a longitudinal study we conducted in the school we found that as soon as we accelerate students' academic achievement, then success in one language transfers over to success in any language.

Our interpretation of these findings is consistent with Genesee (cited in Collier, 1989), who concluded that older students are efficient second language learners in late French immersion programs because their ability to abstract, classify, and generalize in their first language may aid in second language acquisition for academic success.

After we implemented the reading program we had modified, we saw some gains. However, we realized that it was not enough. It just wasn't enough.

Creating a Functional Community

According to Dr. Comer, schools need to "reinvent a functional community." A functional community means that adults relate well to adults and children, and children relate well to children and adults. In a functional community, when children relate to children, it is always under the supervision of adults. That's what's been severed in our communities: adult supervision of children. Furthermore, children are not communicating with adults, and adults are not communicating with children. In schools that are not functioning, adults are not talking to adults about the children, either.

When I was growing up, we knew that any adult was going to intervene if we behaved inappropriately. Nowadays, adults will see young children breaking bottles and just keep walking by. But when children come to this building, they realize that all adults in the school community are going to take the time to support them and also to correct them. So, we're reestablishing, reaffirming that all adults have a responsibility to embrace all the children.

On many different layers, the school is creating community. Consider the Family Interactive Center, located just beyond Freedom Square. As you walk into this fairly large room, you see couches arranged in a semicircle, fresh coffee and rolls in the kitchen area, computers, work areas, the parents' library. Parents with infants and toddlers gather on the couches and exchange parenting tips. Parents learn to use computers. Workshops are held on nutrition, the social services, and the history of public schools. I wanted the parents to know about public schools and the history of parental involvement in schools. The Family Interactive Center helps families to understand the society that they live in and to understand the practices that support their children's education. Focus group discussions are held: For example, parents of children who are on the honor roll talk with parents of children who are not on the honor roll. The steering committee recruits parents to support schoolwide literacy initiatives.

In the Center, informal relationships develop that are powerful and meaningful. I told the parents, "There's the phone. When it rings, who's going to pick it up? We're not going to pick it up. So if you decide not to do anything, then that phone is going to ring and no one else is going to answer it." English language classes for the parents are organized. The Family Interactive Center is becoming a hub of the neighborhood. Teachers will say to students who are acting inappropriately, "I know that your mother is in the Family Interactive Center. Should I ask her to visit our classroom right now?"

Within the school you will also see the Yonkers Spectrum School Health Program, a free, comprehensive health service run by St. Joseph's Medical Center, The Westchester County Health Department, and the Yonkers Public Schools. The Family Interactive Center spearheads social family events that are important to the fabric of the community. Neighborhood family events and informal networks have to be reestablished and reaffirmed because they support and protect all children regardless of their individual family condition. The framework of the Comer Process helped us understand how all the parts of school life should mirror all the parts of the community. Consider the issue of governance, how decisions are made. In a community, a representative group makes decisions. However, tradition-ally in schools only the principal makes decisions. The Comer Process helped us organize ourselves into teams. In our society, few work in isola-tion any more. Today we have a high-tech, information-rich economy. This means that people need to communicate with each other and work collab-oratively.

We opened lines of communication to tackle the essential questions. Are people born with intelligence or do people get smart? If a group of boys and girls go into a classroom and they're successful and intelligent, why is it that when they go into another classroom, they're disruptive? It's not the boys and girls. We have to feel comfortable talking about that if we want to commit ourselves to making sure that all the children learn.

Aligning Our Goals for Students and Staff

We took a sober look at our staff development plan. We aligned staff de-velopment with the goals and objectives of the Comprehensive School Plan. We made the connections and the conversation changed—obviously a teacher could no longer go to a staff development event to learn the Macarena. I said, "If the Macarena doesn't support the Comprehensive School Plan, then I'm not going to okay it."

Every member of the school community is encouraged to continue learning and developing—every member, without exception. For example, the chair of the School Planning and Management Team, Marixa Gonza-lez, is a parent and teacher aide in the school. I asked her to do something she had never done before: to make a presentation to 200 people on the re-design of schools that needed improvement. She presented, and I just helped by flipping the charts. Then I summarized and we sat down. When a lady stood up and said, "I'm a teacher aide and I have not heard any-thing about teacher aides this whole morning. Where do we fit in this?" I was able to respond, "You know Marixa Gonzalez, the person who spoke to you? She's a teacher aide." People had assumed that she was a teacher or had an advanced degree.

A feature of the Yale School Development Program is the process of aligning curriculum, instruction, and assessment in order to determine whether there are gaps. We formed a curriculum alignment committee com-posed of teachers. They looked at every single piece of material that was used in the school, both teacher-made and vendor-driven. And they found gaps in the areas of mathematics and reading comprehension. We identi-fied the materials needed to support all of our students in achieving on the New York State Pupil Evaluation Program (PEP) assessment. In addition, the school has an Advisory Board composed of a judge, two state legislators, and representatives from local businesses, industry, and banks. The Advisory Board works with staff and children in modeling the Micro-Society after real-life situations. The students realize that our curriculum is very powerful. They understand that they need to learn it well in order to resolve problems in their community. We are very excited about the school because what we have created here and continue to enhance is a fully functioning prototype of the healthy, just society in which we hope all our children will spend their adult lives.

Reference

Collier, V. (1989). How long? A synthesis of research on academic achievement in a second language. *Tesol Quarterly*, Vol. 23, No. 3., pp. 509–531.

CHAPTER 5

Shared Ownership

Parents as Partners in Education

Jeffie Frazier

Photograph by Laura Brooks.

Educators who truly welcome parents find that the benefits are virtually limitless. A nationally recognized educator describes the roles parents play in her top-performing, inner-city school, and she details how other principals can create the same relationships in their schools.

On October 6, 1995, a headline in the *New Haven Register* read "Helene Grant Masters Mastery Test: Despite Poverty, Most Kids Ace Reading Goal." The article reported that state education officials had visited Helene Grant School because they were "very interested in trying to find out what works," according to Connecticut State Education Commissioner Theodore S. Sergi. The school, he observed, "has phenomenal reading scores . . . while also having a significant portion of poorer students." According to New Haven Superintendent of Schools Reginald Mayo, "The difference seems to be that everyone has the same goals and they understand what they are—that's good, school-based leadership."

Another description of the school appeared in *Reclaiming Our Nation At Risk* (Lloyd, Ramsey, & Bell, 1997). Dr. Comer appears in the book as if he is testifying before a Citizens' Commission on school reform. The authors identified "Best Practices" in fifteen states and eighteen cities. The following description of Helene Grant appears in the "Best Practices" section accompanying Dr. Comer's "testimony."

> This one-story building, with its broken playground equipment and a bell that was once the signal tower for the fire department, is in the middle of . . . neighborhoods plagued by gangs, drug dealers and shootings. Situated between two housing projects and flanked by two churches, Grant is one block away from the juvenile detention centers, a high school, community shopping plaza and Police Sub-Station. . . .
>
> Like other Comer schools, Grant has stressed children's holistic development—that children be taught social as well as academic skills. Grant has emphasized putting children's needs first by coordinating all available resources. It involves the total school community—teachers, parents, counselors and others, even students—in school-related decisions that are made by consensus. . . .
>
> Criteria for tracking improvements include standardized tests, teacher-made tests, student self-assessment, even absences. The number of absentees, for example, dropped from 30 to 40 students daily to between 5 and 7. The Connecticut Mastery Test, a standardized test, measures achievement in reading, writing, and math skills. . . . More than 63% of all students scored above the state goal in reading on the Mastery Test. These are amazing reading scores, especially when compared with the citywide average of between 15% and 20%. (Lloyd, Ramsey, & Bell, 1997)

My goal has always been to do all I can, as well and as often as I can, for the young boys and girls I work with. My job as an educational leader is to prepare youngsters today to be the productive, caring adults we want to see tomorrow.

Dr. Comer's School Development Program encourages a collaboration of the home, the school, places of worship, and the community to support the life of the school. At Helene Grant School, we've proved that this concept really works: When you have all of those forces connected—each reaching out a hand—a school becomes a well-organized, safe, and exciting place in which all our children, all their parents, and all the teachers and administrators can learn and grow.

Now, no matter how well I attempt to plan life at school, parents are still the most important influence on children. Therefore, one of my aims has been to get very close to parents—bringing them into our school to help us and, at the same time, helping many of them to become better parents. A lot of the parents of my students belong to gangs. I have not been afraid to go out into their culture and learn about those gangs in order to understand my students and help them succeed.

I put in long hours at my school, and I find that my teachers do, too, right along with the parents. We are inspired by our vision of what our children can accomplish, and we're already making that vision come true in elementary school.

All Children Can Learn

I know that all children can learn, and I know that with the right attitude all adults can help their children learn, even if they are not well educated themselves. Let me tell you a story about that.

> When I was a high school student, my mother was at work, so my grandmother had to proof my homework. I remember one assignment in particular. When my grandmother proofed that assignment, she gave it back to me within minutes, and she said, "You look it over again because I think there are a couple of mistakes in it."
>
> I went back, and—sure enough—there were several mistakes in it. When I gave it back to her, she looked at it for a few minutes, and then she gave it back to me saying, "Look it over again. There are some more mistakes in this paper."
>
> I redid that paper three times that night, and when I finished, it was correct.
>
> Three years later, I found out that my grandmother couldn't read!

When people tell me, "The parents can't do this because it's not in their environment," I point to my grandmother. Through me, my grandmother influences every single child in Helene Grant School even though she could not read a single word. We can all be educational leaders—not just the principal, not just the teachers.

Principals and teachers are so busy trying to get those test scores up that we have forgotten how to love the children and how to communicate with them. But at Helene Grant School we work with all three of the As: Attendance, Achievement, and the Attitude that school is important. And parents are an integral part of our success with all these As.

There's another A: Anger. We have to get angry at stereotypes so that we can raise our own expectations and get encouragement from our entire society. I was so angry with some representatives from the State Board of Education when they asked me, "How are these boys and girls excelling on the Connecticut Mastery Test?" That wasn't what they really wanted to know, and I knew it. They wanted to know, "How did those black boys and girls excel on the Connecticut Mastery Test?" They just wouldn't come right out and ask me that. So I asked it for them, and then, before I answered it, I simply said, "Why don't you take a little visit around my building? When you come back to me, I think you'll have the answer."

They did tour the building, and then they had another question: "Why aren't these boys and girls hanging from the rafters? You're in an inner-city school, you're in the heart of Dixwell, where there are fights and shootings every night. How is it that these boys and girls are so well behaved?" I said, "Would you just show me the teacher in this room?" They pointed out a person, but it was not the teacher, it was a parent. Everywhere they went, they saw parents in the building. That's the key to our success.

When you get parents involved in the life of the school, you increase children's chances to succeed. Many parents can't finish their job at home because they are working. By the time they get home and try to prepare a meal and try to go over homework, they are at their wits' end and they lose their patience. So we provide other parents to do that. Some of those parents already have the skills to support the children. Some of them don't. So the teachers and principal set the example for those parents right here in the school.

The School Planning and Management Team can't change what goes on outside, but we can make the inside of our school as comfortable as possible and full of opportunities. If we see a light that says it's possible to make a change, then we go for it. We do that by offering workshops for parents, by supporting them as they work for their G.E.D., by inviting parents on trips, by showing up in the community and inviting the community into the school. We do that by knowing every child as an individual and establishing a relationship with every parent. And the benefits are tremendous, not only for the students, but for the staff. Each principal is just one individual. But each school community has many, many parents, and those parents have many, many ideas. When you're working with a group of youngsters, every parent has ideas about what the children should achieve. So just look at all the ideas we can take and use when we talk to parents and work with parents!

Parents as Partners

The very first thing that's needed to go from zero parent involvement to meaningful parent involvement is that the principal must feel comfortable with parents and treat them with respect. Principals may be fearful of parent involvement because of what they've heard other people say about it. I suggest that principals get to know one parent at a time. Start with the PTA president and try to work out some things with that person—small things like, "What can I do to help you? What would you like to see me do that I'm not doing in this school?" and then go on from there. Then you solicit that parent's support and say, "The next time you come and talk with me, bring another parent." Make sure you're available outside the door first thing in the mornings. I recommend a "Meet the Principal" session around 8:00 A.M. Invite parents in for coffee and open up to them about your expectations of yourself, of the students, and of them. And then just listen to them. Explain at the outset, "We're just going to meet for an hour. If we find we still have concerns or interests, then we need to set up another meeting." I guarantee you will not cover everything in one hour, but that day you set up the next meeting. Then the word starts flowing around about what each person needs, what each person can do, and that the principal is not so bad after all.

Another way to make parents feel comfortable, especially when you want to have them work with the students, is that you offer miniworkshops to them—at least one in the morning, one right after school, and then one in the evening. This way you catch parents who drop off kids in the morning, who pick them up in the afternoon, and who work during the day.

Whenever you run a workshop, make sure that you give the parents an A for their effort. Then they are proud and have a good feeling about themselves and school. Whenever it's appropriate, invite the kids in to stay with the parents during the afternoon and evening workshops. If they can't find baby-sitters, you have to provide them. I use my area's junior high school and high school students to baby-sit in a room in our building. In the afternoons, we sometimes use senior citizens to baby-sit for a bit. It works.

Once the parents are comfortable coming into the building to talk with you, why not have a teacher just happen to drop in and say, "Oh, Ms. Frazier, I need this child to read to someone alone. Can anyone in here help me?" Even if parents are uneasy, they'll help when the teacher explains what she wants. Also, you can look to the parents' talents. Maybe there's a parent who knows how to knit or crochet. Ask if she can come in for ten minutes to show something she made and explain how she made it. Maybe she can set up a knitting class.

Because a lot of parents won't feel comfortable in the beginning coming into a classroom during the regular school day, have an after-school class where, for example, parents can teach cooking or help students with their multiplication tables. Then the teacher can invite them into the classroom.

Encouraging Teachers to Welcome Parents into the Classroom

When teachers understand the neighborhood in which they work, it makes a difference. If teachers are afraid to be there, they shouldn't be there. If teachers are afraid of parents, they shouldn't be there either. Parents are human beings, just like teachers. Each has to appreciate that about the other. The best way to do this is to have them working side by side to benefit the children.

I find that teachers are willing to take on extra hands. When they don't feel comfortable with it, I set up a miniworkshop and explain it: "No one is spying on you. Everyone is here to offer a helping hand. It will make it easier for you. When we add parents as teacher assistants, you'll be able to reach more children and do more individualized work."

On a typical day in our building we have twenty-five parents in our nineteen classrooms. They stand watch to make sure their children are starting the day properly. They go on trips with the class. Some just hang around to see if we need some help. For instance, one little girl didn't have a uniform on, so a parent helped me out by taking her to her home to change. One parent explained about a trip to another parent. When our librarian was busy bar coding our library, she needed a lot of help reading stories and doing other tasks. Parents run the copying machine. For at least the first hour of the day, you will see parents walking around asking what they can do to help.

We have a quiet and orderly school, and the parents help to maintain that order. All of us work together all the time. And boys and girls understand, as do teachers, that we come to school to learn and that although there will be some noise, we can tell the difference between noisy learning and noisy, disorderly behavior.

Parent Involvement Supports Everyone

Parent involvement benefits a school in so many ways. For example, we needed a playground. Our SPMT, which includes parents, decided that they would go through the proper channels to obtain a playground. One parent had a friend who was an architect, and the architect designed a playground for us that met the School Board's specifications. So we were able to present that design to the Board without waiting for the Board to find a designer for us. I constantly patted that parent on the back and told her how grateful I was for her effort. Many times, a parent can accomplish things quickly that would take the principal a much longer time to do.

When parents are comfortable becoming part of the life of the school, it helps in other ways, as well. Let's take, for instance, a parent who says, "Well, I don't want my child in this teacher's room because this teacher is mean." When the parent is comfortable in school, you can take him aside and say, "Other parents have been in the class helping out. Let's ask them what's been going on and how your child is behaving." Before the situation becomes a problem, it's eliminated—by one parent talking with another.

Another example is that parents can provide adult supervision for teachers who need a 2–5 minute break: They read a story to the class, or take them out for a walk, or do another activity with them. The parents are more valuable than they realize.

Teachers also learn about the children better when they know the parents. When parents have worked in the classroom, they seem to share more with the teacher, and the teacher can more readily understand why a child acts up and then help both the parent and the child. For instance:

Parent: I told him ten times to clean up his room!
Teacher: Well, when you told him to do that, were you looking at him?
Parent: No, I was in the kitchen. I was. . . .
Teacher: Well, you know what I found that I need to do? I need to look at him when I'm talking to him because I need to find out if he's listening. Also, that's a way that can I show him that I'm listening to him.

In this example, the parent and teacher share both the frustrating experience and the solution. Parents need to tell the teacher when they have taken the child to the doctor to have the ears and eyes checked. It's not necessarily something that the teacher will pass on to a school nurse, but the teacher needs to know. When the teacher is assigning seats in the classroom, it is important for her to know whether a child needs to sit in the front row. Someone in the family to whom the child was close may have died. In our school, parents come in and let the teacher know. Sometimes a parent may have been very friendly in September and October. All of a sudden in November the parent stops coming into the building. The teacher will notice a change in the child's behavior. She'll contact the parent to find out what's happening.

When the teachers and parents have this ongoing, open relationship, it makes for a better learning environment.

Welcoming the Community into the School

Community support also does wonders for the learning environment. Our school has extremely beneficial relationships with several community groups.

There's a church right on the corner. The church adopted us many years ago. When we want to have a bake sale, they donate all of the ingredients, and all we have to do is bake and sell them. They also send people over to buy, and they advertise for us. It's like a family.

We're close to the Elks Lodge. Most people think that the Elks Lodge is a place where people go to drink and have a good time. They're surprised when they find out that some of the men at the Elks Lodge helped to design Interstate 95 and other highways and were officers in the Navy. Sometimes they put on their Reserve uniforms and come to school and talk to the students about the history of the wars they fought in, military service, and what it's like to be a working man.

The owners of the stores near the school watch out for us, and that prevents vandalism of the building itself. If they see someone strange around, they will call the police. We also find that their relationship with us prevents things from happening in the stores because the boys and girls know that the person in the pharmacy will tell me if a student goes into the pharmacy and does something he or she has no business doing. The pharmacist also helps the children. If he knows that medication has run out and the child's parent has not come in, he'll call me and let me know. Then I'll have the nurse send a message to the parent.

Our neighborhood extends a great distance. One morning around nine o'clock I got a call from a New Haven resident saying, "I found a little girl up on Prospect." Prospect Street is about half a mile from the school. The man didn't know the little girl's name. He knew she was one of my students, however, because she had on her green and white uniform.

School Uniforms

There's a story behind our uniforms, and it shows what wonderful things can happen when parents and the community consider themselves to be an integral part of the school. Inner-city youngsters pay a lot of attention to clothes. We found that it was getting in the way of the children's learning. For instance, at one point, some of the girls wanted to wear red skirts, but one of them didn't have a red skirt, so they all decided to stay home. Also, I don't think we realize what the effect is on elementary school children when parents insist that they dress a certain way. For example, a little kindergarten girl comes to school with a yellow dress on, and she has about twenty yellow barrettes in each braid. She loses one, and she's crying all day because she lost it almost as soon as she came to school. She's crying all day because she knows her mommy's going to get her when she arrives home because she lost that barrette. When we decided on a uniform dress code, we took all of that away so that the children could think about learning.

Another thing we noticed was that parochial school students seem to have an air about them that says, "I can learn." We wanted to show our community that you can learn in a public school setting just as well.

The key for us at Grant School was the parents. In 1988, the parents decided that the children were going to have uniforms, even though we were late getting started. One parent asked, "Why can't our kids wear uniforms?" The parents just took the ball. We went to talk with School District Superintendent Dow. He thought the idea was fantastic, and said that he had been thinking of it, too. He was just looking for a school. That summer, I was away for eight weeks on fellowship in Africa and didn't get back until late August. When we went to uniform companies, they said it was too late to order in bulk. But the parents were determined.

We chose our colors carefully. White is for innocence; green is for growth. These are young, pure minds that we have. And we're steadily growing here. It is so important that we develop these young minds and make them grow and expand in the right direction.

My sorority, Alpha Kappa Alpha, has members who live in the Wallingford and Meriden area. They asked me if I was aware of the fact that some very small outlets and companies actually made outfits for larger companies and larger stores. My sorority sisters did the legwork and found a company in Wallingford, Connecticut, which used to cut out very expensive clothing for Laura Ashley. When they heard about our problem, they cut out all the dress patterns for us for a dollar! When one of the owners of Horowitz Brothers, a clothing store in New Haven, heard that public school students would be wearing uniforms, he thought it was a fantastic idea and sold me the material at a discount. My sorority gave us $300 to pay for material for needy children. The Elks Lodge also gave us money.

The parents, along with senior citizens and people from my church, sewed the uniforms (Helene Grant has 451 students!). They set up an assembly line: They measured the youngsters in the lunch room, cut the fabric out, and sewed in their homes, in the senior citizens' building, and in the school. Teachers sat with them and basted the pieces together so that the sewing machine operators could just sew along the thread. One of the leaders was Mrs. Jessica Dortch, a grandmother who had three children in our school at that time. Many times we were at her house, sewing, at three and four o'clock in the morning. Mrs. Dortch even made my uniform.

Help has come from all over. A lady in Milford said, "I'm sending in money for you in case a child can't afford a uniform." Dr. Borenstein, a medical doctor working with the state, brings in loads of good clothes three or four times a year. We usually take out the white shirts and gray or green pants to use for uniforms, and put the rest out front for parents just to pick up, free of charge. And when children graduate, their parents come back with good pants, sweaters, blouses, and shirts and donate them to the school.

Now we work with uniform companies. Whenever they offer me something that's beneficial to the parent, I take them up on it. Discount stores, like Caldor's and Bradlee's, have decided they're going to sell the pants and white shirts because they realize that uniforms are in. One discount store came to us with an offer for a bulk sale, and we're going to be able to get them even cheaper. We let our parents know now that they can buy uniforms during the summer, so they won't have any excuse for not having them. Parents who work at Sears and T.J. Maxx and Marshall's let us know when the $8 and $9 shirts go on sale for $4.99, and the parents go and buy them.

If a child cannot afford a uniform, we have plenty of extras in a little room here in school. We set up a plan so that they can buy a uniform. They might not give any money or pay the full amount, but they must make an effort to make payment. We work with them to help them do that.

Strengthening Community

As you enter our school, you can see a picture of Helene Williams Grant on the wall. Above the picture hangs a plaque, which says in part:

Helene Williams Grant

May 1, 1919–October 20, 1961

Helene Williams Grant was a Black woman of beauty, and of valor, who dedicated her life to the cause of public education. She was the first and only classroom teacher in Connecticut to receive a citation from the State Board of Education for her pioneer work as a reading specialist in the development of materials and techniques for remedial reading.

As a woman of action, she recognized the concept and potential of the community school. She played an important role in the building of the first community school, Winchester. Her role was not limited to just the classroom, but also as a teacher of parents and of the neighborhood. Mrs. Grant served the Dixwell community all her life.

We continue Helene Grant's work, using the ideas of the School Development Program to guide our thinking about how to relate to parents and help them feel comfortable. We have learned from Dr. Comer that it is an integration of home, school, place of worship, and community that determines what takes place within a school. And when a school community has all of those forces connected, reaching out a hand, it makes everyone's job easier.

References

Schuster, K. (October 6, 1995). Helene Grant Masters Mastery Test. *New Haven Register*, p. A1.

Lloyd, K. and Ramsey, D., with Bell, T. H. (1997). *Reclaiming our nation at risk: Lessons learned: Reforming our public schools*. The Terrel H. Bell *Knowledge Network* for Education Reform, pp. 220–222.

CHAPTER 6

Preregistered for Success

The Comer/Zigler Initiative

Barbara M. Stern and Matia Finn-Stevenson

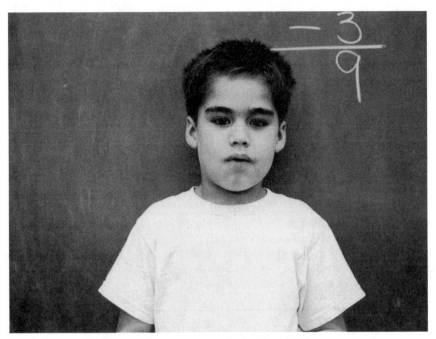

Photograph © 1999 by Michael Jacobson-Hardy.

How soon can SDP notions begin to influence children's development, and how long can the best early childhood education continue to support students and their families? The answers are "before birth" and "throughout school," according to two naturally allied programs that have combined to form an exciting, comprehensive school reform initiative.

It's 7:30 a.m. Three-year-old Antoine is skipping into the Bowling Park CoZi (Comer/Zigler) Community School in Norfolk, Virginia. His mother is dropping him off for preschool on her way to work. She will pick him up again at 5:00. In between, Antoine will have been fed breakfast, lunch, and an afternoon snack and have a full day in a language- and experience-rich classroom with other three- and four-year-olds from his neighborhood.

It's 8:00 a.m. Four-year-old Jessica enters the same school hand-in-hand with her mother, who is on her way to a G.E.D. class down the hall from Jessica's preschool class. During the day, Jessica's mom will spend some time volunteering in Jessica's classroom and will join her for lunch in between her own studying.

It's 8:00 a.m. Mr. Spence, grandfather of Tyrone at this same school, is on his way to the Family Breakfast Club. This club meets monthly to discuss books they are reading and share pieces of prose and poetry they are writing. Mr. Spence has been writing poetry since he became involved in this club and is looking forward to sharing the following poem with the group:

Children *by George B. Spence*

> When your girls act up or your boys disobey
> Just remember to always say,
> "They are my children."
> No need to belittle or cast any doubt
> Because in the end good will always come out.
> Instead of saying, "You can't" or "aren't,"
> Try saying, "You can," and "You shall,
> For you are my children."

It's 10:00 a.m. Mrs. Jones answers the door to Angie, the parent technician from the same school who has come for her monthly visit to see how 7-month-old Jonathan is coming along. During the visit, Angie will talk with Mrs. Jones about what developmental milestones 7-month-olds are typically passing and suggest ways to support and nurture their development at home. She'll play some games with the baby and perhaps leave some toys that Mrs. Jones and Jonathan can play with later. She'll also invite Mrs. Jones to the next parent workshop at the school that will be attended by other new parents participating in "Parents As Teachers," and inform her of other events at the school she might like to attend with Jonathan.

What Is a CoZi School?

It was at Bowling Park School in Norfolk, Virginia, that the feasibility of combining the School Development Program with Edward F. Zigler's "The School of the 21st Century" was first explored in 1992. The idea was suggested by Michael Levine, a program officer at the Carnegie Corporation of New York who was familiar with both programs and saw the potential benefits for children and families through their combination. Other Comer/Zigler, or CoZi, schools are now operating in North Carolina, Connecticut, Missouri, and Kansas. Because the School Development Program is described throughout the rest of this book, we concentrate here on describing "The School of the 21st Century" and highlight why combining it with SDP makes such good sense for children and their families.

The School of the 21st Century

The School of the 21st Century (21C) brings a variety of child care and family support services under the roof of the neighborhood school. Rather than waiting until children are entering kindergarten, the school reaches out to families beginning in the last three months of pregnancy and provides needed support services beginning at birth and continuing until the child is twelve years old. The 21C model assumes that children have the best chance for success when a number of systems work together: the family, the educational system, the child care system, and the health care system. The goal of 21C is to coordinate these systems, make them available to all children, and start as early as possible.

21C includes two child care programs and several outreach services. The first child care component is full-day, year-round care such as the one Antoine and Jessica attend for children ages 3, 4, and 5. It opens as early as 6:00 a.m. and stays open as late as 6:00 p.m. It is a safe, nurturing, and stimulating place where adults encourage learning through play, exploration, and socializing with other children. The second child care component is before- and after-school and vacation care for school-age children. This nonacademic program offers children a relaxed setting in which to play, do their homework, and make choices about joining in other activities. It also offers parents the chance to meet each other at the school and attend school activities and social functions with their children. Support and guidance are offered to new and expectant parents like Mrs. Jones through home visits that begin in the last three months of pregnancy and continue until children are 3 years old (based on the Missouri Parents As Teachers and other home-visitation programs).

An information and referral component informs parents about child care, health care, and other community services they may need. Another outreach service supports and trains family day care providers in the school neighborhood in order to improve the quality of care they give to children who will someday be coming to the school. Many 21C schools also have a nutrition component (which educates children and parents about nutrition and assesses and improves school food services) and a health component (which provides health and mental health services, usually in collaboration with other agencies).

These basic components ensure a full array of services for children and families, and permit the continuous care and support that is the basis for learning. The strength and ultimate potential of 21C stems from its integration with the education system. The model embraces and acts on the view that learning begins at birth and occurs in all settings, not just within the traditional classroom. When all those settings are enhanced, children's outcomes improve. 21C is also convenient for parents who are juggling work and family responsibilities. The school no longer is just a building delivering formal schooling during limited hours. The school becomes a one-stop shop, or a community hub, where formal schooling, child care, and other services are provided together and coordinated.

Service Components of 21C

Child care services:

- all-day, year-round child care for children ages 3–5
- before- and after-school and vacation care for children ages 5–12

Outreach services:

- family support and guidance through home visits to new parents, beginning in the third trimester of pregnancy and continuing until children are three years old
- support and training for family day-care providers in the school's community
- information and referral services for all families in the community
- nutrition and health

Additional services:

- adult & family literacy
- teen pregnancy prevention

- on-site prenatal services
- intergenerational programs
- social services

As of 1998, there are close to 600 Schools of the 21st Century operating in fourteen states. Each program varies slightly. After the school community conducts a needs assessment, it designs its own program according to its particular needs and the resources it has available. Once the program has stabilized, communities often add such other components as adult education, job training, teenage pregnancy prevention, and family literacy. However, all 21C schools share a common goal, the optimum development of children, and they all adopt a set of principles that guide the implementation and operation of the program.

The School of the 21st Century is grounded firmly in the belief that all families must be able to get the support they need, and all children must be able to get the child care they need. This conviction has given rise to a set of guiding principles:

Child care must be accessible for all families, regardless of their income. The program provides universal access to child care. To achieve this, we use a sliding-scale fee system based on family income. Subsidies for middle- and low-income families will still be needed, and these may be made available from government and private sources and through local fund-raising and in-kind contributions from the school system.

Programs must be of high quality. Research has proven conclusively that high-quality child care programs are positive experiences for children and nurture their development, whereas poor-quality programs can harm children and inhibit their growth. 21C programs maintain high quality through qualified and trained staff, high staff-to-child ratios, small groups of children, and a stimulating, developmentally appropriate curriculum.

Programs must view each child as a whole person, addressing social, physical, emotional, and intellectual growth.

Employees must enjoy a professional and supportive environment, including training and adequate pay scales that acknowledge the important role employees play in influencing children's development. (High staff turnover is probably the greatest roadblock to quality child care.)

Schools must foster a partnership between parents and schools, encouraging parents to be involved in all aspects of the program and visiting as often as they like.

Programs must be noncompulsory. Each family must be able to decide which services, if any, to use.

An Answer to the Child-Care Crisis

Today's families barely resemble those of thirty years ago. One quarter of all children now come from single-parent homes, often headed by a mother who lacks financial resources to raise a family. The number of families with young children who are living in poverty has increased significantly. Rising rates of divorce, dual-worker families, increased mobility, and difficulties in getting health care have added further stress to the lives of children and affect their ability to perform well in school.

The most dramatic change, however, is the large increase in mothers working outside the home (U.S. Department of Labor, 1988, 1993). Never before has there been such a demand for child care, far exceeding the supply. This problem has been well documented in the press and elsewhere for many years, but so far it has not resulted in a national child care policy or system. Each family is left to face this struggle alone, usually patching together a number of arrangements for their children, and often without the traditional supports of an extended family.

The child care problem has several interrelated dimensions: cost, availability, and quality. Parents may pay anywhere from $1,500 to $10,000 a year for child care depending on the quality of care and the age of the child. It costs more to care for younger children, for example, because infants and toddlers need more one-on-one care and a smaller group size. Families that can pay often hire a "nanny" or use an expensive child care center. Low-income children fortunate enough to obtain a slot in a Head Start program or another form of subsidized care are likely to receive good child care. However, for working poor and middle-income families, the chances of finding good child care are less sure and vary widely depending on where they live (Galinsky et al., 1994; Helburn et al., 1995; Whitebook, Philips, & Howes, 1989).

Quality also varies widely and ranges from care that enhances growth to that which is merely custodial and may, in fact, inhibit growth. In a nurturing environment, children play and socialize and are cared for by adults who interact with them in positive ways and attend to their individual needs. In a custodial environment, on the other hand, children wander aimlessly around the room or watch television. There are often too many children for any one provider to attend to, so the children receive little, if any, adult attention and supervision. Sadly, every study done on the quality of child care nationally—whether in family day care homes, in the care of relatives, or in child care centers—has found consistently dismal results. These results are alarming because the experiences children have in these early settings are critical to the way they view themselves, their sense of security, their attitudes toward exploring and learning, and their readiness for an academic program at age 5. It is well understood that a high-quality preschool program can provide children with the foundation for later school success and can change their outcomes in later life (Berrueta-Clement et al., 1984; Schweinhart, Barnes, & Weikart, 1993). Therefore, it is a matter of national importance to ensure that all children, regardless of where they happen to live or their socioeconomic level, have access to high-quality care during these critical years.

The School of the 21st Century was conceptualized by Edward F. Zigler in 1987 as a solution to this national child care problem (Zigler & Finn-Stevenson, 1989). He reasoned that locating child care and family support services in the one resource that every community has—the neighborhood school—made good common sense. In this way, the child care system could be linked to the education system, and all parents could access high-quality services in one trusted place, at a reasonable price.

Combining the Benefits of 21C and SDP

Combining 21C and SDP builds on the strengths of the individual programs and extends the benefits associated with each. SDP's goals are to support the child's growth along all the developmental pathways and to create a strong and inclusive community with a high degree of parent involvement. Having access to younger children and their families through 21C services makes these goals easier to reach. SDP's focus on improving academic and social achievement is also enhanced through the combination since, with children are more likely to begin formal education ready to learn and to benefit from schooling. At the same time, the SDP process provides a structure for planning, implementing, assessing, and modifying the program. The School Planning and Management Team (SPMT) incorporates the components of 21C into its Comprehensive School Plan. The SDP guiding principles of consensus, collaboration, and no-fault decision making help ensure that the entire community accepts the program and that the components become an integral part of the school, as opposed to add-on services that are simply housed in the same building. The SDP teams include representatives of the various 21C components. The concerns and observations of the child care staff and parents of preschoolers become part of the adult dialogue at the SPMT, Parent Team, and Student and Staff Support Team, and thus their fiber become part of the tapestry of the school.

The Case of Bowling Park

Bowling Park School was chosen for the first implementation of CoZi for several reasons. This school demonstrated a need for the 21C services, had a principal and central office with a commitment to providing early childhood services within the school system, and already had firmly established the SDP. Therefore, the three SDP teams were already in place to give information and to elicit feedback, to plan the program, to build support in the community, and to make the many necessary decisions. Also, the Comer philosophy was already part of the culture of the school. Expanding the school's mission to take on more responsibility for the children's well-being was widely accepted by the school staff.

The school is located in a public housing community and serves approximately 500 African-American children. It qualifies as a Chapter I schoolwide project because more than 75% of the children are eligible for free or reduced-price lunch. The school's principal, Dr. Herman Clark, is well known in the district for being innovative and undeterred by the traditional boundaries of the principal's role. He has earned and enjoys a great deal of respect and support from faculty, students, and parents.

In April 1992, the school's paraprofessionals went door to door in the neighborhood to find out what each family needed in the way of child care and family support and how interested they were in having these services provided in the school (the majority of parents in the housing project who had young children wanted to participate). The paraprofessionals also collected information about what services families were currently using. This personal approach to collecting the information proved very effective and also began to build support and enthusiasm for the program in the neighborhood. Almost immediately, parents began to call the school to inquire about enrollment. Thus, the planning period was shortened, and plans for implementation began. Of the almost 200 parents living in the housing project who had young children, 98% of those who responded said they would use child care services at the school, and 81% stated that if their children received full-time care at school, they would use this time as an opportunity to finish their own education, attend job training, or find a job. It became clear that everyone would benefit with CoZi.

Between the fall of 1992 and the fall of 1995, under the leadership of principal Clark and CoZi coordinator Lorraine Flood, and with the technical assistance of the CoZi staff at Yale, Bowling Park opened four preschool classes serving three- and four-year olds, a before- and after-school child care program, a summer vacation care program, a home visitation program for parents of newborns and toddlers, an adult class leading to a G.E.D., a health clinic, and a family literacy program. Funding has come from a variety of sources including federal Chapter I funds, a state department grant, in-kind contributions from the school system, private foundation grants, and parent fees. The fees are based on a sliding scale; when parents cannot pay, CoZi schools make arrangements for state child care subsidies and some schools also have scholarship funds to which local businesses contribute.

What has CoZi done for Bowling Park? Upon entering the building, visitors will see parents and grandparents in every corridor and classroom, volunteering, attending meetings and activities, dropping off and picking up children aged anywhere from birth through age 12. They are all part of the school, which has become the community center. Teachers report greater job satisfaction because they see that more of their students' needs are being met and that parents are becoming more involved in the school. Kindergarten teachers are noticing that the students who attended the CoZi preschool are better prepared for kindergarten. In addition, attendance rates have improved and test scores have steadily risen. On the Iowa Test of Basic Skills (ITBS) for grade 4 Mathematics in 1995, Bowling Park scored at the 46 percentile; a year later, at the 88 percentile. In Reading, Bowling Park scored at the 44 percentile; a year later, Bowling Park scored at the 87 percentile. For grade 4 Language in 1995, Bowling Park scored at the 47 percentile; a year later, at the 86 percentile. In the words of Lorraine Flood, "CoZi focused the school on something wonderful—Children!—because that's what child care does: It focuses on children. It focused us on the developmental approach, and when that becomes part of the structure, it becomes part of the philosophy."

What Is a CoZi School Like for Teachers?

Since 1983 when the United States National Commission on Excellence in Education's *A Nation At Risk* was released, most educators have been engaged in "school reform" of one type or another. Teachers in CoZi schools have moved away from a narrow focus on either curriculum reform or school governance, however, to the understanding that schools can assume more responsibility for the very foundations of learning: attending to the needs of the whole child starting from the very beginning. Whether they are members of the SPMT, on one of its subcommittees, or teaching in the classroom, teachers are internalizing new notions about the role of the school and who "belongs" within its walls. Now included in the definition of school participants are infants, toddlers, and preschoolers. Their "team" now includes parents, child care staff, and other service providers, all of whom can help them understand and serve their students even better.

Although many of the programs in a CoZi school operate independently of the academics, teachers' acceptance and support can make or break these programs. At our national office at the Yale Bush Center in Child Development and Social Policy, we convened a panel of teachers to develop guidelines to help teachers benefit from their school's participation (Bush Center, 1995):

- Be open to the changes occurring in your school, whether or not you had a hand in bringing them about.
- Support the guiding principles on which CoZi is based.
- Promote the program—act as an ambassador to the community.
- Attend meetings and participate in communication opportunities.
- Incorporate the program philosophies into the classroom—focus on all developmental pathways and the principles of consensus, collaboration, and no-fault decision making.
- Make referrals for students and parents who benefit from support services.
- Be a team player.
- Facilitate interaction between older and younger children.

Ideally, CoZi teachers should see this model as one that allows them to take some of their other "hats" off and focus on their area of expertise—teaching. With the addition of child care and other support services, children are in a better position to do well in their classrooms. The early interventions permit any developmental delays to be detected earlier, and in many cases special education services can be minimized later on. In sum, the program enlarges the safety net around children and increases the chance that they will do their best.

An unanticipated effect of CoZi is what we are calling the "trickle-up effect" of developmentally appropriate curricula. Kindergarten and first grade teachers in public schools have been feeling pressure in recent years to make their classrooms more academic in the traditional sense, often going against their best judgment and knowledge about how children learn. But CoZi schools have high-quality preschool classrooms, rich with manipulative materials and opportunities for children to make choices and "work" through play and social interaction. This helps kindergarten teachers feel more professional confidence about setting up their rooms and curriculum appropriately during the two months between the end of preschool and the beginning of kindergarten. There is no reason why their classrooms should look very different from each other. At Bowling Park, we noticed a big change in the look of the kindergarten classrooms after the preschool was implemented. Gone were the desks in rows! In came tables and interest centers! Also, when early childhood professionals are at the SPMT table for schoolwide planning, their early childhood developmental perspective broadens everyone's view of children. Successful schools enjoy good relationships with parents. Successful students have parents that are involved in their education. A significant benefit for teachers in CoZi schools is the chance to affect both of these factors. The staff of a CoZi school has five years to get to know children and families before kindergarten even begins. These years are an opportunity to establish strong, positive relationships that will benefit the academic and social performance of children as they progress through school and contribute to a positive school climate.

What Is a CoZi School Like for Parents?

Parents at Bowling Park report that the school is an open, welcoming place that enthusiastically invites their participation. They can begin their involvement in the third trimester of pregnancy by participating in the Parents As Teachers (PAT) home-visitation program, as has Mrs. Jones in the opening scene. If they choose to participate, their children have first priority for slots in the preschool program. If they work, go to school, or are in job training, like Antoine's mother, their children can have child care services at the school. Adult education and a family breakfast club are also available to them, as well as parent workshops and exercise classes. Health care services are available to children and their parents in the school health clinic. In sum, their CoZi school, in addition to providing formal schooling for their children, works at creating the conditions they need to be the best parents possible for their children, with less stress influencing their family life.

For parents who have not had a very successful school experience themselves, this type of school offers them a second chance. During the preschool years, before there is any attention given to "academics," school personnel and parents have the time to get to know one another, to learn to trust one another, and to overcome some of the negative feelings they may have about schooling. These relationships will serve to bolster the school experience of their children. Antoine's mother depends on the school to take care of him so she can work. Her good feelings for and trust in the school will help Antoine feel positive about the school. Jessica sees her mother in school as she goes about her day, both in her own classroom as a volunteer and as a student in the G.E.D. class. This can only increase the bond Jessica and her mother have with the school and reinforce the message that the school is there for both of them. Seven-month-old Jonathan will spend the next several years becoming familiar with the school and school people before he begins kindergarten. The monthly visits from Angie, the parent technician, will be the bridge for this family.

Parents who are striving to improve their own situation and who feel aided by the school in the attempt will be better able to provide the support their children need to thrive. The following observation from a Bowling Park preschool teacher illustrates the two-generational potential of CoZi:

> I had one little boy in my preschool class, Orlando, whose mother was enrolled in the G.E.D. program. During the day, Orlando would see his mom at school, doing her work, eating her lunch and taking breaks just as he did. She would often pop in and say, "Hi," and to get and give the hug they both needed and deserved. It was great to see her attitude change from general depression to such a positive note, once she had a focus and a direction. (Bush Center, 1995)

The staff members at Bowling Park have seen this change in attitude with many parents as they've become more comfortable in the school through participation in the various programs. One such parent, Pam Winstead (1994), with the encouragement of the CoZi staff, received job training and eventually became employed as a secretary. She wrote the following article about her experience in the school for the *CoZi Monitor*, a quarterly bulletin that highlights poetry, prose, and thoughts of Bowling Park parents, students, and staff:

Parent Involvement at Bowling Park *by Pamela Winstead*

As a parent, I want the best of everything for my children, especially in terms of education. I think I have found the best in Bowling Park CoZi Community School, located in Norfolk, VA. Bowling Park has offered both my preschooler and my "pre-preschooler" a head start otherwise not available in a public school setting.

The CoZi Preschool program (ages 3–5) has given my son a chance to learn many things he may not have been exposed to in everyday life. By his going to school at such a young age, we found he had a communication problem. It took his teacher to recognize this, because I didn't. The problem was addressed and my son has improved a great deal. Had my son not started school early, he may have fallen behind later.

My seventeen-month-old daughter is involved in the Parents As Teachers Program (birth-three). She is getting an even bigger head start than my son. If she has any developmental problems, they can be detected before she reaches preschool.

The school's environment allows everyone to feel welcomed and wanted. The parent technicians design workshops that are both enlightening and fun. The workshops give parents a chance to be on the school grounds and keep abreast of what really goes on in the school. School personnel also have a chance to "grab" us if they need help with anything.

As parents with the same focus in mind (our children), being in the school has given us a chance for fellowship and for sharing a lot of common and not-so-common interests. We have a parent advisory board, a parent support group, and a family breakfast club.

Since I am in the school so often, I get a chance to observe and talk to a lot of the older kids. They feel good about coming to school. They love their teachers and are very enthusiastic about everything they do in school.

Principal Clark has found that increasing parent involvement in Bowling Park since the advent of CoZi has brought other benefits. When the school is in need, his parents are right there for him. Early in the implementation, for example, there was some public criticism of CoZi by representatives of a conservative organization. For days this group—none of whom were from the local community—picketed outside the school with inflammatory placards questioning the intent of the program. Finally, the Bowling Park parents decided to "picket the picketers." They succeeded in discouraging them from continuing with their picket line. Dr. Clark believes that the program has bonded his parents to the school in a way he has never seen before, and feels that their loyalty and support is a direct result of CoZi.

The Model Partnership

The school reform models of Comer and Zigler both are concerned with the optimal development of children. SDP offers a process for mobilizing the adults in the community and bringing about change. 21C offers needed services that enable children to build the foundation they need to take advantage of the school program and that enable families to function with less stress. Together they extend the definition of the school by extending the services it offers and extending the school community.

The power of the combined model lies in its comprehensiveness, its multigenerational potential, and its capacity to level the playing field. High-quality child care is an essential part of the foundation of school success, but it can be prohibitively expensive and available only to a limited few. Therefore, school readiness itself has become an equity issue. Providing high-quality child care as part of the public education system gives all children an equal opportunity to benefit from the experience.

Providing child care and family support services in those critical first five years and linking them to the school through the SDP process also has the potential to prevent school failure. Problems can be detected earlier, as with Pam Winstead's son. Special education labeling and services can be reduced if problems are detected and addressed earlier. Parents can be enlisted as partners in their children's education, another ingredient for school success. The difficult transition between preschool and school can be virtually eliminated with CoZi because children are getting "ready" in the very school they are getting ready for. It is likely that Antoine, Jessica, and Jonathan will barely notice a difference from preschool to kindergarten when they cross that threshold.

The CoZi collaboration is an example of several systems of support coming together under one roof in a "caring community." In the words of James Comer, "A caring community committed to development is critical, not only for education but for the future of society" (Comer, 1996). With the enormous difficulties facing children, families, and public schools today, no one system can solve these problems alone. The familiar African proverb states, "It takes a whole village to raise a child." We need to expand our vision of the community needed to face these challenges, get more of the villagers around the table, and start the process earlier.

Postscript: A New CoZi School *by Barbara M. Stern*

This chapter was written while I was the manager of the CoZi Initiative at the Yale Bush Center. During those five years, I helped a number of school districts implement the CoZi model and met inspiring educators and community members all over the country who were passionate about making schools more comprehensive in meeting the needs of children and families. I was often envious of the people I worked with in the field and wished for my own opportunity to make this model live and breathe in my own school. I finally decided to make that move and took the principalship of a public elementary school in Connecticut. As I near the end of my first year there, I've just received word that my school will be receiving funds for a School of the 21st Century Program. I am looking forward to using my experiences at the Yale Bush Center to guide me as I face the challenge of providing leadership for my own CoZi school.

References

Berrueta-Clement, J., Schweinhart, L.J., Barnett, W.S., Epstein, A.S., and Weikart, D.P. (1984). *Changed lives: Effects of the Perry preschool program on youths through age 19*. Ypsilanti, MI: High/Scope Press.
Bowling Park. *CoZi Monitor*. Summer/Fall Quarterly 1994, Volume II, No. 2.

Bush Center. (1995). *The School of the 21st Century/Family Resource Center: The teacher's role.* New Haven: Yale Bush Center.

Comer, J.P. (1996). Comer on creating caring communities. *SDP Newsline,* Vol. 4, No. 4.

Flood, L. (1997). Personal communication.

Galinsky, E., Howes, C., Kontos, S., and Shinn, M.B. (1994). *The study of children in family child care and relative care.* New York: Families and Work Institute.

Helburn, S., Culkin, M., Howes, C., Bryand, D., Clifford, R., Cryer, D., Peisner-Feinberg, E., and Kagan, S. (1995). *Cost, quality, and child outcomes in child care centers.* Final Report. Denver: University of Colorado.

Schweinhart, L.J., Barnes, H.V., and Weikart, D.P. (1993). *Significant benefits: The High/Scope Perry Preschool study through age 27. Monographs of the High/Scope Educational Research Foundation, 10.* Ypsilanti, MI: High/Scope Press.

United States National Commission on Excellence in Education. (1983). *A nation at risk: The imperative for educational reform: A Report to the nation and the Secretary of Education, United States Department of Education.* Washington, D.C.: National Commission on Excellence in Education.

U.S. Department of Labor, Bureau of Labor Statistics. (1988). Labor force participation among mothers with young children. *News,* 88–431.

U.S. Department of Labor. (1993). *Employment and earnings.* 40(1). Washington, D.C.

Whitebook, M., Philips, D., and Howes, C. (1989). *Who cares? Child care teachers and the quality of care in America.* National Child Care Staffing Study, Child Care Employee Project.

Winstead, P. (1994). *CoZi Monitor.* Summer/Fall Quarterly 1994, Volume II, No. 2.

Zigler, E., and Finn-Stevenson, M. (1989). Child care in America: From problem to solution. *Educational Policy, 3,* 313–329.

CHAPTER 7

Why I Will Succeed and Why I Must Not Fail

Erwin John and Iman Jameelah

Erwin (left) with Dr. Comer. Photograph by Laura Brooks.

Erwin and Iman are part of several interlocking collaborations that support them and propel them toward a bright future. Among the collaborators in these endeavors are mothers, teachers, and after-school programs designed for children like them.

Why I Will Succeed *by Erwin John*

I talk with my mother. I told her that I was thinking about becoming an obstetrician. She said, "As long as you set your goals, I will always be there to guide you."

I also talk with my sixth grade teacher, Miss Touré. She helped me get into an after-school program called "I Have a Dream." I had Miss Touré for two years—fifth and sixth grade. In the fifth grade, she told me that I could join an after-school program, but I didn't believe her, so I didn't go for the interview. She told me that I'm a very good student and I could do it. She believed in me, so I started believing in myself. In the sixth grade, I just decided to go for the interview.

The program meets every day after school from 4:00 to 7:00. We do our homework and get help in certain areas that we need help in. And Miss Touré still phones every once in a while to check up on me to see how I'm doing.

Miss Touré asks, "Do you still feel that you want to be in the program?" At a certain point, I didn't feel like it, so I told her, "Not really." And she said, "Trust me on this one. I will help you out. All along the way, I will always be there. So any time that you feel like dropping out of the program, just give me a call before so I can give you another reason to stay in." Our phone conversations are about 20 minutes. She will talk for a good time and I will listen; then I will talk and she will listen.

She keeps saying that she is proud of me. She told all the teachers at my old school how good I am doing and that she is real happy for me. So I was feeling that I should keep on doing this so someone will always be proud of me.

Why I Must Not Fail *by Iman Jameelah*

I'm the first child in my family who is going to college. There was a lot of pressure on me. Since I was young, I've been a straight A student. If I came home with bad grades, it was like I let everybody down. The one fear I had was failure. I could not stand to fail. For someone important who cares about you, like your mother, to be disappointed, that's the worst thing in the world.

CHAPTER 8

I Can Fly

Christine Emmons, Belinda Carberry, and
Members of the Isadore Wexler School Community

Photograph by Laura Brooks.

A Yale researcher and the principal of Isadore Wexler Elementary School sat down with
staff, parents, community volunteers, and students to reflect on the transformation that
has taken place over the last several years. Their thoughts ranged widely over all aspects
of life at Wexler, but their efforts and hopes are probably best realized in the statement of
one child, who said, "There's really nothing else to say about Wexler. It's just a good
school."

On the day that the renovated gymnasium at Isadore Wexler Elementary School was dedicated in honor of Sylvia P. Hare, who had been the physical education teacher at the school for over 37 years, the children gathered in the gym with teachers, parents, and well-wishers. The children's rendition of "I Believe I Can Fly" seemed to be an appropriate metaphor for what was taking place at the school: an attempt to soar toward a vision that they see in the near future. This is the story of how Wexler learned to fly.

This chapter is a first-hand report drawn from interviews and focus groups conducted in 1997 with the principal, staff, parents, and students of Isadore Wexler School, which is situated in a low-income community in New Haven's inner city. Wexler is attended by about 440 students in pre-kindergarten through fifth grade. In 1997 about 87% of students were African-American, 11% were Hispanic, 2% were White, and 0.5% were Asian-American. Wexler has created a Family Resource Center, which provides "comprehensive, integrated, community-based systems of family support and child development services linked to public schools." The Family Resource Center is grounded in Dr. Edward Zigler's concept of The School of the 21st Century: that strong support services for parents and children beginning from birth facilitate healthy development and learning.

The focus groups and interviews brought together members of the school community who worked together. Members of the School Planning and Management Team (SPMT) shared their experience of how the management of the school has changed through their efforts. Members of the Student and Staff Support Team explained their role, how it intersects with the role of the SPMT, and how the renewal of the Comer Process affects the way they work. Staff members and parents who work in the school on salary or as volunteers discussed their beliefs and perceptions of relationships in Wexler. And fourth and fifth graders spoke to us about their strong positive feelings about school and themselves. They spoke of The Raising Up Club, which motivates students to be disciplined and dedicated learners, of how they are being included in school life as decision makers, and of the fact that their voices are being heard. In addition, three members of the staff who were not currently on committees reflected on how the changes taking place in the school affected the entire staff. They described Wexler staff as very warm, accepting, and helpful. They noted that now that their staff development reflects the Comer Process, it is no longer unfocused and instead has enabled collaboration and consensus.

Penetrating the Culture of the School *by Belinda Carberry*

When I came to Wexler in 1992, I felt that I had to get control and change the culture because the system wasn't working for the children. Student scores on the Connecticut Mastery Tests were low, and student behavior was out of control. The teachers were complacent and pointing fingers at the administration and everybody else, not believing that the problem lay within the school. They felt that we needed to get someone to come in and fix things. So I had to get people to realize that they themselves had to change.

When at first I couldn't penetrate the culture at the school, I wondered if I was the problem. If you don't understand the culture of an organization, you can feel that you're not an effective leader. But once you start looking at all the players in your school, you can figure out the networks: why you can't get past one person, how one person may be connected to somebody else, how there may be a sore feeling between another two people. The networking was unbelievable at Wexler. Staff members had close relationships outside of school—for example sorority sisters, cousins, marriage connections—of which I was completely unaware. The network analysis that I learned at Columbia University really helped me figure it out.

Through faculty meetings, SPMT, and just one-on-one dialogue, I found out that the staff had been through a lot. There had been several principals in the past several years, each of whom had a different personality, different goals, and a different management style. The faculty had come to a point where they felt neglected. The facilities were deplorable, parents were apathetic, and staff felt that their professional development needs were not being met. I had to show them something really special if I wanted their attention and support, so in the summer of 1994, I lobbied to have the building painted and more lights put in. The teachers' lounge was painted. There had been a huge hole in the wall that made it look as though we were going through World War III. The hole was plastered up. The custodian kept the floors clean and buffed. When the lights came on, the teachers said, "Oh! Okay!" and they stopped complaining about the building.

For a while I didn't have anyone to help me to implement the changes. I found a few people who knew that the school was in serious trouble, and I got them on my side. Change was very gradual—there was a lot of pain, a lot of accusing, a lot of just ignoring. Finally, staff members realized that I was there to make changes and that changes were being made. When you make changes, you make some people defensive and you make others happy. Over time, you attract people who want to help. When we finally got the right mix of people, our school really became a beautiful place.

Parents Energize the Whole Process

When I came to Wexler I found eight parents who had been my students in high school, and they wanted to do something. They became our Wexler parent patrol. They came in the morning and assisted the kids with arrival and dismissal. They began to invigorate the PTO, and it wasn't long before we were able to get other parents to assist in the school. That made teachers take a second look at parents.

In the past, the teachers had complained that parents didn't care. But now we had parents hanging around my office and helping me out. When the Family Resource Center was established, I set up a little parent room, and we had parents available at any moment to go to assist in the classrooms and help around the school. Some teachers were really warm and open to parents. The parents energized the whole Comer Process at Wexler because teachers began to see that parents did care. Parents do not come in fussing and cursing and wanting to fight any more, and very rarely do parents come in so cantankerous that we can't deal with them.

Now parents are in the school every day. They answer my telephone, work in the classrooms, help in the cafeteria, assist with arrival and dismissal, and copy papers for classroom teachers. The parents are holding our third annual Snowball Dance for the kids, and they're planning a big Gospel Festival. Parents are involved at every level: planning, making decisions, organizing social activities, and participating at parent events.

The Comer Renewal

In 1992 we called ourselves a Comer School, but we were not faithfully implementing the model. Around 1994 there was a renewal of the Comer Process in the New Haven Public Schools. Our staff began attending the School Development Program (SDP) training at Yale. I had received training in the Comer Process when I worked at the high school level, and I knew I needed some type of governance structure to help me manage the various school activities and make certain that everybody on the staff collaborated and was involved. I changed the structure of the School Planning and Management Team (SPMT) by getting a new facilitator, Sheila Brantley, who was trained in the renewed Comer Process. Serving as the facilitator from 1995 to 1997, she has done a marvelous job of bringing people together.

Those of us who went on the first wave of Comer training had a rare chance to become a team away from the school. We learned that staff from other schools were experiencing the same problems, and we compared notes. Sometimes we found that our problems were not as bad as we had thought because some other folks had worse problems. In addition, we had time to share with one another. It was almost like a spiritual awakening: We learned for the first time what other people from our own building were like. We came back from the training as friends, and we had a shopping bag of new ideas to share and to implement on behalf of kids and parents.

The training had a big impact on many staff members. They began to feel better about themselves. They could compare notes and say, "Well, I'm not that bad!" or "I've been doing that!" or "I can even make it better!" It's a good thing when people can build on what they have been doing already.

I strongly believe that we decided to become a site-based management school because we felt that we could really collaborate, communicate, share ideas, and make a difference together. Site-based management is about ownership and empowering the staff. Because we were faithfully replicating the Comer Process, we felt that we could apply to become a site-based management school. We had a governance structure through which, we felt, we could accomplish anything. Currently we are changing the curriculum by getting parents' input and by selecting and purchasing textbooks and equipment that better meet the needs of our students.

We have a very strong Student and Staff Support Team. We talk about issues arising out of the SPMT meetings. For example, we facilitate support for students with special needs—not just students with special education needs but students traumatized by having witnessed violence. We look at individual cases and also at global issues, and we know how to find resources for families and children; we know exactly where to troubleshoot. We meet every other week, discuss all the kids and families who need help, and develop action plans.

One of the easily noticeable things that we have generated at Wexler is more smiles. People are into hugging now. It's really a happy place. It's not perfect: We still have a lot of work to do, but we have more people on board. Those of us who have been trained believe in the Comer Process. We know that it's important for the SPMT to work collaboratively, that it's important for educators to keep parents involved and make them feel good. We have a few people on staff who still believe the SPMT is not working. Even with this team meeting twice a month, there are times when I have to make decisions to get things done, and we have a few people who still have problems with that. They are the ones who have not been to the Comer training.

Training has played a very important role in changing the culture of the school. I've been a part of it at each stage with the staff, learning with them, experiencing how to let go and let them have some say, but I still think they respect me when I have to do it my way, because they know that I understand the process and I believe in it.

We will have a nearly new building in the year 2000, thanks to the $8.2 million we have received from the City of New Haven for renovation. Staff members from the SPMT have become the building committee, and we are dreaming about our new school and what it should look like. At the beginning of 1998, we obtained a computer lab and Sony Playstations for all third and fourth graders, with software aligned to the Connecticut Mastery Tests. The New Haven Housing Authority and the New Haven Board of Education funded the Sony Playstations. We also now have a Science Discovery Laboratory with science kits, and the library is on line so that students can use the Internet. Monthly staff development workshops on math and science were provided by the Connecticut Academy of Science, Math and Technology in collaboration with Southern Connecticut State University.

Wexler is going to be an information retrieval center for kids where they can go to a technology center and work on the Internet and then go to the science lab and work on experiments. They'll do their writing in the computer lab. Wexler is turning into a constructivist environment in which kids are playing with their learning—not just using paper and pencil. I love to see them building and creating and able to articulate. We're going to have a *wow* school.

Life in the New School Culture *by Members of the Wexler School Community*

How the School Planning and Management Team (SPMT) Changed the Management of the School

Ralph Esposito (staff developer): I've been at Wexler School for eight years, during which the School Planning and Management Team has transformed itself. Right now our SPMT includes staff members, parents, and a variety of community workers. The Team has been the pulse of the school. Our main focus is to keep children first. Our chairperson helps set the agenda for the Team. Our recorder keeps the notes, which are then distributed to the staff. Our time keeper makes sure that we don't go off on a tangent. Our facilitator makes sure that everyone is involved and that everyone has an opportunity to contribute to the topic that's on hand.

The SPMT handles a variety of issues through many subcommittees. For example, we have an academic committee, a budget committee, an audiovisual committee, an attendance committee. The principal is a guide and resource person for us, and the SPMT makes most of the major decisions of the school. We work under the principles of consensus, collaboration, and no-fault.

Deborah Davis (family advocate, Family Resource Center): The SPMT has representatives from the Student and Staff Support Team and the parent group as well as the community, so if folks want to bring something into the school, it comes to the SPMT first. Then the information gets to everyone: teachers, administrators, community, and parents. We know that whatever planning we are doing is going to enhance the quality of life for our children. That, in turn, affects the community. So if a child is succeeding, it's because the family has been touched by it, and if a family feels good about what's going on, it radiates in the child and it also radiates in the community.

Gloria Nobles (first grade teacher): I've been at Wexler for twenty-eight years. All that time, I've felt that I had something to say, but no one was listening for many years. Now, because I'm part of the SPMT, people are listening.

We are a site-based managed school, and we are handling big money. We're basically managing the school. I think the main thing is that we feel good about having a say in what happens with the finances and the other aspects of the school because we know best what needs to be done here. We could not have taken on the responsibility without the SPMT.

Teasie Blassingame (third grade teacher): There was a time when I really didn't want to think about what was going on. There were principals here who wouldn't let us take on issues. They always said that they were in charge and we were just little people. But Mrs. Carberry knew a lot about the Comer Process. After she got here, people were invited to become a part of the SPMT, and they were willing. We have representation from almost every grade level at our meetings.

Gloria Nobles: The SPMT discusses issues dealing with the Comprehensive School Plan. If the topic is not child centered, then we don't discuss it.

Sheila Brantley (special education teacher and SPMT chairperson for the first three years of renewal): The SPMT looks at the Comprehensive School Plan to see if we are following it and if we're on target. Then we decide who is going to take what action. We can make sure that children, decisions, and projects don't fall through the cracks.

Deborah Davis: Mrs. Carberry's roles are shared with the SPMT. When one person has a thousand jobs, only ten get done. With the SPMT working as well as it's working, the thousand tasks are all addressed.

Ralph Esposito: It goes back to the idea of the village again. No one person has the burden of coming up with the right answer. We're a team. In the past, teachers were isolated in their classrooms. Now there is collaboration and sharing across the whole staff. We come to a consensus about the need first; then the committee follows. That's resulted in more productive work.

Gloria Nobles: A powerful example of the effective use of the SPMT occurred in 1996. It was evident at the beginning of the school year that we were going to lose Mrs. Carberry. She was going to be placed in another school. In the past, we might have said, "Oh, that's terrible!" and that would have been that. We would have kept quiet and accepted whatever decision was made. But this time a group of teachers felt so strongly about it that they said, "Hey look! We're in a process here, and you're taking away someone who is helping us move along that process." Teachers, staff, and parents all went to the superintendent, and he changed his mind at the eleventh hour and allowed us to keep our principal. We didn't threaten. We were positive and professional, and showed the superintendent how the SPMT was a vehicle of expression for the whole school. I give great credit to Dr. Mayo for recognizing that, because he's in the position where he could have said, "Forget it, guys! Go back! I'm the superintendent!" But he was committed to the SPMT and the Comer Process, and he sat and listened, and we convinced him to let us keep our principal.

Community Involvement

Ralph Esposito: Because we now have a large SPMT with a variety of people, we have access to greater resources for the children. When we discuss their needs, we bring in outside agencies such as Project Hope, Varick Church, and the Yale Child Study Center Outpatient Clinic. For example, we discovered that the children in the early curriculum needed listening skills. When we found a program that would help them, Varick Church came in and helped us pay for that program. We have used it during the summer for two years to help prepare our children for the Connecticut Mastery Tests, and we have seen their scores improve. When one of our committees proposed the Science Discovery Laboratory to Dr. Mayo, he approved $3,800 worth of supplies. To improve science instruction we're now in a partnership with Science Park and Kodak Corporation. Our committee wrote a proposal and received a $50,000 grant to help develop one of the first science discovery labs at the elementary school level in the state of Connecticut.

Teasie Blassingame: Volunteers from Yale come and perform science demonstrations for kids during and after school.

Hazel Johnson (community volunteer): My husband comes over from Varick church and reads to the kids twice a week. I'm here all the time to do anything that needs to be done. They know that I am always here to support them in what they are doing. My husband and I now run a grandparent program for the school.

Teasie Blassingame: For the Snowball Dance, Mrs. Johnson was in here decorating the gym.

Ralph Esposito: We used to assume that we need money when we need support and resources, but I think even more important is the support we get from the community. For example, Mr. and Mrs. Johnson come in and they're smiling and happy and always supportive. That's a morale boost for me. I know I'm not in here alone.

Parent Involvement

Deborah Davis: Parents are in the classrooms not just to make copies but to sit with groups of children and assist them with their math or language work. They are hired and paid for four hours a day, but quite a few of them are here long past the time. They remain in the classrooms or assist wherever they are needed. That has made a strong impact because, once again, it's not the top-down theory where you're being dictated to; it's the whole community working together. We have the parent room, where we have another program going on for half of the day, but the parents have ownership. When parents come in, teachers are greeting them with a lot of hugs; there is a lot of conversation and good feeling. The teachers are calling parents, saying, "Your child had a wonderful day today. I just wanted you to know that."

Sheila Brantley: This week two parents brought their child's homework in because the child had forgotten it. I made a point to reinforce the positive action to both parent and the child.

How the Student and Staff Support Team (SSST) Addresses Children's Needs

Belinda Carberry: The Student and Staff Support Team (SSST) looks at the global concerns of the school and at individual student and staff concerns. We address the health needs of the children and their families, and support them through crisis interventions. When we first started, we had the principal, the nurse, the social worker, the school psychologist, and a few other staff members. But for true collaboration, we began bringing in community people to support us, such as social workers from the Yale Child Study Center outpatient department and members of Project HOPE, a local counseling group working with children and families in crisis.

Sheila Brantley: A representative from the SPMT sits on the SSST, and vice versa. This way each team is kept informed about the activities of the other. If the SSST representative can't be present at the SPMT meeting, she will give me a hand-written report or ask that I mention the current SSST activities. At the SPMT, we don't discuss individual students with whom the SSST is dealing, but we do clarify for staff members how they can refer a child to the SSST.

And we deal with global issues. For example, I went to a conference in Washington a couple of years ago on breast cancer and was shocked by the statistics for African-American women compared to White women. I said to myself, "You've got to do something." So I took the initiative to get trained so that I could make a workshop presentation on breast cancer to our staff and parents in the Family Resource Center. Olga Streater, our school nurse at that time, formed an asthma workshop in which doctors and nurses came in after school and parents and their children could come and learn more about asthma. We also help parents understand about Ritalin. If other team members see a need, they ask, "What can I do to help?" No one sits back and waits for directions from the top. The information is truly coming up from the bottom.

Deborah Davis: Two summers ago, to address the discipline problems that we experienced at the close of that school year, we held a focus group during the summer: Mrs. Carberry, a couple of the parents, a couple of folks from the community, and I sat down and really focused on discipline policy. Out of that came our Pride Center, which is our version of in-house suspension, where the child has the opportunity to work on the eight steps of conflict resolution with an adult—one of our parents who has been trained by Centra Hall and Christian Alexander, clinicians from Project HOPE. The teachers also had input in that because they shared information on Project Charlie (a social development program) and from other trainings that they had received.

Judy Murphy (school psychologist): Last year, the Family Resource Center sponsored a job fair as well. We invited many outside agencies because we wanted to offer the community a lot of resources.

Sheila Brantley: For the whole renewal process, focusing on mutual respect within an organization has allowed an atmosphere in which people can approach each other and say, "Here is the situation. Now, what can we do?"

Jim Maturo (special education coordinator): When we had disruptive students everybody clamored for them to go into special education. Now we have a more comprehensive approach that refers children to other support services before being referred to special education.

Belinda Carberry: One of the challenges for me has been to make certain that the services for each child are coordinated. It took awhile for us to determine how to do this well.

Deborah Davis: We have folks sitting at this table who are comfortable enough to go beyond the walls of this building to provide services to children and families in the community. Parents are also becoming more accountable for their children's behavior and participation in school. It's been a long, long time since I've seen parents fighting or screaming in the hall.

Sheila Brantley: The Family Resource Center has led workshops for parents and parent professionals on a variety of topics including team building and communication: How do you work with your teachers? How do you communicate? Everyone has been very appreciative.

Belinda Carberry: We've hired a lot of parents and trained them on the computers. They have been able to come in and work before and after school. We have lunch mothers and about eleven or twelve parents in the classrooms. When I first told the staff about the Comer Process and that we were going to start the Comer training, I drew a funny-looking umbrella with many spokes and I said, "We need the SPMT to keep these spokes up if this umbrella is going to be functional." I think that image helped folks see that there is a humungous job to be done here at Wexler. I think that's when people started to take responsibility and start the Family Resource Center, revitalize the community school, reach out to the community people who wanted to help us, and welcome CoZi and the Family Campus. (Family Campus is an initiative started by the mayor of New Haven, the president of Yale, and the superintendent of New Haven Public Schools to "promote the healthy development and educational success of all New Haven's children.")

No-Fault Has Changed the School Culture

Sherman Malone (a clinician with Project HOPE): I think that no-fault is the hardest principle in the world. In the larger social environment, finding fault with somebody else is often used as a substitute for taking responsibility yourself. But our school has developed beyond that.

Sheila Brantley: No-fault helps people to see that a problem is not a reflection on them personally, even if it's their child who is acting out and upset. "It's not personal" is such a difficult concept for people to understand as they move toward solutions. I have worked hard to get the children in my classroom to understand no-fault, consensus, and collaboration. Sometimes they will even throw it back at me! A student will do something totally inappropriate, and I will say, "I can't believe you did that!" and they will say, "No-fault, Mrs. Brantley!" and that's good, because it helps me focus on the behavior. Then I say, "All right. It's the behavior that we are dealing with," and I think, "It's not personal."

Deborah Davis: It also eliminates the baggage and the wasted time of going through who is to blame. When no-fault is established from the very beginning, then the field is wide open for solutions.

Sheila Brantley: Consensus is also a matter of honoring the person that has an opposite opinion or a different goal. They have the right to their opinion. You're just asking that they hear you describe your whole picture, that you hear about theirs, and that you thank each other for your opinions so that you can see a balance. In the very beginning in our school, consensus diffused the feelings of some people who were very set in their ways. Now they give their opinion, get a fair hearing, and give a fair hearing.

Parent Involvement Has Changed the School Culture

Patrina Covington (parent assistant): The whole community has access to the school for their needs.

Ida Greene (parent assistant): Wexler is a learning station, and it's where parents and teachers can come together one-on-one to solve problems. I feel comfortable with the staff, with the principal, the teachers, and everybody that I come in contact with.

William Bellamy (PTO president, security guard, parent): I myself went to Wexler and graduated from here. I can definitely say that there has been a change over time because now people are coming more and more together. They're not just teachers. They're not just parents. They're a community.

Patrina Covington: Now we are reaching out to the parents to get them to come into the school, to attend PTO meetings and different events, to associate with the teachers and the principal and staff, not to be afraid of them, and to relax. At one time it was very hard to get the parents involved. Now we have meetings to try to think of things that would be interesting for the parents. If you don't have something interesting, the parents may stay away because, I think, they are afraid. They might say, "Well, I shouldn't be there except for emergencies with my child or if I have a meeting with the teachers." Regular involvement in the school is one of the steps to becoming a parent assistant. This is our first year of the parent teacher aide program. The children see us in the classroom and they respond to us. Most of us are from the neigh-borhood, and the children say, "I know them!" It seems to me like it's a more relaxed atmosphere.

William Bellamy: Getting parents to attend the PTO is a problem. Sometimes we have a big turnout, sometimes not.

Emma Rodriguez (parent, now part-time paraprofessional): But when we have fundraisers they all come out and help.

William Bellamy: In the past, parents would just come in and drop their child off and keep right on going. Now we stand around and grab a news-paper, we converse about what's going on. More parents are starting to come into the school. When parents or teachers see that a child is not in class or that something is wrong, they will attend to that even if it's not "their business." They will stop and say, "What are you do-ing? You know better than that."

Troy Long (parent assistant, substitute teacher): Parents also support substi-tute teachers. When a substitute comes in the kids say, "Oh. We're go-ing to have a nice day today." But if I see the substitute coming down the hall with a line of talking kids, I'll stop and say, "Hey, what are you supposed to be doing?" and they will straighten up.

Emma Rodriguez: We adopted that village model for all of our kids whether we are the teachers or parents. "It takes a whole village"—we enforce that here.

How Student Feelings Have Changed

Floyd Haywood (student): Mrs. Carberry asked each of us to write down what we want for the new school. I wrote down that they should have a bas-ketball court, a swimming pool, a playground.

Natrice Williams (student): Teachers help you when you need help. If you don't get what the teacher is talking about, she will come over and ex-plain it to you privately. If you do get what she is saying, she still comes back over to see if you are on the same track that she put you on. When you get good grades, you get to be in the Raising Up Club, and you get special privileges, like going ice-skating. [Any student who raises his or her grades to the next highest level also becomes a member of the Raising Up Club.]

Terrence Biggs (student): If you have an F, you can't be in the Raising Up Club.

Cheryl Hargrave (student): If you have good grades and don't have good be-havior, you can't be in it.

Natrice Williams: You can't be in it if you fight, get suspended, or curse at the teachers and talk back.

Terrence Biggs: I don't pick on younger people anymore.

Natrice Williams: We have to set an example for them so they won't try to fight every five minutes.

Terrence Biggs: If I get in trouble at Wexler, they give me a counselor to talk to me. If I tell him something important, he can't tell nobody unless I want him to. And if I got kicked out or something, he could help get me back in a different program.

Cheryl Hargrave: There's really nothing else to say about Wexler. It's just a good school.

Translating Theory into Reality

Louise Gugliotti (kindergarten teacher, not on a committee): One of the changes is greater focus on being team directed and working collaboratively. We have had retreat-type activities with the emphasis on implementing, revising, and polishing the Comprehensive School Plan. The thrust of the past overnight retreat was also to get the grade levels working together, special and regular education teachers working together, and really checking out whether the Comprehensive School Plan met the students' needs and the city curriculum framework.

Marcia Herring (special education teacher, not on a committee): The special education department now works cooperatively with the grade levels. It is integrated into the mainstream. We have meetings together and go on field trips together. Special education planning and services are no longer stuck in a closet. At Wexler, special education is accepted as a part of the school. I try to work with the second grade. We do the same science and social studies units. We share videos and other materials. I am going to a workshop next week on inclusion, so we will be able to include the special education children more with the regular education children.

Debra Liburd (fifth grade teacher, not on a committee): Yes. In order to work collaboratively, you have to get together to talk with one another. I think that retreat did that very nicely.

Louise Gugliotti: The curriculum per se has not changed as the result of the Comer Process, but the thrust has changed. [Changes in the curriculum have since extended to content as well as thrust. The Essentials of Literacy Program, Saxon Math, and the Rigby Reading Program are all currently being implemented at Wexler.] The curriculum is now presented in any way that the child can grasp it. Staff members make sure that the curriculum is presented in such a way that it is a positive, successful experience for the child no matter where the child is academically.

Debra Liburd: I notice that everyone at Wexler has manipulatives in their classrooms and particular objectives that help with concept formation, and that's great.

Louise Gugliotti: Prior to the Comer Process, it seems like we just went through the same thing over and over again but no action was taken. I see a little bit more action going on now.

Marcia Herring: We have the Family Resource Center now. We have the new library. We didn't have a library for years. There were books there that were older than I am! We also have a Media Center.

Louise Gugliotti: We got the money for the library through a Library Power grant. Last year was our documenting year, so there was a researcher at the Library Power committee meetings all the time.

Marcia Herring: Parents came in and worked in the library. They also redid the whole Media Center. They did painting and carpentry and created activity centers for the children.

Louise Gugliotti: We can also order things that we think are customized for our children's needs. We have to be responsible for the budget and doing all the things that come with it. It's a lot more work, but we can have a bit more say in how our school is going to function. However, it's not as customized as I had envisioned it to be. I thought that we could say, "At Wexler we need to have smaller class sizes because of the experiences that our students come with," and so far that hasn't happened. That's something that I'm hoping may result from site-based management.

Marcia Herring: Another major thing that has happened is that the second through fifth grades now have a parent assistant for four hours a day. It is wonderful having parents in the room, seeing what's going on and being able to help.

CHAPTER 9

Making a Good School Better

Norris M. Haynes, Cheryl McKenzie-Cook, and Wendy Piggot

Photograph by Laura Brooks.

In 1994, SDP was adopted by the premier school of the Republic of Trinidad and Tobago, the Queen's Royal College, and soon will be implemented in twenty-six schools in that island nation. Despite differences in culture and school structure, the SDP has much to learn from QRC's experience with the program.

Trinidad and Tobago is a Caribbean nation of 1.2 million ethnically and culturally diverse people of African, East Indian, Chinese, Middle-Eastern, and European backgrounds. The islands' religions are also quite diverse: Roman Catholic, Anglican Episcopalian, Methodist, Hindu, Muslim, Shango, and Spiritual Baptists (the latter two are indigenous religions with African roots), and an assortment of other Protestant and evangelical groups. Trinidad and Tobago is the most southerly of the chain of Caribbean Islands, just seven miles from the Venezuelan mainland. It is 1,864 square miles in area. The economy is among the strongest in the Caribbean and less dependent on tourism than that of other Caribbean islands. The country produces oil and natural gas, and has one of the world's largest deposits of asphalt. Trinidad is internationally known for being the birthplace of calypso music, soca rhythms (a combination of soul music and calypso), the steel band, and a very special brand of carnival, as well as for being the home of the hummingbird and the scarlet ibis.

Over the past thirty years or so, the availability of quality elementary and secondary education for all of the country's youth has been of national concern. New approaches to education, therefore, always interest our educators. This chapter tells the story of SDP's first three years in the capital city's leading secondary school—the Queen's Royal College.

The Queen's Royal College: Background

Based on the British system of education, the term "college" in Trinidad and Tobago means a middle-and-high school that includes Forms 1 through 5, which in the United States is equivalent to grades 7 through 12. At the end of Form 5, students take either the General Certificate of Education, Ordinary Level examination, which is prepared by Cambridge University in England, or they take the Caribbean Examination, which is prepared through the University of the West Indies. The school also includes two years of pre-university preparation in what is called a "Sixth Form, Lower and Upper Levels." These two years are equivalent to the freshman year of college in the United States. At the end of the Upper sixth year, students take the General Certificate of Education, Advanced Level examination, administered by Cambridge University, England, which determines who may matriculate in the local university as well as who receives the prestigious and highly competitive National Island Scholarships. It is often the case that students with the General Certificate of Education, Advanced Level are exempted from having to take the SAT for admission to an American University.

The Queen's Royal College (QRC) is one of the more prestigious public middle-and-high schools not only in the Republic of Trinidad and Tobago but throughout the Caribbean. It was the first school outside the United States to adopt the School Development Program. The school serves a representative cross-section of students from various socioeconomic, religious, and ethnic groups. The elegant and beautiful school building is a 127-year-old German Renaissance structure located on the western perimeter of the Queens Park Savannah. Rising above the skyline is a majestic tower, and superimposed on the tower is a big, faithful clock whose melodious chimes have signaled the beginning and ending of the school day for over 100 years. This structure, truly a national treasure, is listed as one of Trinidad and Tobago's historical monuments.

Historically an all-male school, QRC in recent years has admitted female students in the sixth Form. The school is very well known for its high academic standards, the large number of National Island Scholarships it has received, and its outstanding record of success in football (soccer), cricket, and other athletics. It has traditionally been among the top three or four schools of choice for many parents and students.

However, the rapid expansion of the State high school system in the 1960s led to the transfer of many of the school's most experienced teachers to administer newly created schools. As a consequence, the academic performance of QRC students showed a precipitous downward spiral, and the school experienced a dramatic decline in its prestige and national standing and a slow decline in its appeal. This concerned many in the QRC community, and they became determined to see QRC regain its former glory.

The SDP at the Queen's Royal College
by Cheryl McKenzie-Cook

Prior to the introduction of the SDP, since about 1987, the climate in QRC had begun to improve through the efforts of many stakeholders. Many structures and practices already in place in the school were similar to those promoted by the SDP. For example: Deans and year coordinators collaborated with the principal in administering the school. The principal also had an established link to the management committee of the PTA, which was very active and provided continuous assistance in fund raising and organizing social events. The alumni group known as the Queen's Royal College Old Boys Association represented a vitally important interest group of past students and also provided some funding assistance. The school also had a guidance counselor who, though part-time, had been able to establish a supportive climate and system for students in need, as well as provide guidance and counseling services to individuals and groups. In addition, over the years, some very successful initiatives, groups, and programs had been developing for the whole child such as peer mentoring and peer tutoring programs, as well as Form level (grade level) teams for supporting students' academic development.

One of these initiatives led to introducing SDP into the school. A Form teacher experimented over a two-year period with class parents and students, the guidance counselor, and a few other teachers on a program aimed at bringing out the obvious potential of the students. The parents were taken through a parenting program to enable them to provide effective support for their children. The students were guided through a program of personal development, goal setting, and study skills. The results were spectacular. The parents and students formed such strong bonds that they became an extended family that looked after students' needs, and the students performed exceptionally at the national exams as well as in leadership roles and in many other co-curricular areas.

Therefore, when I first heard of the SDP, it was with absolute confidence in its likely success that I sought to find out more. I was joined by three other enterprising, enthusiastic women who were determined to make a difference to the national education system—Esla Lynch, Allison Hamel-Smith, and Gloria Nelson. We found our way to Yale, where we met Dr. Norris Haynes, the research director of SDP. Imagine our surprise and joy on discovering that Dr. Haynes was, one, Trinidadian, and two, an alumnus of QRC! It took very little persuasion to convince him that he absolutely had to help his country of birth and his old school to put this program in place. Dr. Haynes said that he felt that he was "embarking on a new journey of professional and personal renewal and growth in a country, an educational system, and schools that in my formative years helped to shape who I had become. I was returning to give back some of what I had received and to share the powerfully transforming ideas and principles developed by Dr. James P. Comer."

Student Development *by Norris M. Haynes, Cheryl McKenzie-Cook, and Wendy Piggot*

SDP is a student-centered program, and thus student progress is a very real measure of the program's success. As Michael Thompson, an ex-QRC student currently in his second year on scholarship at Yale University, says about the SDP:

> Before SDP, the principal and senior teachers would make all the decisions and *then* they would inform the parents and students of what the decisions were. There wasn't any system where students could actually suggest things. I guess prefects [student advisors appointed by staff] had the opportunity to

complain if decisions made were not working, and *hopefully* the senior teachers and principal might take these complaints into consideration and change things, but it was unusual that someone would actually come and address the students and parents about it and get feedback from them. Now students are finally part of the decision-making process.

A lot of kids in high school go off track and start getting involved in everything from drugs to promiscuity, and there's only so much that a teacher can do. In most cases, parents have far more influence over their kids than a teacher would, so with the parent's involvement a problem has a better chance of being solved.

The QRC students have shown encouraging signs of inspiration and leadership. The first two student representatives on the SPMT, who were products of the pre-SDP experiment, set the pace together with their classmates. They were comfortable with their obviously equal status on the SPMT, and very ably represented student concerns. Their challenge was to ensure that information flowed easily and quickly to and from the students, particularly those in the lower school, and they accomplished several truly significant achievements. For example, they successfully argued on behalf of the Upper Sixth Form students that an examination at the end of the Christmas term was not in their best interest. Also, senior students gathered and presented to the SPMT an analysis of student needs that resulted in rooms being assigned for after-school study. Training in conflict resolution, leadership, and co-counseling was conducted for senior students. Students from the school were more and more outstanding as representatives of the national and international student voice.

Two outstanding examples of student empowerment and leadership are the hockey team's remarkable success and the formal inclusion of music in the school's academic program. The school has always prided itself on its achievements in most local sports, but there had been no hockey for some time. Teachers, parents, or Old Boys usually coach and manage these teams, but for some reason, there had been no one to mentor the hockey program. Then, in 1996, a new teacher expressed his willingness to do this. The team was doing well in the national competitions when the teacher/coach left the school. That seemed to be the end of that. But no, there was on the team an extremely talented 15-year-old player who decided that he could not allow all the effort to be wasted. So he stepped forward, filled the breach, and trained, coached, and captained the team. Many players were older than he was, but they had no problem with his assuming the leadership. As of this writing, the team has won the national competition for several years.

Student empowerment has also affected the music program. Music theory is part of the school curriculum in the first three years. However, what the students consider as real music is the 100-member Scout Band, which is considered the best school orchestra in the country, provides many members of the National Youth Orchestra, and regularly sweeps the instrumental class prizes of the National Music Festival. In the Band, the older students teach the younger ones, and the musical director is usually a senior student.

With a fine understanding of their new voice in the school, two very talented senior students, one of whom was then the musical director of the Scout Band, successfully demanded that they be allowed to take music as part of their official academic program. This was the first time that this had happened in the school, and it sparked a number of the other students to demand of the administration that they, too, be allowed to take the Cambridge University GCE Music exams as part of their official program. The question, of course, was: Who would teach all these people? The staff member who teaches music was already stretched to the limit. The students arranged a compromise with the music teacher, so that he would teach the theory and they would continue teaching each other the practical! Between thirty and forty students are now involved in this program, studying music in addition to all their other subjects.

The finest example of the new student consciousness is the newly revamped Student Council—the Student Empowerment Association (SEA). Early in the implementation of the SDP, a Student Council was started. The school already had a well-established prefect body drawn from the senior students. Problems developed because there was no working model to use as a comparison and because the general body of students were not sold on the benefits that could come through such a Student Council. Some of the prefects were not willing to give the younger ones an equal voice. In 1995, however, some of the senior students decided that they needed to take affairs into their own hands. Without the knowledge of the adult stakeholders, they discussed the matter with all the students in the school—including even the youngest—and came up with this new organization, which has representatives from each class and each year so that all the students now have a voice. They then presented this *fait accompli* to the administration and the SPMT. Every week the SEA holds meetings at which students' concerns are discussed, matters brought up at the SPMT are examined, and students' input is sought. All SEA representatives, even the 11-year-olds, have equal status. Recently, when because of exams and graduation the student representatives on the SPMT resigned, the SEA voted to replace them with two students of their own choice instead of with the holders of the official positions of head prefect and president of the Student Council, which had been the previous system. They have been so effective in voicing student concerns that staff began to feel uneasy about this new empowerment. Fortunately, the SEA has been stoutly defended by the principal, the SPMT, the newly vocal Old Boys, and enough staff members to ensure both the survival and impact of the collective student voice.

Closely linked with this new movement is the publication of the school newsletter. This started off as an effort of the public relations subcommittee to open the lines of communication between the SPMT and the stakeholders. One of the parents working on this subcommittee, who is a communications specialist, persisted in seeking the views of students. Suddenly, nobody quite knows how, the students have taken over the publication, to the great delight of the subcommittee. The only input from the adult stakeholders is that they edit the articles' style, print the newsletter, and occasionally write a guest article. Adult stakeholders are often interviewed by the students, however. Now it seems that the adults have to get their own newsletter!

This reawakening of the student voice offers the greatest hope for improving the school and is most pleasing to all those who have been struggling for the last few years. Most of all, though, it pleases those Old Boys who feel passionately that this represents a resurgence of the role that the school played in its glory days, of providing models of excellence in all fields and particularly in the area of national leadership.

The QRC Foundation

The catalyst for much of this renewed passionate interest in the affairs of the school is the work of the QRC Foundation. It has been painfully obvious for some time that lack of funds is the stumbling block to all the grand plans for refurbishing and retooling QRC. The QRC Foundation was specifically set up to address this need. The first goal the members set themselves was to reduce the school's dependence on the government for funding for recurrent and infrastructural needs. We needed to get major funding, but we had no previous experience in doing this. However, there are parents and Old Boys who certainly have the expertise. The Foundation decided that the first move would be to hold a number of social events that would achieve several objectives at the same time. The events could provide funding for urgently needed repairs to the plant (first of all to the staff facilities), for training for all the stakeholder groups, for equipment and materials, and for salaries for extra staff. Even more important than this was the impact on the social climate through bringing the entire QRC community together to allow for achieving the SDP philosophy of "family togetherness."

The musical concerts were deliberately planned to feature the very best professional artists, known nationally and internationally, with the intention of marketing QRC to the general public as the center of excellence in all areas, including the very best in Trinidadian musical culture. The concerts always start with a fifteen-minute segment featuring student musicians, as a reminder that *they* are the ultimate beneficiaries of the SDP program.

Ainsley Mark, a former government senator, an Old Boy of the college, and chairman of the QRC Foundation, describes a true SDP environment as a result of the concerts: "There's a new spirit in the place. People you haven't seen since they left the college three decades ago are there, reminiscing. There is a coming together, there is an understanding of the problems of the school, there is a willingness to assist."

Parent Involvement

The promotional activities of the SDP have definitely heightened parent involvement in the school. For example, at the very beginning, it was thought necessary to collect some baseline data since there were no systematic procedures in place for collecting, collating, or using data other than academic scores. Undaunted by the absolute lack of experience or funding for even the paper (far less for extra personnel) but armed with loads of enthusiasm, a group of parents and students administered school climate surveys to students, parents, and staff. Parents paid for the paper; the cost of the printing was donated; parents distributed questionnaires to other parents; students administered questionnaires to the student body. The parents were so involved and eager that the response to the questionnaires was overwhelming. Other examples abound. Dr. Haynes conducted a whole-day seminar for staff. To allow the school to remain in session, parents, senior students, and interested members of the community volunteered to help, and everything went very smoothly. As a result, parents have continued, on a limited scale, to volunteer their help in the classroom.

Around the same time, the annual October Affair was held. This is a fund-raising/social event coordinated by the PTA but organized at the class level by the teachers. Because of teacher nationwide industrial action (strike and performing the minimum of work acceptable) at that time, the parents decided to take a greater role and undertook much of the organizing. The event was very successful.

Parents have also organized study groups for the students and workshops and seminars for themselves, and—in family groups—they have refurbished and painted some of the classrooms.

The Old Boys (Alumni)

Bringing the family closer together has resulted in several marvelous initiatives by the Old Boys. For example, the school now has several new computers, which will go a long way toward ensuring that the students are equipped to face the twenty-first century. A fund has also been launched to restore the beautiful, historic, but crumbling Hall. In many ways the Old Boys are now enthusiastically involving themselves in the life of the school, and more and more of them are trying to get their sons into the school.

The enthusiasm extends even to the Old Boys abroad. For example, Dr. Brian Harry, an Old Boy who lives in the United States, where he is an organizational management specialist, offered his experience and expertise to facilitate change and assist the school with strategic planning. Realizing that staff buy-in was a tremendous challenge and was critical to the success of the SDP, he used his vacation time to come down to work with the QRC staff. He succeeded in motivating and assisting staff to come up with personal and professional action plans and promised to help them write a proposal for funding. This has generated a renewed feeling of enthusiasm and hope among the staff.

Public Profile

The massive marketing and promotion that is done nationally to promote the QRC Foundation concerts and the general public relations program about SDP have given QRC a very positive, high profile in the media and, consequently, in the minds of the general public. The media have been very good to us. They all say how much they admire what we are doing. Gloria Nelson, parent and SDP facilitator, sums up the effects:

> Wherever people meet you—in offices, in the supermarket—they are telling you, "I want my son in QRC." If you read the sports pages on any day, chances are that you will see somebody from QRC making the headlines. In the *Junior Express Newspaper*, QRC is always among the schools highlighted for youth achievements. The school with the most talked about activities right now is QRC.

Challenges

Although these achievements have been very heartening, it takes time and resources to bring about significant change in any system. We have faced many formidable challenges as we attempt to change traditional attitudes, beliefs, and behaviors. For example: It was evident from the start that the Ministry of Education was very supportive of the program, but this support was not cemented by conferring formal authority on the SPMT or the designated in-house program facilitators. This led to some uncertainty about the way in which the SPMT and facilitators could or should operate within the school structure and thus to some skepticism, resentment, and opposition from some stakeholders. Experience shows that substantially more time and effort should have been spent on communicating the intent of the program and on sensitizing all stakeholders, *particularly the teachers.* From the beginning, the teachers should have helped to develop and structure SDP at QRC. Our failure to do this resulted in a prolonged buy-in period and a possibly avoidable, emotionally exhausting experience for many of the stakeholders.

David Simon, one of the teacher representatives on the SPMT from the start of the project, analyzes the challenges this way:

> Teachers found it difficult to understand why it was important to have people outside of the teaching community involved in the whole process of education or why we needed to import a *foreign system (SDP).* Moreover, effective communication has been a major challenge, which unfortunately has led to a great deal of mistrust within the school community.
>
> In my opinion, what the Comer Process allowed us to do was to put a proper structure to the things (such as parent involvement, peer mentoring, and coaching) that we had always had in place (these were now part of an organized way of operating, based on a consensus view of what was best for students and the school as a whole). However, the threat of familiar ways of operating being changed or taken away could be one of the reasons why individuals were so fearful. I guess that change is always going to trigger fear in some individuals.

The Principal's Perspective *by Basil Jordan*

Because change is often frightening to people, one has to think: How do I change the attitudes of all these people, all these stakeholders? In particular, how do I change the teachers, who are such an integral part of this process? Unless one can get their attitudes right at the beginning, it becomes extremely difficult for the Comer Process to succeed. This was really our major problem.

Several key ingredients, issues, and considerations related to implementing SDP should receive special mention.

Getting the Major Stakeholders Ready

The staff decided that it was going to take its own time to make its own change. We understood quite clearly that the staff were not ready for the change and immediately started to prime the staff to make them ready through staff seminars, group meetings, and meetings with psychologists.

From my point of view, while these were useful, success could be related only to the environment that existed. People who were unwilling to change found faults with the seminars and other initiatives. It got to the point that we were wary of suggesting or arranging further activities for staff.

My purpose was helping them to let out all this bottled up resistance. The Comer Process worked beautifully whenever it was given the opportunity to be put to the test. There was a marvelous blend of energies and spirits and minds. So I think the staff decided it was going to take its own time and make its own change. I don't think that any entity can change before the time is right. Therefore, I have to own that the first mistake must have been our anxiety to implement the Comer Process *now*. We should have got the staff ready. I recommend that everyone spend the extra time to get the major stakeholders ready. In other words, I would hasten slowly.

The Parents Fit in Beautifully

Our PTA was our most developed extracurricular organization. In the Comer Process, the Parent Team is one major element of the SPMT, and our parents fit in beautifully. They were more ready than anybody else. This was an advantage in that there was one group that was willing to get things going but a disadvantage because the slower-moving staff became somewhat uncomfortable with the level of energy and motivation that the parents demonstrated. Managing this healthy tension and converting it into positive, collaborative energy is a typical challenge in the process of change.

I Don't Think the Old Boys Have Been the Same Since

The Old Boys Association has been a very supportive group throughout most of the years that they've been around. However, the Association, which was very interested in helping establish SDP at QRC, originally represented a very small subgroup of Old Boys, and they did not have a very good link with the school. One could say that the Comer Process pulled them into the family; they couldn't be halfway in and halfway out. They began to see clearly what other family members were doing, what the PTA was doing, what other Old Boys were doing. This gave them dynamism. The Comer Process does not allow you to be a supporter from without. You've got to join hands, feel the pull, become so much a part of it that it becomes a part of you. The Old Boys Association became involved. In addition to that, a number of Old Boys formed a QRC Foundation. I think that the energy of all of these groups together—their physical, spiritual, and emotional energy—made it possible to imagine the unimaginable. Before, we were so restricted. Suddenly our hopes and dreams didn't appear ridiculous because of the linkage of all these groups. So we're really talking about a lot of good things happening.

The Students Gave Us All the Support We Could Need

Students are extremely aware, much more so than most people understand. They understood a lot of the difficulties that we had. They understood a lot of our inability to get things going. Some were influenced by negative teacher attitudes, but by and large they gave us all the support we could need. When a few more things are put in place, the student body is going to be changed almost overnight because they're ready for it.

Teams and Committees: Too Much, Too Soon

The Student and Staff Support Team has played an important role in pulling together counselors and psychologists. Quite frankly, I'm disappointed that it hasn't gone further, but viewed in another way, it *is* one of the two major groups that at least got off the ground (the other being the SPMT). I was disappointed that we didn't get a games committee moving. Games play an important part in the extracurricular life of the school, and sports is often the area where you can reach many whom you can't reach through the purely academic methods. I think the major problem in many of these committees was again the way we introduced it, in that too much was happening too soon. Even though it isn't working as it should be, the social climate group has hosted a number of events that have revitalized the school. People look forward to the next event at QRC. Foundation events, for example, have gotten better, more sophisticated, and more beautiful and it's all just part of this new movement that has been inspired by the Comer Process.

The Biggest Gains

When one looks at it, we've had so much to gain. I think we have just touched the surface because the biggest gains are the personal gains in which each individual feels more secure, more understanding of the system, and more understanding of life. There are immense possibilities for what we can do for teachers—for example, trainings and sabbaticals. We just need to get the teachers to the point of understanding the tremendous implications and positive spin-off for them.

The Comer Process advanced the system of Parent Core Groups. These formed links between the groups of parents of each year's students and have provided a mechanism through which parents can be mobilized at a moment's notice to organize activities. In essence, each year group should have a set of parents who can look after students' needs on the six developmental pathways. We do admit that at this stage all the groups have not benefited to the same extent. Some are stronger than others. One hopes that in time the stronger can pull in the weaker and the whole system can then move forward.

Cheryl McKenzie-Cook, of course, has to be especially thanked for the work that she did with a particular group of fifth Form students before we had heard about the Comer Process. As a result of this, these boys became perhaps some of the most socially and academically well-rounded students in the school. By the time the SDP was actually introduced, when they had got to the sixth Form, they truly wanted to give back some of what they had gained.

Some Lessons Learned *by Norris M. Haynes, Cheryl McKenzie-Cook, and Wendy Piggot*

One interesting challenge that we have had to face is adapting to our culture a process that was developed for a different culture. In the case of the SDP, this is vital since so much depends on culture: the way things are done, individual perspectives, and traditional relationships among stakeholders. We tried at first to do things exactly as described by the Yale model. Three years or so later, these are some reflections on the process:

David Simon, a teacher representative on the SPMT, observed:

> Because of our history, the whole idea of collaboration and of all stakeholders having equal voices is the most important cultural challenge. If you go back historically, we have always had clearly defined leaders and followers. Nowadays we find some teachers who cannot deal with students giving their views openly.

Chairman of the QRC Foundation Ainsley Mark, on the other hand, sees the greatest difficulty as arriving at decisions through consensus:

> Given the difficulty of making decisions through consensus, I feel that we will have to go back to having a chairman who will listen to people but firmly guide the process. I think that the way we manage meetings has to be more reflective of how things are done here.
>
> We have never done a school plan because traditionally we have never associated managing a school with following a plan—in terms of developing our budget, in terms of setting priorities, and in terms of how we use resources: from where, and to do what, and so on.

In spite of these reservations, it must be remembered that the school already had a long tradition of some collaboration and consensus decision making. It was however, framed by the overall authoritarian structure within the national culture. The future challenge for us will be to encourage stakeholders to rethink, reassess, and recognize the benefits of a more open communication and decision-making structure as well as more effective planning.

One interesting cultural difference is the level of parent interaction in school. There is still a widely held belief among parents in Trinidad and Tobago that since education is so important their duty is to do whatever is necessary to help their children succeed. This is particularly so in QRC, where the parent input has always been high. Since SDP was introduced, this interaction has increased at all levels.

As parent and SDP facilitator Gloria Nelson says:

> Hitherto, you had some parents coming out and assisting, and some who felt that they had something to give, but there were others who felt, "I can't be like them because I am not educated, I don't have the financial wherewithal, and my thoughts and ideas would not be welcomed." Now, from the time they enter Form One, they are told, "Look, this is where you can help: There are three or four levels of parent involvement, and you can fit into any level where you feel comfortable. They have taken that to heart. Most of them fit into one or another of the levels, and they come out and do their part.
>
> And it's across the board. We have found that some of the best ideas have come from people who are of lower economic status because they understand the needs and wants of their kids and their own needs and wants. People are coming forward to do things to assist the school without feeling out of place.

Our future efforts will have to focus on revitalizing the parent core groups and realizing the tremendous potential of this coordinated resource. All in all, we will have to step back a bit, invite much wider participation in the planning process and focus more intensely on staff preparation.

The View Ahead *by Norris Haynes*

SDP has helped tremendously in getting Queens Royal College back on track. Ainsley Mark refers to the revitalization at QRC as "turning this old battleship around." The analogy to a battleship is an important one when one considers the legacy that QRC has had in producing success even in the face of overwhelming odds. Mr. Mark is devoted to seeing the College recapture and restore its record of success and valor, both in the academic and the social development arenas. The Foundation should go a long way in helping to provide for systematic, enduring, financial, and moral support for the school's mission. With an air of excitement, he makes it clear that his personal goal is to see QRC rise to the top again. The most gratifying aspect of the turnaround at QRC—as we find in SDP schools all over the United States—is the sense of vitality, achievement, and wholeness among the students.

A national implementation team has been established. It is led by Mennen Walker Briggs, a school supervisor at the Ministry of Education, and includes Cheryl McKenzie-Cook, Norman Lambert, Gloria Nelson, Esla Lynch, Allison Hamel-Smith, Jennifer Lavia, and Rose Bereaux. The members were trained at Yale and represent a cross-section of professionals driven by their commitment to improve education for all children. In volunteering their time to conduct training workshops about SDP for twenty-six school principals, they are now influencing school reform across the country.

Returning to Trinidad, my birthplace, and to the Queen's Royal College, my alma mater, to introduce and help shepherd the SDP process has been one of the most gratifying experiences of my professional life. It was Dr. Comer's powerful idea that adults who care enough can learn to nurture, support, guide, and challenge children to be the best they can be. Seeing these ideas transcend cultural and geographic boundaries has strengthened my faith in the universality of the human capacity to do good.

PART II

Professional Development and Consultation

Bringing the Program on Home

Jonathon H. Gillette

Once a school community has decided to become an SDP school, the real work begins. It is one thing for a group of adults to want to act collaboratively in the best interests of children. It is quite another thing for those adults to actually collaborate toward that goal. Schools are already very busy places, and the basic demands of the day can be exhausting.

How does a school make a transformation? Part of the answer lies in creating new systems of support for change: professional development and on-site coaching, follow-up, and consultation. Members of the school community need to learn new information, connect that information to what they already know, learn new behaviors, and find reinforcement for those behaviors. All of this requires skillful outside help—help that is rooted in a deep knowledge of SDP theory and practice and a deep knowledge of the particular context of that school.

Part II of *Child by Child* offers a look at that outside help, starting with SDP's national professional development academies at Yale (Chapter 10, "It Takes a Whole Person"). Designed to support implementation, these learning sessions offer essential information and—just as important—provide experiences in doing collaborative work. They also connect local reformers to a larger support network.

Chapter 11, "The Comer Facilitator in Action," and Chapter 14, "Making a Personal Commitment," examine the world of the critical on-site change agents who support principals, teachers, parents, and others as they learn to apply the Comer Process. "The Comer Facilitator in Action," which describes facilitators' experiences in Maryland's Prince George's County, helps answer the question, "What do facilitators actually do?" From a view of a daily planner and from specific examples of activities, we gain a concrete sense of their day-to-day work. "Making a Personal Commitment," which describes facilitators' experiences in Chicago, gives us a sense of the personal challenges of entering a school and creating change— and not being the focus of attention.

Chapter 12, "Charting a Course for Student Success," tells the story of building the Detroit school system's capacity to implement SDP. Although the large grant that supports this effort has been the envy of many, this story reminds us that even with fiscal support, the complexities of building collaborative partnerships can be daunting. This honest account of the struggle to align three very different institutions provides important information about the kind of skills and flexibility that are necessary for large-scale change.

All of these chapters echo the themes of the Comer Process. To make a difference for children, adults must make significant and sometimes difficult changes in themselves, develop relationships with others who are different, and commit to a process of life-long learning. None of us can take these actions by ourselves because they are not about the self. They are about the relationship of the self with the community. And in the process of developing that relationship, we model for our students the same resilience that they need in order to thrive.

CHAPTER 10

It Takes a Whole Person

Professional Development in the Yale School Development Program

Jonathon H. Gillette

Photograph by Laura Brooks.

The adult learning team is clearly struggling. They have been together now for three days and still find working with one another a challenge. Their task is to outline developmental stages based on a presentation and materials in their notebook. It is a group task, and their process is anything but smooth. Finally, one member, a long-time principal from an urban school system, gets up in frustration and says, "I came here to learn about teams, not to be on one!"

Child by Child: The Comer Process for Change in Education. Copyright © 1999 by Teachers College, Columbia University. All rights reserved. ISBN 0-8077-3868-9 (pbk.), ISBN 0-8077-3869-7 (cloth). Prior to photocopying items for classroom use, please contact the Copyright Clearance Center, Customer Service, 222 Rosewood Dr., Danvers, MA 01923, USA, telephone 508-750-8400.

We continually ask ourselves: "What is the best way to teach the School Development Program? What does it take for people to learn how it works and how they can become part of it?" We ask this question because learning about the SDP is not simply a cognitive process. Somewhere along the line people must experience SDP to genuinely understand it. So we have developed a series of structured steps from print information to national training events that enable people to both think about and experience the Comer Process.

In designing ways to teach the SDP, we have been faced with a number of challenges. When you walk into a successful SDP school, much of what makes it successful is not visible—unlike specific classroom instructional reform. Dr. Comer makes the analogy to a beautiful float in a parade: The School Planning and Management Teams and all the other structures and relationships in the school are like the wheels under that float. When things work well, you don't see the wheels; what you see is simply a beautiful school passing in front of you, because those wheels hold the float up and move it forward. Training people to support schools and move them forward is like uncovering the sides of the float, examining what's underneath, and learning how to build and then drive it. That requires not only seeing a school, but also opportunities to talk with practitioners about how they are working and what differences they see.

It is a challenge to communicate the comprehensiveness of the SDP and to make clear the importance of the process as a whole. In the education world today, you can attend specific seminars and trainings on a wide range of topics including parent involvement, school-based teams, coordinated or integrated social services, and school improvement planning. Each is a topic of considerable breadth and content. Yet the SDP is each of these and more. How do we do justice to each component and not overwhelm our listeners? Further, how do we reinforce over and over again that the value is in the connections between the parts of the SDP as much as in the individual parts themselves?

Yet another challenge is communicating the parts of the SDP theory that come from outside the field of education. This is difficult not only because the material may be unfamiliar—few school people know about organizational development and child and adolescent development—but also because it may feel overwhelming. "Our job is hard enough and you want us to do more? Know more?" Thus it is vital to find ways to use the new concepts to help teachers and parents make sense of what they are currently experiencing in schools. It is vital that the SDP frameworks are not just new materials but useful lenses that give them ways to better solve local challenges. This then requires an interactive setting in which information and experiences are shared and re-examined.

Finally, we have the challenge of keeping our training staff close to the real, messy world of schools. Once out of a classroom or school context, it becomes too easy to "should" on people. We attribute too many of our own past successes in schools to our own brilliance and forget the complexity of events that supported those triumphs. Therefore, we require all of the staff that present the SDP nationally to be continually involved in several SDP schools. That humbling reality helps us remain open to the ongoing dialogue with learners that is so vital to the success of our program.

Initial Contacts

How do teachers and parents learn about the SDP? How do they get their school involved? How do they begin the process of implementation? Each of these is a series of specific steps.

People learn the basics of our program through print material. We have a number of print materials available, including this book and *Rallying the Whole Village* (Comer, et al., 1996); a video series, *For Children's Sake*; and our *SDP Newsline* (http://info.med.yale.edu/comer). Anyone can call or write to the SDP at Yale and get information packets. Then it's up to that person to share those written materials with people in their school or district. At a minimum a whole school must become involved; however, we prefer participation by a cluster of schools in the district, so that schools can support each other as they grow and develop. An individual person or group can begin a local campaign to have people learn about the Comer Process using some of our information packets; by attending keynote addresses given by Dr. Comer, Dr. Joyner, and other members of the national staff; and by viewing videotapes, which can be ordered from us at Yale. People are moved by the keynote addresses—they reawaken in educators the reasons why they went into education in the first place and they reawaken in parents both their righteous anger and their hopes.

One of the unique qualities of SDP as a reform process is that it directly acknowledges how much feeling there is in the everyday interactions of people in schools. If we do not work with the feelings of the professionals on the front line, they are going to become hardened against the feelings that they need to have, or to withdraw from their work, or to become less motivated to take on appropriate challenges. So in disseminating information about the SDP—even in the keynote addresses—we are already modeling the ways of interacting that support our school reform process.

As the school or schools begin to digest the materials, we ask them to go through a "discernment process" and collectively begin to make some decisions: How does this Comer Process address the important issues and challenges our particular students face? In developing an interested community in this way, they have already begun to live the Comer Process of collaboration.

Site Visits

The next step is to visit one of our "demonstration" school sites. We don't designate schools as "exemplary." We don't believe in exemplary schools. I remember too well reading groups labeled "the bluebirds" and "the robins," and if we're talking about schools and individual children and adults developing without labels, why should *we* label schools? Rather, we're aware that people want to see schools that are in different stages of implementing the Comer Process and also in different geographic regions. Therefore, a demonstration school has to be willing to:

Decide whether to become a demonstration school. The SPMT members say that showing their school is an opportunity to explain to others what their work is, which has a way of deepening their own commitment. But showing a school takes time. Do they want to spend that time on another school, or do they need to do work with their own school?

Share the underside. It's in the struggles and failures that schools can learn a lot that's important. The visiting school people want real dialogues. They don't want to just have a presentation that is all nice and clean or all "smoke and mirrors."

Share all their data, no matter what the data have been, no matter what the data are. In doing this, they give their visitors a true picture of what their first steps were and how they have progressed, no matter where they are in the implementation process.

We have a Regional Training Center in Prince George's County in Maryland and demonstration schools in Prince George's County, in Cleveland, in Guilford County, North Carolina, and in Dade County, Florida. That's a wide range of contexts from very urban through somewhat urban to almost rural in some parts of Guilford County and Prince George's County. So people can see an SDP school whose context matches that of their school.

The school visit itself is designed to engage experienced practitioners in a discussion about the Comer Process with other practitioners who are considering embarking on the process or may already be into the process at some level in their school district. There's very little theoretical overview, but there's a lot of nuts-and-bolts conversation. It's parent to parent, principal to principal, teacher to teacher, community person to community person. "What did you do?" "How did this happen?" "What are the things that you learned?" "How was national SDP useful?" "What else in your district has been useful?"

From investigating and identifying with another school in a similar context, people can see how the SDP framework may suit them. They begin to ask, "If this is the solution, what is my problem?" and "Here's my problem; is this really the solution?" We work hard to make sure that these site visits provide specific examples in specific, concrete contexts so that school people and parents can have direct experience and end their visit with a fuller knowledge of the process and a sense of the challenge of applying it. Over the years in school reform there have been enough "magic bullets" and powerful, charismatic presentations of new programs that spread because of marketing rather than critical analysis of school fit. We want to make sure that our site visits give people a clear sense of their next few years with SDP so that they won't look back later on, as they have so many times in the past with other initiatives, and say, "That turned out not to be the right thing for us."

The root issue, it turns out, is not raising the money to get computers into the school or which math curriculum to use. The root issue is becoming galvanized about our children and about what is in the best interest of children. During these site visits, people really begin to see that good education is a human relations issue. SDP helps people develop knowledge in other areas as well, but the most important component of the process is a set of very specific interpersonal skills. By the time people go back to their own schools from a site visit, they've seen other educators in action using those skills and they've seen how far they've managed to move their schools.

Orientation

After the site visit, people who are interested in learning more attend a three-day orientation, which meets for two days at a regional training center and for one day at a school. It combines the site visit with a broader overview.

From the very beginning of the orientation, beginning with the bus ride to the training center, we take every single possible moment to model what can happen in a learning community. In Prince George's County, for example, the Comer facilitator has people on the bus meeting and greeting up and down the aisles for the hour and a half ride to the Piney Point conference site. By the time they reach their destination, people who had been a little anxious are relaxed with each other and excited about what's coming. They are already getting to know each other, beginning to exchange addresses, beginning to ask questions—"Why are you here?" "What are you interested in?" "What strengths and ideas do you bring that I may learn from?"—beginning to build a learning community.

The orientation itself contains much more extended dialogues and specific skill-building activities. It also uses an instructional design that is part of all our national events: *adult learning teams.* We assume that people come to our trainings with a wealth of knowledge, skills, and experience. Adult learning teams are a means of tapping into that knowledge and giving participants a forum in which they can connect to the Comer Process and contribute to it. The format is similar to the cooperative or group learning activities model in many classrooms: Participants are assigned to a group of six to eight people at a round table. The set of activities for each day is structured so that participants take in information and then do an exercise that applies that information.

An adult learning team requires working collaboratively. You can lecture people about collaboration, but when they actually *need* to collaborate in order to learn, they have a personal experience of how much richer their learning is because they have truly listened and shared with each other. In addition, training in collaborative teams gives people the vehicle to talk about what's important to them, rather than what's important to the presenter. The teams are always mixed, by role and by geographic location, so participants are learning with people they don't know, people who have different roles. They have to practice reaching across and creating a working relationship. By the end of the time they've been in those teams, they have priceless experiential knowledge of being equal team members, whether they're superintendents, principals, teachers, support staff, or parents. In working together, they have learned the collaborative power of the Comer Process. Some people find this to be totally new. They're used to being the boss, or being able to go off and close their classroom door and accomplish things on their own, or simply doing what they've been told to do. The adult learning team, therefore, is not just a tool to bring in past experiences; it's a vital means for people to experience equality and mutual respect. Later on, when they're back in their schools, implementing the process and getting frustrated trying to get a group of people to work together, they can refer back to their adult learning team and replicate their own experience. We also find that many people go back to their own faculty, get their faculty into teams, hand them some Comer material, and create dialogue groups right from the beginning of the implementation process.

National Leadership Training

Now that they have some knowledge of the Comer Process, schools and districts can begin to implement it. In order to ease this complex undertaking, additional staff development events have been designed specifically to support school- and district-based implementation. Designed and produced by the Yale staff, these sessions enable a key team of school staff, parents, and central office allies to learn more about the SDP, gain a greater set of skills, and create plans for making implementation a reality back home. From the very first activity, members face the challenge of consensus, collaboration, and no-fault, when they're working on a process or a problem.

The team members come as students to the national trainings and go back as leaders to their own schools and districts. At home they help work with their colleagues, who have very little time. In a sense, the fully trained team is like my preacher, who spends all week studying scripture and comes to the pulpit to give me some lessons about it. I take time on Sundays to listen and learn, and then I think about it for the rest of the week.

In addition, SDP needs these local leaders who have in-depth knowledge, who spend time thinking about what the possibilities are for their schools, and who make connections in their schools. Each time the local leaders come back for the next training, they are actually sharing their knowledge with SDP schools across the nation because the Yale staff members take the new knowledge out to the school districts in which they work. So new knowledge is continually circulating from the national office to the local districts and schools, from local schools and districts to the national office, from district to district, and from school to school.

At the SDP's national professional development academies at Yale, as many as twenty districts will be represented in the same training, as opposed to one or two districts at a regional training. That broad context gives people many opportunities to network and share. One of the things we do is a "share fair" at which people put up newsprint displays that say "I'm proudest about . . ." and "I'm desperately seeking help on. . . . " We encourage people across contexts to share their success stories and to help people in the areas that they're struggling with. The Yale staff can give general guidance, but the best exchanges often are those among the participants as they swap information about how a particular best practice in one school or system matches a need in another school or system.

Week One: Leadership Training 101

In the first training, which usually takes place in April or May, the Yale staff members present the overarching framework of SDP and our best new information about practical applications within each of its components. This occupies the first three days. On the fourth day, we guide applications. For example, all the parents go off and work on how they will take this information back to their schools and what parents' roles are in an SDP school. We don't want people to leave feeling very enthusiastic, get back to their school setting, and then say, "What was it I learned? I don't remember any specific application." So an expert facilitator supports parents as they think about how specific ideas will work back home in their own school. For example, participants learn the basics of child development when they learn the six developmental pathways. Here's a typical dialogue within an application group:

Principal: Well, how do I take the first step with these pathways? I don't have any idea. My teachers are already so overwhelmed with all the mandates that they're currently given.
Facilitator: What are some of the mandates that you're under?
Principal: One of the things that we're mandated to do is a character education program.
Facilitator: How would that character education program fit the six developmental pathways?
Principal: Oh, I see. So if I go back to the group that's in charge of character education, I could introduce the six developmental pathways there, and that would extend their ability to work.
Facilitator: And that's just one entry point of applying the six developmental pathways.
Principal: I get it. Okay. Well, how do I go back and even tell my staff about it? Who should do that? How do I get the people who came for training last year to meet up with me? How do I connect in with some of their work?

On the last day of training, there is a sharing of specific take-home activities and a celebration of the fact that people have learned, have had some important experiences, have named some of those experiences, and are now ready to go back and try some very specific things. The key here is that each member of the Yale staff who is presenting at the training is connected with a group that's returning home. For example, people who came from Cleveland know that they'll see me back in their district next fall and that I'll be checking in with them, supporting them, and helping them connect what they've learned at the training.

They also know that we're all going to come back to Yale in February for a second week in which we do a couple of very specific things: (1) We share what worked and what didn't work; and (2) We get a sense of what the next steps are. Then it is time to address the school's culture, tying SDP into what's going on in the classrooms. Therefore, child-centered planning is the focus of that second week of training.

Week Two: Leadership Training 102

We hold the second week of the Leadership Training in early February so that schools will have had time to struggle with some of the early elements of implementation. We want to be able to talk about their experiences as well as deepen their knowledge and skills. Early in the implementation process, schools often find it possible to change some structures but see little, if any, shift in school culture. The 102 training is specifically targeted at deeper knowledge of the cultural change elements of SDP.

Thus the content of the week is the SDP framework known as Child-Centered Planning. Central to that framework is the role child and adolescent development plays in teaching and learning. The SDP requires a change in the way people understand what goes on in schools—a cultural paradigm shift—from an emphasis on cognitive testing to an emphasis on development as a basis for achievement. After an exposure to the child-centered framework, one entire day is spent deepening knowledge of development and one entire day is spent integrating that knowledge with a school improvement planning process. Simultaneously, there is an emphasis on developing the interpersonal skill of giving and receiving feedback. Of all the skills that help a team go forward, comfort with feedback is the most critical. If people haven't had any comfortable, respectful experiences of giving and getting feedback, they either don't know that it's possible or they don't know how to do it. So the whole second week of training is designed to give people in-depth experiences of feedback. Again the participants are in adult learning teams, but this time it's different: Each team is watched by a process observer who gives feedback every day about how the team is operating.

On the first day, teams do a set of activities, and the feedback is generally pretty gentle: "I noticed this; I noticed that." It's descriptive as opposed to judgmental, and it takes on only a couple of issues. As the week progresses, the team members begin to give feedback also, and the process observer gives more detailed responses, pointing out times when group members have difficulty, and encouraging participants to do the same.

On the fourth day, the process observer joins the group for the entire morning for a review of the week. Never before have the participants had that much time to delve into the operations of a learning team. That morning elicits rich experiential learning about giving and receiving feedback, as well as passion about the Comer Process. When these team leaders return to their home schools, they are much more knowledgeable, skilled, confident, and energized.

Principals' Academy

The third national leadership academy held at Yale is the Principals' Academy. Principals are in a unique position, so all principals come to this academy having attended the Leadership Training 101. During 101, they are with their school's team and learn as much as their own school's facilitator. Because of the demands on principals' time, we don't always require principals to come back in February for Leadership Training 102, though we're finding now that many choose to come.

Participants typically come to Principals' Academy in the July after their first year of implementing the Comer Process in school. There are two very specific reasons for this. First, the concepts taught in the Principals' Academy sound simple before you try to live them. After you've been under pressure, on the line, responsible for a building, and at the same time trying to be collaborative, the concepts have a richer resonance. Second, it is hard for principals to be able to see that SDP is not just about governance but is deeply connected to instructional issues. Spending a year in the process prepares principals to share more deeply at the Principals' Academy.

Again, the structure is adult learning teams. The content for the week is specifically devoted to understanding oneself, one's personal leadership style, and the demands of the Comer Process. For many principals, the training stirs up a lot of feelings of inadequacy, so we provide a lot of support. Some of them look at "star" principals who lead SDP schools, and they think, "I could never do that." But that may be simply because they're looking at someone whose style is not their style. Pat Howley, an SDP implementation coordinator, has used the Myers-Briggs Inventory, which describes sixteen different styles. We have had exemplary principals in every one of those styles. A principal can be very extroverted or very introverted and still run the process well. Principals need to be affirmed in their own style even while they're being encouraged to stretch, and we make a commitment to support them in their journey toward making a learning community that's based on true collaboration.

The second, essential element of the Principals' Academy is discussion and activities focused on instruction and curriculum alignment. Instruction is not a separate reform entity; it is critically connected to the SDP process. At the academy, principals are introduced to the balanced curriculum process, one that aligns curriculum from grade to grade and with city and state requirements, all the time keeping children's and adolescents' needs in the forefront and balanced via the six developmental pathways. As a result, their understanding and commitment to the process deepen profoundly.

Subsequent Training

Some of our principals and facilitators return to Yale the next year for a second level of training. The principals move from the structured setting to one in which they work in a self-guided study group process and focus on some particular content; for example, how to help make connections between all the activities that are happening and the SDP process. Important issues emerge. The principals call upon senior staff to come work with them throughout the week, but they manage their group themselves. This has been remarkably successful because at that point principals don't need to be told anything. They need to work with issues that are important to them.

During the same week, the facilitators do a similar kind of self-guided study group to deepen their knowledge of how different schools are applying the process. Then they can share that knowledge in different districts, offering the specific content expertise that people need. Conversation in facilitator groups sounds like this: "What's another good conflict resolution process?" "What's another good problem-solving process?" "I've got a school that can't come to closure on issues. What are some techniques to help them collaborate on a decision and stick to it?" "I have a person who's very bitter and difficult. What are some strategies for getting to that person, even though she's a brilliant teacher?" "I have some kids who are really needy in this area, and I can't find a community resource that matches them. Do you have any ideas?" Facilitators trade specific strategies, all of which strengthen their own personal experience of the Comer Process and, therefore, implementation.

Supporting the Whole Person

In every week of training, from the orientation session through the most advanced work, if school people are not deeply moved, we've missed the ball. It's not unusual for tears to flow at our trainings. That's because participants are moved from the center of their being. If we're not working with the whole person in each school—if we're not helping them work with the feelings they have about children as well as the thoughts they have about schooling and about themselves—then we're unable to tap into the power that is right there: the human power.

It is feelings that get in the way of schools' operating better. Sometimes we're told that SDP is "touchy-feely"—as if that were easy! In fact, those words—touching, feeling—point toward the most difficult aspects of school teaching. How do we come to grips with a passionate teacher who discovers every week that many of her children have been physically abused? What do we do with her feelings? Are we to act as if those feelings are not affecting her? And if we act as if those feelings are not there and are not important, what are we in the business of doing? Touching and feeling are not gratuitous. They're central.

This is a human enterprise. Schooling requires teachers to touch their students deeply, which requires them to open up to the experiences that their students bring to school. And we all know what is happening to kids. How dare we not address and support the psychosocial, emotional elements of interactions in schools, by giving teachers and administrators an opportunity to express their feelings, by honoring their feelings, by working with their feelings?

All of us should be able to work in a supportive environment. When reformers barge in, ignoring other people's feelings, telling them what to do, and never listening to their experiences, it's as if they are trying to open a drawer with a sledgehammer. People feel assaulted.

Listening isn't easy. I have come to tears many times just talking with people in schools because their feelings overwhelm me. But if we don't acknowledge those feelings and work with them, then SPMTs will just be dead, mechanistic management. The lifeblood of the Comer Process is that people can be heard, can share, can be supported, and can know that they're not alone in dealing with the tremendous challenges that require expert effectiveness, on the line, every day.

The key to change in any school is people's ability to have hope, not fantasy. Real hope creates energy, a feeling that anything is possible. People gain that sense of hope through their connection to a larger movement and from seeing things happen in places where other people said they could never happen. That's what a movement is about.

This larger connection provides resilience in the face of numerous setbacks, and there is no school in the SDP that didn't have early setbacks. It ain't easy! The national movement supports the local school leadership, and the continually arriving new members of each school group are reminded that they can do it: "It does happen. It takes time. Talk to these people. It has worked here."

In all of our teaching experiences, in all the ways people learn about the program, we have tried to model every element of the process. It is a rich, co-constructive process, and it takes all parts of the human experience to make it work. It involves people really talking and listening to each other all the way along the line, sharing their expertise and insights—committed partners in this essential endeavor to make schools as good as we can imagine them to be.

References

Comer, J.P., Haynes, N.M., Joyner, E.T., and Ben-Avie, M. (1996). *Rallying the Whole Village: The Comer Process for Reforming Education*. New York: Teachers College Press.

For Children's Sake (http://info.med.yale.edu/comer).

SDP Newsline (http://info.med.yale.edu/comer).

CHAPTER 11

The Comer Facilitator in Action

*Jan Stocklinski, Beckie Roberts, Sheila Jackson, and the
Comer Staff of the Prince George's County Public School System
in Maryland*

Photograph by Laura Brooks.

*The facilitator is an essential part of the SDP, embodying the guiding principles,
supporting individuals and teams, and feeding back to other facilitators across the
nation ideas and solutions that individual schools develop for themselves. This chapter
follows SDP facilitators in Maryland's Prince George's County through a typical week
in several schools, as they use their expert skills as collaborators, mediators, mentors,
and inventors.*

A Personnel Vacancy: Facilitator of the Comer Process

Description: Specific duties will include but not be limited to:

- Coordinating the implementation of the School Development Program in 3–7 schools
- Program planning in conjunction with the Comer Process director, Instructional and Pupil Services supervisors, principals, and area supervisors
- Working with School Planning and Management Teams to develop and assess Comprehensive School Plans
- Working with Student and Staff Support Teams
- Working with PTAs and their Executive Boards
- Planning and implementing staff and parent in-service training at the school sites as well as countywide
- Infusing cooperative learning into the instructional program
- Assisting in/and working with the research and evaluation component of the Comer Process
- Modeling demonstration lessons

Figure 11.1: Personnel vacancy notice for a Comer facilitator.

Of the 178 schools in Prince George's County, Maryland, 100 are at various stages of implementing the Comer Process. Thirteen facilitators provide direct service to 44 schools in the "Comer Network." The other 56 schools are called "Comer Affiliates." They have the opportunity to participate in all countywide Comer training events, but they do not receive direct facilitation.

The facilitators themselves receive extensive training locally and at Yale University as well as ongoing support from SDP's national office. Their mission is to support the implementation of the Comer Process by helping all individuals and teams develop and grow well, keeping children as their focus. Modeling is key to their success in schools. This is a huge undertaking, and yet people accept the challenge and excel. When we have interviewed applicants for the job of facilitator (see Figure 11.1) and asked them about the impact the amount of time required for this position will have on their family life, they have responded: "I met with my family before I applied. They encouraged me to apply and understand the demand." "I have been a teacher all my career. I already work for hours every night." "I have supportive family and friends."

Once on the job, facilitators sometimes include their children in our activities. At annual retreats, the children of facilitators often help out with logistics. At evening School Planning and Management Team meetings, the children of facilitators often read and do their homework or work in the school library with the children of teachers and parents.

The Facilitator's Role in Staff Development

In Prince George's County, Comer facilitators lead many different types of staff development:

- annual district retreat for SPMTs (1,100 participants)
- six Comer orientations (48 participants per trip)
- three half-day workshops for school secretaries (40–50 participants per workshop)
- three day-long trainings for the in-house facilitators (50–60 participants per training)
- five-day class for parents, instructional and support staff (secretaries, custodians, cafeteria workers), and community members (50–75 participants)
- weekend advanced training for demonstration schools
- ongoing staff development in schools
- coaching staff and modeling demonstration lessons.

A Week in the Life of a Facilitator

What follows are the actual experiences of several facilitators during a single week in 1997. The week is in no way unusual, and we have all done versions of what is reported here many, many times. But to focus our story, we are writing as if Jan, one of the authors, did it all. It's a fair way to present the life of an SDP facilitator—any one of whom will tell you that he or she, in fact, does do it all, every single week.

To start writing this chapter, we all opened our day planners. We invite you to peer over our shoulders and take a look as well (see Figure 11.2). Then read on as we point out, specifically, what each entry really means.

Sunday Afternoon: Develop the Week's Schedule

With her day-planner on her lap, Jan organizes the upcoming week. Talking aloud, she says, "I have five schools to schedule this week. One of my middle schools has an after-school School Planning and Management Team (SPMT) meeting on Monday, and the high school has its SPMT meeting on Wednesday afternoon. The only trouble is that I have a 7:30 AM SPMT meeting on Wednesday at one of the elementary schools, so I'll go there before

I report to my second elementary school. I have a Student and Staff Support Team (SSST) meeting on Thursday at my third elementary school. A teacher has just passed away at my second middle school and the funeral is Friday, so I'll be there then to support the building when a large number of faculty will be out. That leaves elementary school number four for Tuesday, which works out well. . . ."

Monday, 7:30 to 9:00 AM: Check in at an Elementary School

At a school, Jan opens the trunk of the car—the "Comer office"—and selects one of the five tote bags; each is for a different school. In the school, Jan meets and greets staff members, students, and parents. She says to a teacher whose body language indicates weariness, "You've had a busy weekend." "No," comes the reply, "I've been greeted with ten things to do at once this morning." "How can I support you?" Jan asks.

In the mornings, Jan troubleshoots problems, checks to see who may need special support, looks for non-verbal language that may reveal the opposite of what people are saying aloud, and greets students with a warm, "Good Morning!" She whispers to a young student who has cut in front of her, "What do you say to somebody when you want to get by?" She calls the PTA president, touches base with teachers, the school psychologist, the guidance counselor, and other specialists in the school; time permitting, she may even phone civic organizations, business partners, and volunteers.

Monday, 9:00 to 10:00 AM: Meet with Principal

Jan meets with the principal for an update on school events and to look specifically at the agenda for the SPMT meeting to be held that afternoon. The principal shares the progress of four siblings who had experienced academic and social challenges in their previous school. The guidance counselor has "embraced" these children, in the words of the principal, providing them with special love and attention, including after-school tutoring. The children are now reading at home on their own. They want to read at home, the mother has said. Jan mentions that this would be good data for the mentoring program. Anecdotes, comments from report cards, and test scores could be used to document the progress of this type of mentoring program and help answer several questions: Does this type of mentoring program work? Do we want to continue it? How does it support the goals in our Comprehensive School Plan?

Parent volunteers have wired the school for the Internet. However, new computers are needed, and a team from the school has been formed to look into funding for them. The principal brings up the challenge of hav-

	Sunday	Monday	Tuesday
7:00			
:30		Arriving and	Meet admin team
8:00		checking in at an	at a **middle school**
:30		**elementary school**	Meet cafe workers
9:00		Meeting with the	Walk the building
:30		principal	and greet people
10:00		Visit 1st grade	Meet 8th grade
:30		Visit 4th grade	academic team
11:00		Meet with curr. &	
:30		instr. subcommitee	Calls, reports, lunch
12:00			Attend SSST
:30		Paperwork and	meeting
1:00		student assembly	
:30		Attend parent-	
2:00		teacher conference	Prepare presentation
:30		Meet with SPMT-	at PTA meeting
3:00	Weekly planning,	chairperson	Travel to **high**
:30	thank-you notes	Attend SPMT	**school**
4:00		meeting	Participate in team
:30			building with 9th
5:00		Meet with principal	graders
:30			
6:00			
:30			
7:00	Work on the	Meet with the	Attend PTA
:30	Newsletter	PTA executive	meeting at an
8:00		board	elementary school
:30			
9:00			

Figure 11.2: Day planner for a Comer facilitator.

ing staff get to the grant office where available grants are made public: The teachers' school day ends between 3:00 and 4:30 PM, and the county office closes around 5:00. Jan says, "I'm thinking that if a team were to go they could split the work and brainstorm while they search. Maybe you could offer flex time for a team to go to the grants office or call the grants office and ask if a person could meet one evening with them."

The principal and Jan look at items on the SPMT's afternoon agenda: an update or sharing of information from each team member ("round robin"), PTA items, volunteer survey summary, staff development for the rest of the school year, special education, and business partnerships. Jan says, "Today, at SPMT, we will be talking about staff development. Will everyone know to bring their copy of the 'needs' survey that was conducted

Wednesday	Thursday	Friday
Meet and greet a visiting school group from another school system at the Comer Office	Meet with a parent	All day staff meeting at the Comer Office
	Help to monitor testing in an **elementary school**	
	Team teach	
	Meet with the 5th grade team	
Teacher coaching		
School Climate sub-committee meeting	Debrief of meeting	
Problem-solving workshop by Student Government Assn.	Staff development committee to plan in-service	
	Attend in-service training on the observation process for Dimensions of Learning	
At home: make calls plan workshops, prepare lesson plans		

at the end of the last school year?" They agree to have all materials available at the meeting.

Monday, 10:00 to 10:30 AM: Visit First Grade Class

At 10:00, Jan enters a first grade classroom. The purpose of this visit is not only to acquaint students with the SDP, but also to model best instructional practices. The students greet Jan with enthusiasm; last year, when they were in kindergarten, she had introduced them to the Comer Process through songs, activities, and poems. In particular, they ask whether she has brought her "magic wand." She used the wand last year to talk about the "ideal" classroom. Each child made wishes with the wand: more sharing, getting along, wishes for their parents.

Today Jan's magic comes from a story written and illustrated by facilitators in the Comer Office called "Comer Kids." She shows the students a picture of Dr. Comer to explain why she is called a "Comer" facilitator. Turning to a picture of a schoolhouse, Jan reads aloud, "Dr. Comer teaches people how to make schools better for children. His program is called the School Development Program."

Then Jan introduces the idea of teams. "A family is a kind of team," she says. "What kind of team work do you do in school or at home?" she asks. After talking about teams with the students, Jan explains the three guiding principles of the Comer Process: Collaboration means we include everyone. Consensus means we solve our problems together. No-fault means we don't blame other people when we try to solve our problems. Together, the class reads a poem about team work and one about talking things through, rather than blaming. Jan ends the period by engaging students in a discussion of these topics, encouraging the children to make connections to their work in school and at home.

Monday, 10:30 to 11:00 AM: Visit Fourth Grade Class

Jan engages the students in age-appropriate team-building activities that will support them in the upcoming Maryland School Performance Assessment Program. The program is designed to assess the performance of the school as a whole.

Monday, 11:00 AM to 12:00 PM: Meet with Curriculum and Instruction Subcommittee

The curriculum and instruction subcommittee has been asked to assess the new math program, but the math teacher is on lunch duty. Jan comments, "Perhaps this is an issue we need to address before we can really look closely at the math program." Noting that the Language Arts Department person is present, the committee discusses developing appropriate writing tasks for the primary grades.

Monday, 12:30 to 1:30 PM: Do Paper Work and Attend Student Assembly

After half an hour of paper work and phone calls, including checking in for messages at the Comer Office, Jan joins the students assembled in the multipurpose room for Perfect Attendance Awards. Given the opportunity to say a few words to the children, Jan closes her comments by saying, "Thank you for modeling that being here every day counts."

Monday, 1:30 to 2:30 PM: Attend Parent-Teacher Conference

As facilitators meet, greet, and work in schools with parents and families, their emphasis is on modeling positive communication to encourage and promote parent, family, and staff involvement. A parent, whom Jan knows, has come in for a conference with a teacher regarding his child's progress. The parent asks Jan to sit in on the conference. In the course of the meeting, the teacher and parent disagree on a course of action, both feeling that they are "right." Jan probes, using paraphrasing and open-ended questions, to reduce the resistance of both the parent and the teacher. She models no-fault problem solving. Through her interjections she keeps the conference student-focused, and they agree on an action plan.

Monday, 2:30 to 3:30 PM: Meet with SPMT Chairperson

Jan and the SPMT chairperson discuss the same agenda that Jan discussed in detail at the morning meeting with the principal. The chairperson had distributed this agenda to all staff members and parent representatives the previous week. Today, the chairperson reviews with Jan questions that she may want to ask, materials she needs, the best seating arrangement for the meeting, and other details necessary to run an effective SPMT meeting. (Jan is also training an "in-house" facilitator. When he is more skilled and confident, he will take over this kind of guidance).

Monday, 3:30 to 5:00 PM: Attend School Planning and Management Team Meeting

Known as an instructional leader, Jan has earned the respect of the school community through team-teaching with new staff and providing in-service training on the statewide student assessments. The school is new to the Comer network, and the nine-member SPMT is in the "fledgling" or "forming" stage. On the agenda: the staff development plan for the year.

A list is circulated to SPMT members that contains staff development needs that were itemized through brainstorming based on an analysis of the school's data. Ideas include in-service training on reading, visits to other schools, coaching on specific cooperative learning strategies, and additional SDP training for the school community. Jan wonders aloud whether these suggestions reflect the needs identified in the Comprehensive School Plan (CSP). She observes that the academic goals of the school are well represented, but such topics as school safety (mentioned earlier in the meeting) are not included. Jan suggests that the team analyze the suggestions to see if they support the goals and objectives of the plan. The SPMT decides to establish a staff development subcommittee to debrief the SPMT after each staff development event and monitor whether these events meet the needs identified in the CSP.

The next agenda item is a debrief of last week's Comer Retreat. Held annually in October for SPMT members, the retreat this year was attended by over 1,000 participants. Each year a new theme is selected by the countywide Steering Committee for this one-day retreat. "Whole Communities—Whole Children: Modeling Matters" was this year's theme. The principal comments that she enjoyed the interactive session called "Teacher-to-Teacher Talk," in which participants explored strategies to add the skills that will be assessed by the state performance assessment into everyday instruction. Another SPMT member says that she found the math session to be very valuable. In that session, the participants learned strategies to promote higher-level thinking in students as well as different approaches for teachers to assess students' progress and to incorporate math into other content areas. A parent mentions that he appreciated the opportunity to spend a Saturday getting to know the staff members and other parents on the SPMT. A decision is then reached on how these learnings will be shared with all the staff.

Monday, 5:00 to 5:30 PM: Meet with Principal

After the meeting, Jan and the principal meet to debrief. One of the issues facing the school is staff development time. There has not even been adequate time to conduct an in-depth workshop on the SDP. They agree to place this issue on the next SPMT agenda.

Monday, 7:00 to 9:00 PM: Meet with the PTA Executive Board

Jan attends the PTA Executive Board meeting to observe and offer feedback on the president's skill as a facilitator. The president, who attended the In-House Facilitation Training Level I conducted by the Comer Office, has been eager for this opportunity. After the Executive Board meeting, the president and Jan meet for half an hour. Jan begins by asking the president for a self-assessment. The discussion that follows includes observed strengths and recommendations.

Tuesday, 7:30 to 8:30 AM: Meet with Administrative Team at a Middle School

The principal and two vice principals meet daily to stay up-to-date on how well the whole school is functioning and to address problems. Jan participates as a part of this team on the days that she is in the building.

The principal begins by expressing concern about some of the teams and their leadership. After some discussion, Jan asks the principal, "How often do you meet with the team leaders? Do you think they have had enough training in the skills they need to be effective team leaders? Would it be beneficial to have a meeting with team leaders to brainstorm their specific job description and assess the skills they feel they need to do the job?" The principal feels that this would be a good idea, and Jan then offers to do the training on effective meeting skills, based on the self-assessment done by team leaders.

Tuesday, 8:30 to 9:00 AM: Meet with Cafeteria Workers

Jan makes every effort to attend each constituency group meeting in the school. During this meeting with the cafeteria workers, she listens to their concerns: The students are very noisy and they constantly touch each other. She encourages the staff members to tell these concerns to their SPMT representative.

Tuesday, 9:00 to 10:00 AM: Walk through the Building and Greet Classes and Staff

Walking through the building, Jan continues to build relationships with members of the school community and can see and hear how they interact with one another.

Tuesday, 10:00 to 11:30 AM: Meet with Eighth Grade Academic Team

This is an interdisciplinary team of eighth grade teachers that discusses how to integrate specific disciplines into one performance-based instructional task (a hands-on activity designed to have students apply what they have learned). The content will be measured on the Maryland School Performance Assessment. Twenty-five minutes have been set aside for a discussion of specific curriculum that must be covered, time needed to cover an integrated performance task, and time needed to plan the task.

Jan lists the different issues on chart paper. She asks, "Can the team first reach consensus on whether or not to do an integrated task, assuming all problems you have raised can be addressed satisfactorily?" The team leader says, "Do we have consensus?" Jan notices a frowning team member and asks if he agrees. He says he needs more clarification on what, exactly, a performance-based instructional task is. Others nod their heads. "Would you like to have an in-service training on performance-based instructional units at the next team meeting?" Jan asks. The team feels strongly that this would be beneficial. "After the in-service, we will be able to determine what resources or information we need to effectively address the concerns we just noted," Jan observes.

Tuesday, 11:30 to 12:00 PM: Make Phone Calls, Write and Read Reports, Have Lunch

Tuesday, 12:00 to 2:00 PM: Attend Student and Staff Support Team (SSST) Meeting

This team is made up of the special education resource teacher, school counselor, principal, psychologist, pupil personnel worker, community special education specialist, and Jan (when she is available). They discuss global issues that have surfaced in the school. Jan asks, "What are the specific data that support the issues we have been discussing?" A thorough review of meeting notes and case studies shows that out of a list of ten items, only five are truly of concern to the school community. These issues will be placed on next month's agenda. Other issues may be sent to other, more appropriate teams.

Tuesday, 2:00 to 3:00 PM: Prepare for Evening Presentation to a PTA Meeting

Tuesday, 3:00 to 4:00 PM: Travel to a High School

Tuesday, 4:00 to 5:30 PM: Participate in Team-Building with Ninth Grade Teachers

The newly formed team of ninth grade teachers has invited Jan for a second session on teaming and team building. As the teachers enter a ninth grade classroom, Jan asks for their assistance in moving the chairs into a circle. In the middle of the circle, she places bright yellow "reminder cards" that read: Collaboration, Consensus, No-fault, and All decisions are made in the best interests of students.

"What do you think your team members should know about you as the team begins to work together?" Jan asks each person. One teacher says, "I understand best when I know the expectations." Another responds, "I understand best when I have the time to think through the problem myself." Jan highlights how important it is to have a feeling of belonging to the team. A teacher talks about the need for quiet when she learns. In response, Jan relates this comment to teamwork: "So you are saying that when the team meets, it is important that there are no side conversations. Is that right?"

Jan asks the team members to complete this sentence frankly: "It bothers me when . . . ." Among the responses are: when team members are apathetic, waste time, are rude, lack important information. Once again, Jan connects their answers to the project ahead: "As you begin to work together, it is important to think about what bothers you when working on a team. Later, we will establish ground rules to govern our team meetings."

After a 25-minute group dynamics activity, Jan suggests that they develop the ground rules. One member volunteers to write the suggestions on a poster-size piece of paper attached to the blackboard. One by one the teachers offer suggestions for ground rules: beginning and ending on time, no side conversations, one-minute comments (no "speeches"), stick to the topic, have a different member record the notes each time, end with concrete tasks and assignments, set the length of the meeting, decide by consensus. Jan then guides the team in categorizing these suggestions into Meeting Guidelines and Dialogue Guidelines. Under Meeting Guidelines, the team places "setting an agenda." "Sticking to the topic" goes under Dialogue Guidelines. Two items don't seem to fit into these categories. "For the meantime, put them into the parking lot," Jan suggests, pointing to a place at the bottom of the paper, "and we'll retrieve them later." The team then shares with Jan that they too frequently rehash topics from previous meetings. Jan responds by showing them a note-taking sheet with a grid on it. The practice at the Comer Staff Meetings, she says, is to record key decisions of each meeting by completing this grid: Topic, Main Decision, Who's Responsible, Timeline. The grid is distributed to team members and kept on file in a notebook.

Tuesday, 7:00 to 9:00 PM: Attend PTA Meeting at an Elementary School

Jan intentionally arrives early for the PTA meeting. She begins to help set up the room and arrange the seats in a semicircular pattern to encourage communication between parents and other participants. On the walls she places chart paper, dialogue guidelines, and the reminder cards. Checking in with the arriving PTA officers, she asks, "Is there anything in particular on the agenda that you would like my assistance with tonight?"

One of the issues on the PTA agenda is how the money gathered in the last fund-raiser is to be spent. As discussion ensues, Jan says, "It sounds like there are a lot of different ideas on the table about how we can best use our fund-raiser profits to support our students and the goals of the Comprehensive School Plan. Perhaps we can chart everyone's ideas and begin to work toward an agreement by prioritizing areas of need." She then guides the PTA through a brainstorming problem-solving process, and they reach consensus on how to spend the money.

Wednesday, 7:30 AM to 12:30 PM: Greet a Visiting School Group

Several facilitators from the Comer Office greet a group of educators and parents visiting from another school system. Since Prince George's County is a Regional Training Center, a satellite training center of the Yale SDP, visitors from around the United States regularly visit to observe demonstration schools in action as well as participate in training offered by the office. A demonstration school is a school that is actively engaged in faithful replication of the Comer Process and is ready to host visitors, share their data with outsiders, and permit visitors to observe SPMT, SSST, and PT meetings. There are usually six such schools.

After a brief orientation and question-and-answer period, the visitors and staff drive to the first school, where they are greeted by students who take them on a tour. After that, the students and visitors meet in a large group to discuss further what they have observed. The students then return to class, and parents and staff meet to talk with the visitors. Typically, visitors observe team meetings and stay for a debriefing. Not only is this beneficial for the visitors, but the kinds of questions they ask frequently cause the team members to reflect more deeply on their own work.

Wednesday, 1:00 to 2:00 PM: Meet with Teacher for Coaching Conference

Jan and this veteran teacher had prearranged a chance to have her observe him in action and then have a talk about his performance. He is clearly enthusiastic. "I'm glad that we've been able to establish a peer coaching program in our school," he says. "It's one of the best decisions to come out of the SPMT for me this year." "You're right," Jan replies. "Peer coaching is so beneficial—it can help all of us to become better teachers. You know, research says that getting specific descriptive feedback and coaching are great ways to help us internalize skills—whether we're in the classroom or on a team."

"Speaking of teams," Jan continues, "you used a variety of cooperative learning strategies when you grouped your students for the different activities. The way you added in the physical team-building activities definitely helped to focus all of that energy that we know our third graders have." The teacher responds, "Since I attended that Comer workshop on child development, I like to try to meet those pathway needs. But I feel like I'm running out of ideas. Sometimes I feel like I'm using the same ones over and over again." "I'd be happy to share some more of my resources with you," Jan says. "Next week, I'll bring some activities I've tried, and maybe we can look at some of your lesson plans together to talk about linking developmentally appropriate strategies with content."

Jan asks the teacher how he felt about other aspects of the lesson. They cover several topics ranging from classroom management style and strategies to an in-depth discussion about effective means of delivering the curriculum.

Wednesday, 2:00 to 3:00 PM: Attend School Climate Subcommittee Meeting

The committee reviews the school's Comprehensive School Plan (School Improvement Plan) in light of the results of the recently administered Process Documentation Inventory and School Climate Survey. The Inventory and Survey were developed by researchers at the SDP's national office at Yale to provide schools with data they can use for planning.

Wednesday, 3:00 to 5:30 PM: Attend Problem-Solving Workshop for the Student Government Association

By teaming with classroom teachers, Jan establishes relationships with students in each school. She works with students in classrooms, cafeterias, hallways, and the community to teach them about SDP and to help them learn, practice, and internalize the life skills and habits that are essential to the Comer Process. Key points of contact are school organizations such as the Student Government Association.

The Prince George's Regional Association of Student Governments is made up of student government officers from schools all over the county. Every year, the Student Government's advisor collaborates with the Comer Office to design and implement training that meets the needs of high school student leaders. On this day, the focus is on brainstorming and problem solving, skills which are required for students to be successful leaders, and on how student leaders can help adult teams value student involvement and input. At the conclusion of the session, each of the more than forty high school student participants leaves with a prioritized list of skills and strategies to share back at his or her school. Their evaluations of the training show that not only is this type of training experience valuable and the networking enjoyable, but also that they already have ideas about their future training needs.

Wednesday Night at Home: Make Phone Calls, Design Workshops, Prepare Lesson Plans

Thursday, 7:30 to 8:00 AM: Meet with Parent

A parent walks in, visibly upset. He begins by stating that he has heard that the Comer Process can help solve problems of school climate, parent and family involvement, and shared decision making. Jan greets him, offers him a cup of coffee, and invites him to sit down. He is clearly emotional as he tells her what happened.

On his oldest child's first day of kindergarten, he took the morning off from work so that he, his wife, and their three younger children could all walk the oldest child to school. As they excitedly approached the school doors, a teacher asked him to drop his child right by the curb, saying, "We'll take him from here. Parents don't come inside. Have a nice day." Later that day, before he picked his son up at the same curb, he spoke to the principal and shared that he felt that the teacher had been rather abrupt to him and to other parents and that such behavior could possibly make parents and community members feel that they are not welcome. The principal replied, "This is what we have always done in order to show parents how to let go and turn their children over to the school."

The parent explains that as the year went on, he made several attempts to become involved in his son's school. He has many skills and resources that he would like to share, yet at every step of the way he has felt unwelcome, mistrusted, and shut out. He feels that the school just wants him to go away until it's time for a fund-raiser or his son's graduation.

Jan describes the Comer Process to the parent. Reminding him that the process is not a "quick fix," she suggests, "Perhaps we can work together to introduce the Comer Process to your son's school as a way to address these and other school concerns." They decide to encourage the principal, a few teachers from the school, and a few more parents to attend the next countywide SPMT Retreat together.

Thursday, 8:30 to 10:30 AM: Help to Monitor Testing in an Elementary School

Criterion Referenced Tests (CRTs) are being administered to the sixth grade students this morning. (With CRTs, student performance is measured against expected standards of academic achievement—instead of their performance being compared to that of others in their age group.) In order to be familiar with administering the semiannual tests and to offer on-site support and subsequent feedback to the teaching staff, Jan helps to monitor the testing.

Thursday, 10:30 to 11:30 AM: Team Teach

Jan models effective skills as a team teacher. One of the new teachers asked Jan to help her introduce a writing lesson that involves helping students make observations. Jan met with the teacher the week before the lesson was to be given, and together they planned a directed teaching activity from the objectives through the assessment and closure. Today is the day when Jan and the teacher are to divide the class into two groups. Jan leads her group to the playground, and the teacher guides her group to the park across the street from the school. Each group records observations of what they see, hear, smell, and feel in their surroundings. When they all return to the classroom they list all the observations, which will be used as details in a writing prompt.

After the students leave for their music class, Jan and the teacher debrief the exercise. "How do you think it went?" asks Jan. The teacher beams as she says, "I've never seen them more engaged. They really enjoyed being involved in an activity in a place other than the classroom, and actually having them use their environment in their assignment (Live Event Learning) helped them see how they should use observations whenever they write." Jan agrees. "Tomorrow," she adds, "would be a good time to introduce the graphic organizer, which shows main ideas and details. That will help them organize information for the writing prompt." "Great idea," the teacher says. "Thanks for all your help."

Thursday, 11:30 AM: Have a Brief, Unscheduled Conversation with the Principal

The principal is new to the Comer Process and has conveyed some not-so-subtle resistance to implementing the process. For example, Jan had been offered a "work space" in a closet that was loaded to the ceiling with boxes.

One time, the principal saw Jan coming down the hall and walked the other way! Not discouraged, Jan has persisted—she's a real pro in the "Velcro method" of staying attached to principals.

Today the principal says to Jan, "I'm going to eliminate the media center specialist position next year." Jan replies, "Sounds like you have given this serious thought. What prompted your thinking?" The principal says, "We need another classroom teacher." "You see no support for instruction through the media program?" Jan asks. The principal responds, "No, I don't." Jan continues by asking the principal, "What are the thoughts of the SPMT on this issue?" to which the principal responds, "I haven't told them yet." Jan suggests, "Perhaps placing this issue on the next agenda as a problem to solve will provide alternative solutions and group support." (As facilitators, we remind ourselves regularly that it takes time, patience, persistence, and support for change to occur).

Thursday, 12:15 PM: Have a Brief, Unscheduled Conversation with the School Secretary

Jan notices the secretary's slumped shoulders and exasperated expression. "You look tired," she says. The secretary replies, "This phone never stops ringing. The office is constantly filled with students, and parents come and go with a thousand questions. How can the principal expect me to get these reports out?" Jan lets her know she's been heard. "Your job is very challenging," she says. "You've got to juggle many tasks at one time and think on your feet." "You're right," the secretary says. "It's hard to stay calm." Jan asks, "Have you and your principal analyzed the reasons students are being sent to the office?" "No, I never thought of that," the secretary answers. Jan starts to brainstorm: "Perhaps we could place this on the SSST agenda since it is a school-wide issue. And about those phones—perhaps you could work with the volunteer committee to come up with some possible solutions. Also, I really would like you to ask your principal about attending the Comer Office's countywide training for secretaries. It will help you work with your school's SPMT and you'll get to share ideas with secretaries from other schools."

Thursday, 1:00 to 2:00 PM: Meet with the Fifth Grade Team

The fifth grade team is having their monthly planning meeting. Their task is to assess the last interdisciplinary unit and start planning the next one. The grade level chairperson opens the meeting by asking a general question, "How do you think the unit went?" The other team members respond with all their observations of the unit and come to the consensus that the unit was pretty successful. Jan makes a suggestion: "Before we start planning the next unit, how about if we look at the test scores from the unit, average student attendance during the unit, and any other quantitative data that we could add to our general observations of this unit." "That might give us a truer picture," agrees the math teacher. "Then we can analyze what worked and what didn't, which will help us plan the next unit," Jan says. The meeting continues with everyone participating in a thorough data analysis.

Thursday, 2:00 to 2:30 PM: Debrief after Fifth Grade Meeting with Chairperson

The fifth grade chairperson meets with Jan to debrief the planning meeting. Jan opens with, "What are your reactions and observations of the meeting?" "I think that I should have structured the meeting instead of just asking for a free flow of observations," the chairperson responds. Jan has some comments and suggestions. "There's value in analyzing teacher observations," she says. "Perhaps charting the observations so that they could be categorized for a closer analysis would be helpful. Then, having another team member pull out the quantitative data prior to the meeting so it could also be recorded might be one way to give structure to the meeting and speed up the process. The analysis that your team did was really helpful. You'll see that when you begin to chart the objectives of the next unit." The chairperson considers this. "You're right. The next meeting will run much more smoothly as a result of our discussion today. Thanks a lot."

Thursday, 2:30 to 4:00 PM: Meet with Staff Development Committee to Plan In-Service Training

The committee consists of six members: primary teacher, intermediate teacher, reading specialist, math specialist, guidance counselor, and a parent. Jan has been asked by this committee to assist them in planning a three-hour in-service training that will address the needs of the students in the school. No other direction has been given. The chairperson of the committee opens by asking the members, "What kind of in-service training will meet our needs?" After some brief discussion of ideas back and forth Jan asks, "What goals have been identified in the Comprehensive School Plan (CSP)?" The committee refers to the CSP and identifies five major goals. Again Jan asks, "Are there already staff development plans cited in the CSP for these specific goals?" Reviewing the CSP, the committee recalls that an in-service training was suggested on strategies that students can use before, during, and after reading. Jan asks, "What data do we have to sug-

gest that there is still a need for this training?" The team examines test
scores, teacher observations, and grades and concludes that an in-service
training on this topic is clearly still needed. Jan says, "What if we analyze
the evaluations from the last in-service training to get some ideas about the
format for this one?" The suggestion is accepted, and the team continues
to plan.

Thursday, 5:00 to 7:30 PM: Attend In-Service Training on the Observation Process for Dimensions of Learning

Dimensions of Learning is an instructional framework for teaching and
learning. The county is currently advocating its implementation in the
schools. In order to support schools, the facilitators participate in as much
staff development as possible so that they can learn what the principals are
learning. Through incorporating specific Dimensions of Learning techniques into their own repertoire (such as employing graphic organizers),
they can model for schools more effectively.

Friday All Day: Staff Meeting at the Comer Office

The thirteen facilitators meet at the Comer Office for their biweekly meeting. One by one, they share their challenges, successes, concerns, ideas. As
a group, they plan and solve problems. They reflect through journal writing. Later that evening or over the weekend, the director of the Comer Office will read the journals and write back to the facilitators. They also plan
countywide staff development trainings, steering committee meetings, and
the annual retreat.

Reflections of a Seasoned Facilitator

On this particular Friday afternoon, Jan also meets with Michael Ben-Avie,
a researcher from the Yale Child Study Center. Interested in Jan's thoughts
on her own life's work, Michael asks, "You have now been director of the
Comer Office for twelve years. Think about yourself twelve years ago. If
you were able, what would you say to your younger self?" Jan reflects and
gives a thoughtful answer:

> I would tell her that time passes quickly when you are engaged in meaning-
> ful work in schools and that each of us is capable of growing personally and
> professionally with the right support and in a positive environment. I would
> also say, "Think about research, data, and evaluation." Twelve years ago, our

superintendent said, "Do it," and we did whatever the task was. At the Comer Office, we gave little thought to collecting baseline data. Today, I know to ask, "If we start this process called Comer, how will we know whether it will work or not? How are we going to evaluate the effectiveness of our work? What do we have in place now that is similar to SDP?" If we had asked those questions twelve years ago, we could already have proven that the climate changes fast. We could have shown the critical importance of relationships.

I would also teach her the importance not only of team building, but also of teaming. Team building refers to promoting relations among the members, including encouraging the quiet to speak and making sure that no one's ideas are mocked or ridiculed. Members get to know each others' strengths and talents. On the other hand, teaming refers to the specific actions that ensure smooth functioning, including assigning roles, paraphrasing each other's statements, devising methods for staying on track, taking notes, and summarizing. It took us a while to realize that teams needed specific training in teaming in order to work effectively together.

I've learned over the last twelve years that the Comer Process is all about change. I really didn't understand that in the beginning. Then I was introduced to the game called *Making Change for School Improvement* created by The Network, Inc., which is a great training tool, and the theory behind moving people and supporting them through stages of change. And the more I understood, the more patience I had with the whole process of change.

So if I were to speak to my younger self, I guess I'd say, "Do your best each and every day. Always work in the best interests of children. Know that *modeling matters*. Recognize that it's an honor to work with a talented and gifted staff. And remember that our work with children and schools is more critical today than ever before!"

CHAPTER 12

Charting a Course for Student Success

University, School Community, and Foundation Partnerships

Alison J. Harmon, Sherrie B. Joseph, and Wilhelmina S. Quick

Photograph by Laura Brooks.

In Detroit, the whole village includes a university, the school district, the SDP, and a generous and civic-minded foundation. They have created a powerful partnership called the Comer Schools and Families Initiative that, in its first few years, has already benefited thousands of children and their families. The Initiative's three facilitators describe its creation and organization.

The Comer Schools and Families Initiative is a collaboration among the Detroit Public Schools, Eastern Michigan University (EMU), the Yale Child Study Center, and the Skillman Foundation. These institutions—school system, universities, and foundation—now relate to each other and the community in new ways. The Initiative has produced remarkable results and has developed so many useful new processes that the SDP plans to use them in all its incoming schools.

We're often asked how the Comer Schools and Families Initiative has made such rapid progress. Some have attributed our steady and strategic progression to the generosity of the Skillman Foundation, whose resources have added to the basic program in each of our eighteen Comer Schools. Abt Associates, the independent evaluator of the Initiative, says that we three coordinators are "central." Each of us has her own view, as well: Wilhelmina's testimony is, "divine order and prayer—lots of it"; Alison's philosophy is, "an investment on a personal level accompanied by the willingness to change oneself"; Sherrie's logical comment is, "Detroit had many of the structures in place when the SDP began implementation." Whatever our individual responses, as a group we're pleased with the progress that's been made in Detroit.

This chapter describes the course that we have charted to lead a group of faithful Comer followers to build relationships to work for and with children. We describe our voyage towards fully using the guiding principles in selecting schools and facilitators; creating the School Improvement, Student Support, and Parent Teams in schools; and involving the community and university as resources for the Initiative. Our journey has not been without incident; therefore, the chapter also illustrates the decisions we made in rough weather, the course corrections we made en route, and how we finally converted from paddles to powerful engines.

The Cartographers

Founded in 1960 by Rose P. Skillman, the Skillman Foundation is a private grant-making foundation whose purpose is to improve the well-being of residents of Southeastern Michigan and, in particular, the Metropolitan Detroit area.

In 1991, the Skillman Foundation began to explore investing in long-term comprehensive school reform to improve public education in Detroit all the way from kindergarten through twelfth grade. Led by president Leonard Smith and program officer John Ziraldo, the Foundation's staff enthusiastically reviewed many program models, corresponded with the directors of the major school reform initiatives, chose the Yale Child Study

Center's School Development Program, approached the general superintendent of the Detroit Public Schools, brainstormed with other district central office administrators, and began to work with key stakeholders to develop a Partnership Agreement.

From the beginning, the strength of the Initiative has been with its stakeholders: the Detroit Federation of Teachers, the Organization of Administrators and Supervisors, the City-Wide School Community Organization, the Detroit Public Schools, Eastern Michigan University, the Yale Child Study Center's School Development Program, and the Skillman Foundation. Using SDP's comprehensive approach to school reform, these groups collaborated for two years to establish goals and objectives and to outline the responsibilities of each stakeholder group in the Initiative.

From 1992 to 1994, representatives from each stakeholder organization formed a working group that is now referred to as the District Planning Team. Team members were introduced to the Comer Process through orientations by James P. Comer, SDP's founder, and Edward T. Joyner, the current executive director of the SDP, and through site visits to SDP districts and schools throughout the country. The site visits allowed the team to identify and hear firsthand what worked and what would present challenges (e.g., it became clear that the district would need to place nurses and social workers in each school and that the SDP facilitator would have to be available full time). Both the orientations and site visits were invaluable in shaping many of the decisions on how to organize the Detroit Initiative. The result of these activities was a contract, signed in 1994 by the heads of each of the organizations, with the Skillman Foundation, which committed a total of almost $16 million to the Initiative over ten years. The Foundation's current commitments (1994–1999) for the Comer Schools and Families Initiative total $12,083,000. This includes $1.5 million for the Abt Associates evaluation. The Foundation may approve up to another $8 million for the second five years of the Initiative at the April 1999 Trustee meeting.

The Partnership Agreement clearly states the understandings and commitments of the major stakeholder groups in supporting the Initiative in Detroit's public schools. It states that funds are for additional staff, professional development, and other expenses selected by each school. It also summarizes the phases of program implementation, which has involved a total of eighteen elementary schools entering the program at different times over a four-year period.

The District Planning Team selected us to be the three coordinators. When we came on board, Sharon Johnson-Lewis, assistant superintendent and chair of the District Planning Team, briefed us. In the following sections, we describe ourselves and how we used the Partnership Agreement to navigate our seaworthy Comer vessel, leading a crew of believers on an expedition to fully implement SDP in the Detroit Public Schools.

The Navigators

The navigators of this journey, according to Abt Associates (1997), are "three resourceful, committed, and experienced Comer coordinators, each of whom brings her own strengths to this endeavor." We met for the first time at the SDP's Leadership Training 101 at Yale University.

Wilhelmina S. Quick had been appointed district coordinator the week before. At the time, Wilhelmina was the principal of a Detroit elementary school that had been recognized by *Redbook* as a school of excellence. Wilhelmina is highly respected in the district for her ability to mobilize community agencies and groups. Her well established internal and external relationships have been a hidden asset to the program's outreach.

Alison J. Harmon, the full-time university coordinator, brings a broad theoretical perspective on urban reform, experience as a coordinator of a school/university partnership, and experience as principal of both an elementary and a middle school. Alison is released from teaching responsibilities at the university and devotes all her attention to assisting the district coordinator in implementing SDP and garnering resources for maximum impact on the schools.

Sherrie B. Joseph, the full-time SDP implementation coordinator, has a unique role based on site in Detroit to organize and conduct training for her constituent groups. She also provides technical assistance to all stakeholders, supporting them in the faithful replication of the Comer Process. A social worker, Sherrie has had many previous SDP experiences including directing the implementation of the Comer Process for the New Jersey State Department of Education.

Our backgrounds and experiences create an interesting dynamic. Wilhelmina, who understands and expects others to follow district rules and procedures, is systematic and efficient. Her bottom line is results. Alison, a dreamer, enjoys academic freedom and autonomy and feels that rules, systems, and procedures restrict people from pursuing the creative ideas that change the way schools operate. Sherrie is process oriented and sees the big picture. Committed to SDP's principles, she models, motivates, and guides others to embrace Dr. Comer's intentions: true collaboration, mutual respect, and trust.

Having on this voyage three co-captains with different management styles has been an ongoing challenge. Sherrie wanted us to be faithful to the process and stressed the importance of meeting to report and give feedback to one another. But Wilhelmina felt that meeting to "process" when we had so many deadlines was not efficient. And Alison wanted to avoid the conflict that might arise as a result of the constructive exchange of perceptions and feelings. Nonetheless, because we are devoted to our work, we have managed to select tasks that best suit our strengths.

Wilhelmina was certainly right about too much work and not enough time. A multitude of tasks has faced us since our first meeting three years ago, and they have taken priority. Within weeks of our first meeting, we were orchestrating the selection of six participating schools. Within two months we had hired six facilitators, and by the fourth month we'd organized and conducted our first three-day retreat for principals and facilitators. In three years, the pace has not changed, although we certainly could have had a little more fun and less stress on our voyage if we had balanced task with process as Sherrie continually suggested. Nonetheless, no matter the pace or level of difficulty, we have always been able to plan and forecast our next steps.

The Ships: The Schools

Before the Initiative, the Detroit Public Schools had many SDP components in place. There already were school improvement teams, prescreening teams, provisions for parent participation, and school improvement plans.

We faithfully replicated the nine components of the Comer Process: the School Planning and Management Team (SPMT), the Parent Team (PT), the Student and Staff Support Team (SSST), a Comprehensive School Plan (CSP), Staff Development (SD), Assessment and Modification (A&M), consensus, collaboration, and no-fault problem solving.

The School Improvement Teams

For consistency, we kept the name "School Improvement Team" rather than use "School Planning and Management Team," although many in the Initiative now feel that "SPMT" signals a much broader management role. One team decided through consensus to change its name to SPMT.

In restructuring the SIT we focused on how the teams were organized and what the teams did. Before this restructuring in each school, Sherrie, Wilhelmina, and the Comer school facilitators conducted an overview of the Comer Process of SDP for the entire staff with the understanding that additional training would follow.

We then worked with each existing SIT to establish procedures and guidelines for restructuring itself. The team was to be more inclusive and reflective of all the adult stakeholders in the school building and the child's life. We identified these stakeholders, formed constituent groups, and developed a formula to determine the number of representatives from each group. In the past, teams often were made up of the "faithful few" volunteers or persons chosen by the principal. Now they would consist of persons chosen by their peers, representing the interests and concerns of a broader group and also accountable to them. This increased the number of noninstructional and support staff serving on teams. It also broadened parent representation since parents from all of the formal and informal parent groups had an opportunity to choose representatives, as well. In Detroit, parents make up at least 25 percent of the SIT. Schools were given action steps to guide this process as well as written guidelines on what was to take place immediately after reorganization.

The Comer school facilitators were trained in how to organize the meetings, what should be included on a typical SIT agenda, team building, and how to organize and use subcommittees. They were then to replicate the training or adapt it to the school's needs, schedule, and level of readiness. We constantly reminded the schools that each should proceed at its own pace, and we ensured that they did.

During the second and third years, training was conducted at the schools and focused on aligning the school improvement plan with the district goals and on organizing subcommittees to support that alignment. In this way teams came to understand that SDP is a way to achieve the district's goals.

The teams and subcommittees have planned a range of student and parent services and activities. Schools and staff members express satisfaction that relationships among staff and between staff and parents are improving, communication within the schools is improving, there is greater emphasis on putting children first, the relationship between school staff and support staff (members of the Student Support Teams) is improving, and parents are more visible in the buildings.

The Student Support Teams

We chose the name "Student Support Team" (SST) rather than SDP's "Student and Staff Support Team" (SSST). Wilhelmina, Sherrie, and the supervisors of the school district's departments of Social Work, Psychological Services, Specialized Student Services, and Counseling collaborated on deciding how to staff the Student Support Teams. We were able to supplement counselors in some schools and arrange for school social workers and school psychologists to serve only two Comer schools each rather than split their weekly assignments between one Comer school and one or more non-Comer schools.

While the support personnel were being identified and assigned, Wilhelmina worked with the principals to identify which additional support personnel would serve on the SST (whose size and composition varies from school to school). This included the teachers of the speech and language impaired, teacher consultants, resource room teachers, and attendance officers. Their supervisors helped them assess their interest and willingness to work differently before they were placed on the teams.

Training has included orientation on the composition, roles, and responsibilities of the SST and on how to use the six developmental pathways to assess needs and plan individual, family, and group intervention strategies. This training was conducted at each school to address the specific needs of the students and families. Sherrie and faculty from EMU also conducted two one-day training programs for all the SSTs throughout the district. To help them create referral forms and processes, the teams received sample forms and ideas both during site visits and from the Intervention Assistance Teams already in place in the Detroit public schools.

The directors and supervisors of the district's Department of Specialized Student Services continue to provide excellent support: There is now a full-time social worker in each Comer school. The district's director of Psychological Services instructed her staff to work within the SST structure by receiving all referrals through the team. The teacher consultants and teachers of the speech and language impaired continue on the SST, even though there are not additional funds for their services. The Attendance Departments have also been very cooperative: About 80 percent of the attendance officers are active members of SSTs.

Wilhelmina and Alison have brought in excellent resources and networking opportunities for the schools such as on-site immunizations, dental health screening, and pre-student teachers and social work interns to provide individual assistance to children referred to the SST. The Skillman Education and Advocacy Program (an organization providing training for parents throughout the city of Detroit) and the Detroit Public Health Department have helped parents create networks. The SSTs have introduced new and expanded interventions such as aggression replacement and social skills development groups, parenting skills interventions, increased tutorial services for targeted students, specialized summer programs for identified students and their parents, and other programs for children who are retained or in danger of being retained.

The Comer Parent Teams

We struggled with how parents should be organized in the buildings during the initial year. Each parent group selected an SIT representative. Staff worked with the existing parent groups to integrate their work into the SDP. We now use the term Parent Team, which makes it easier to organize our parent program, bringing representatives from all parent groups in the building into an organization that coordinates all their activities and directly supports the SIT.

Much of the initial effort with the parents focused on acquainting them with the Comer Process and on selecting and supporting parent representatives on the SITs. Comer coordinators and facilitators also worked with existing parent groups such as the PTA and Local School Community Organization (LSCO) in such areas as team building, organizational issues, trouble shooting, and providing staff support for planned parent activities.

Facilitators hired to involve parents in their children's education have made remarkable progress in planning parent activities, participating on the SIT, and becoming a part of the school family. They restructured the parent volunteer programs in their buildings by creating a Volunteer Request Form and volunteer assignment sheets and by broadening the number and types of volunteer opportunities available to parents. They have planned some excellent parent and parent/staff activities including a Thanksgiving Feast for the entire family, a series of parenting skills workshops on such topics as discipline and self-esteem, a parent appreciation dinner with teachers serving as the waiters and waitresses, a teacher appreciation dinner as a way for parents to reciprocate, the establishment of parent resource areas, and much more.

The Harbor

University Partners

Eastern Michigan University's main role in the Initiative is to provide resources—sometimes even before school teams are in full operation—so that the Comer Process can be fully implemented. EMU pinpoints the schools' needs, locates the services, negotiates the cost of delivering the services, and finally, provides the services.

To find out what was needed, Alison surveyed the District Planning Team members and had the School Improvement Teams fill out a Resource Survey. Both the District Planning Team and the school teams wanted re-

mediation and enrichment programs for children, staff development focused on child development theory and schoolwide discipline, health services for families and children, advocacy awareness and volunteer programs
for parents, and child and family intervention strategies for the student
support program. Alison looked first to EMU and then to neighboring universities and agencies to meet these needs.

The Skillman Foundation made an additional grant to support EMU
in providing services to the Comer schools, and EMU and other collaborating organizations have made in-kind contributions of materials and services.

Dr. Jerry Robbins, dean, and Dr. Robbie Johnson, associate dean, at the
College of Education, provide administrative support for Eastern Michigan University's role in the Comer partnership. Dr. Robbins and Dr. Johnson represent the initiative through the district planning team and as
liaisons between the university and Detroit Public Schools. Dr. Robbins
represents Dr. Shelton, the President of Eastern Michigan University, at the
executive level of the Comer Initiative. Both Dr. Robbins and Dr. Johnson
attend various functions for the Comer Schools and Families Initiative, including on-site visits to monitor progress, and visits to Yale University to
participate in events intended to maintain the integrity of the project.

On EMU's campus, Dr. Robbins is actively involved in the development of the annual budget to meet the objectives of the project. Dr. Robbins and Dr. Johnson promote the Initiative, and provide administrative
oversight for the Skillman Foundation grant. They act as liaisons between
and among departments, provide leadership to advance systems change
within departments to sustain the initiative, and support the activities of the
university coordinator to facilitate an ongoing development of processes
that will sustain the partnership between EMU and the Detroit Public
Schools. In addition, Dr. Johnson's academic services role provides support for the undergraduate teacher education practicums and internships
that form the core of direct service resources provided by EMU to Comer
schools.

Alison and Dr. Mary Homann, the university facilitator, recruit, train,
schedule, and place university faculty and students in Comer Schools. They
also identify community organizations and agencies to work, preferably
as volunteers, with EMU in providing educational, mental health, and physical health services to the children and families in the schools.

Curriculum Support. Seventeen university professors have part-time
assignments in the Comer schools. Faculty from the Departments of Teacher
Education; Special Education; Leadership & Counseling; Health, Physical
Education, Recreation and Dance; Nursing; and Social Work provide direct services to the children, parents, and teachers in the Comer schools.

Three professors teach curriculum methods, social behavior in schools, and reading methods to undergraduate students on-site in Comer schools. Two professors conduct a nursing seminar on-site in a Comer school. Two professors provide oversight for nearly 200 undergraduate teacher education interns placed with participating Detroit school teachers. One professor works with Sherrie to coordinate the parent facilitator training, and another professor coordinates the social work intern program. Six professors provide site-specific staff development and guidance in the areas of child development, parent advocacy, schoolwide discipline, and collaborative leadership. Two professors have received grants to support teachers in some schools as they include hands-on science in the classrooms and sessions on nutrition awareness for children and parents.

University Student Involvement. Undergraduate and graduate students from the College of Education and College of Health and Human Services may become involved through course assignments or by volunteering through campus service groups. These students are assigned to work with small groups of children or one-on-one with children identified by the school's SST. Three days per week for ten weeks during each semester (Fall and Winter) the undergraduates are transported by bus and vans to the schools. Preparation for the day's field experience actually begins en route to Detroit. Those who can provide their own transportation are scheduled on the other two days of those weeks.

Undergraduate reading and curriculum methods and community nursing courses are taught at five of the schools. Students enrolled in these courses are required to spend one full day per week at the school site. Students enrolled in the methods courses teach demonstration lessons to an entire class or small groups of children. Students enrolled in the community nursing course organize community projects to promote healthy living and partner with classroom teachers to provide instruction using the Michigan model for Comprehensive School Health Education.

Nearly 200 undergraduate teacher education interns were assigned to the Comer schools during Year 2 of implementation: Two teams of six to ten undergraduate students each served children in each of the ten Comer schools throughout the year. The interns led tutoring groups, helped organize schoolwide literacy activities, taught language arts skills to small groups of children in the classroom, and assisted classroom teachers in record keeping and routine classroom management tasks. Also, during the same year, 12 social work students completed their internships in the schools.

Additionally, we have formed a collaboration with two neighboring universities in support of the pre-student teacher component. In Years 2 and 3, Oakland University assigned approximately 72 undergraduate students and Wayne County Community College assigned 28 undergraduates to the Comer schools. The students from all of the universities tutored children, organized small groups for improved social interaction, taught mini-lessons, and/or assisted the teacher with classroom management or instruction.

Medical Partners

Mary Homann, the university facilitator, and Lisa Brown-Williams, the district's supervisor of Physical Health and Safety, work collaboratively to provide the Comer school children and their older and younger siblings with health services. Mary organizes health clinics to vaccinate children at each Comer school at the start of the school year. Follow-up clinics give booster vaccinations one to three times throughout the school year. Since 1995, 3,540 immunizations have been administered to children on-site in Comer schools. Additionally, physical, vision, and hearing exams were administered in the spring of 1996 and 1997 during Kindergarten Round-Up at several Comer schools.

The Children's Hospital of Michigan sent pediatric resident physicians and Detroit's Health Department provided the vaccines for each of the immunization clinics. Nurses from the Initial Health Care staffing were hired for each clinic.

Abt Associates' Second Year Evaluation of Detroit's Comer Schools and Families Initiative reports, "Detroit has recognized the value of social work and undergraduate teacher education internships as well as the support from EMU faculty; participating schools rate the services received very highly."

As coordinators, we have seen the mutual benefit of the partnership between the district and the university. We are learning from and with one another. University faculty members help us with staff development, mentoring, and coaching special discipline or content areas (e.g., reading, team building, classroom discipline). Their involvement in the schools frees us up to attend to other areas. EMU students provide a direct service to the children in the Comer schools, giving teachers the support they need to do things differently.

Community Partners

Like the university, the Detroit community was eager to get involved in the Initiative. Both Drs. Comer and Joyner had addressed community forums. The media provided good coverage of the Skillman Foundation's press conference announcing the Initiative. The various departments in the school district and the community-at-large inquired about the Initiative and about their role, as well.

Wilhelmina organized a Resource Fair that attracted a number of neighborhood community groups and agencies. These groups offered a range of services: parenting skills, health screening, family counseling, after-school programs, asthma assistance, vision care, etc. The Resource Fair was an excellent way for us to avail ourselves of the multitude of services in the geographic areas surrounding the schools.

Wilhelmina also appealed to churches, businesses, and community organizations to form partnerships with the Comer schools. One church congregation adopted four of the schools and provided the children with mentors, after-school tutoring, and scholastic recognition. A local business provided free eye exams and glasses for selected children in two of the Comer schools. A community hospital provided physical exams for children and health education seminars for parents in a number of the Comer schools. Community interest about the Comer schools continues to be high, and community support remains an immeasurable asset.

The Log of the Voyage

In Year 1, immediately upon our return from the SDP Leadership Training 101 in New Haven, CT, we met to develop our work plan for the Skillman Foundation. Determining the tasks was the easy part. Coming to consensus on how to accomplish them was extremely difficult. In one day, we were able to determine that our objectives for the first year would be to select the teacher and parent facilitators, organize the school teams, orient the key stakeholders at the district and school levels. However, it took many meetings to determine who was to do what, when, and how.

Finally, by consensus, we decided that Sherrie would focus on providing the leadership for training the facilitators, stakeholders, and constituents rather than begin work on the objectives for the whole school system. Wilhelmina would attend to the day-to-day operations of the program in Detroit, namely engaging in the preliminary work for selecting the facilitators and schools and student support personnel. Alison assumed the leadership for producing joint reports, planning the first Comer Kick-Off, a district-wide staff development program, and arranging placements for pre-student teachers and social work interns.

Then it was easy to develop strategies and activities to achieve the first year's objectives. The activities we established have become the model of an SDP school system's first year. They are:

- a process for selecting schools that includes representatives from each of the district's stakeholder groups: administrators, teachers, non-instructional staff, support staff, parents, community representatives
- a process for selecting school-based facilitators
- a three-day orientation retreat for the principals and facilitators
- twice-weekly professional development meetings with the facilitators, including process journals and logs
- monthly information meetings with the principals
- weekly visits to each of the Detroit Comer schools to observe the team meetings and give feedback to their members
- professional development activities for team leaders and members
- site visits to existing Comer schools
- attendance at SDP Leadership Training and Principals' Academy at Yale.

A brief description of each activity follows.

Selecting Schools

The Partnership Agreement stated that a total of eighteen schools would enter the Initiative in four cycles over a four year period. Six schools were selected during the first year of the program (one from each of the six geographical areas of the district). To be selected, schools had to show: economic need of the students and families; need for programmatic resources; an appreciation of and respect for collaboration among staff, parents, and the community; a willing participation from the teachers, noninstructional staff, and parents; and no affiliation with other school improvement reforms. Additionally, each school's administrator and team had to write a narrative explaining why they wanted to be a part of the Initiative.

Applications were distributed at a districtwide information meeting. Three weeks later, interested schools submitted their applications, which were reviewed and rated by subcommittees from each geographic region consisting of District Planning Team members and the coordinators. The subcommittees screened these applications according to the established criteria, looking for no-fault language and strategies in applicants' descriptions of their schools' needs and approaches to addressing those needs. The subcommittee members also looked for signs of progress toward collaboration: Were the state-mandated school improvement teams and district Local School Community Organizations formed, meeting regularly, and viewed as an integral part of the school program? Was the principal committed to collaboration and consensus? Each subcommittee discussed the merits of the three applications ranked first, second, and third in their geographical area and then recommended them to the District Planning Team for further consideration.

In the second and third years of school selection, the District Planning Team recommended a pool of qualified schools rather than a ranked preference list. Through our own District Planning Team assessment, we decided to visit each school selected by our team to get a better assessment of the school's climate and culture. The site visits took place before the recommendations to the area superintendents. Each team was given a rating scale to be used in the selection process and some sample questions for the principal, SIT, and parent and community representatives. When the three finalist schools were chosen, the scores for both the paper screening and the site visits were given to the area superintendent for consideration and selection.

Selecting School and Parent Facilitators

After we selected the schools, we began to select school and parent facilitators. The Skillman Foundation had granted time-limited funds for the school facilitator (full time for Years 1 and 2 and half-time for Years 3–5). The half-time parent facilitator in each of the Comer schools is funded for the duration of the project. However, principals have the option of purchasing facilitators' services using their school's resources, and one school has done so.

School Facilitator. The duties and responsibilities of the school facilitator as outlined in the Partnership Agreement are to:

- provide leadership in planning the school improvement approaches with teachers, parents, and students
- coordinate the human material resources that are focused on student needs in a comprehensive, collaborative school-based improvement process
- initiate and maintain the active involvement of all school community stakeholders with emphasis on active parent involvement
- emphasize the principles of collaboration, consensus, and no-fault problem solving in working with constituent groups pursuing the school objectives and goals.

The district's nine-month employees were on vacation when we began the selection process for the first six school facilitators, so it was not possible to post the positions. However, the Detroit Federation of Teachers (DFT) supported our request to use an alternate selection process. DFT vice president Carol Thomas was a member of the District Planning Team, and the DFT shared in all decisions about the design of Detroit's model of the Comer Process and plans for implementation. Carol traveled with the District Planning Team to visit Comer schools and districts in other parts of the country and knew first-hand about SDP's benefits. She, like all stakeholders in the Comer Schools and Families Initiative, believed in and promoted the principles of SDP. Through her influence, the DFT was also convinced that the Initiative should begin implementation in the fall of 1994. Therefore, the teachers' union was willing to grant the dispensation.

Using the alternate process, each area superintendent recommended three teachers for consideration as school facilitators. Teams consisting of three Comer school principals, the district coordinator, and a representative from the personnel office conducted face-to-face interviews with the applicants. The principal of the school seeking a facilitator sat on the team. The district coordinator and personnel office representative served on all teams. Each interviewing team made its selection and subsequent recommendation to the respective area superintendent for approval.

After the first year, announcements for the school facilitator positions were posted. All teachers in the district were encouraged to apply if they met the eligibility criteria of being a member of the DFT; being a teacher or a student support professional; having a bachelor's degree with a current Michigan Elementary Teaching Certificate; and having three or more years of elementary school teaching experience. All applications were screened by the personnel office, and applicants who met the minimum requirements were placed on an eligibility list. From this list, Comer school principals could choose candidates to be interviewed by the school's Selection Committee, a subcommittee of the SIT. With approval from the SIT, a final selection was made.

Both selection processes (in the first and subsequent years) have produced very capable and talented school facilitators. Five of the fifteen school facilitators were teachers in their school before the Initiative implementation began, and we've repeatedly discussed whether an insider or outsider is likely to be more effective as school facilitator. We have not modified the criteria for selection regarding an inside or an outside teacher.

Our assessment has been inconclusive. When interviewed by Abt Associates, one Comer school principal described the benefits of an outsider teacher:

> There are real advantages to having an external person. It gives everyone a clean slate; the person is unbiased; the person gets to know everyone equally well. If the person comes from within, she/he is already part of a group; and there are perceptions to undo.

A school facilitator who is new to the school wrote about the issue in her journal:

> I'm feeling like a person in the middle, right now. I know who's in what group and how each group stands on this issue. They all want to hear my opinion. I don't have an opinion. I just want what is best for the children. Thank God I haven't identified with any group, because [it] could get messy. I don't know the history . . . and I don't need to know. I wonder if my fellow facilitators feel like I'm feeling now.

Parent Facilitator. The role of parent facilitator as outlined in the Partnership Agreement is to involve parents on three levels:

- supporting their child's educational development
- supporting the school's program
- participating in decision making.

Parent facilitators also help bring more parents into the school and create programs to meet their needs. School teams believe that the work of the parent facilitator is important in making parent participation an integral part of the school program, so the parent or community member filling the position must be visible and respected in the school and community.

Wilhelmina spent countless hours in meetings with District personnel officers and representatives from the local bargaining unit for noncertified staff in creating the position, negotiating the salary, and determining the appropriate classifications. We three coordinators developed the job description together. The job description was posted in each SDP school and at each area office. Children took it home with a notice that applications for the position were available in the school's office. Any adult who meets the qualifications for the position (high school diploma; lives within the school's geographic boundaries; has a child within the school or if not, currently an active volunteer at the school) can apply. All applications are screened by a district personnel officer, a representative from the City-Wide Parent Organization, and Wilhelmina. After the screening process, a pool of eligible applicants is created for each SDP school and interviewed by its SIT or a subcommittee.

Principals' and Facilitators' Retreat

In August 1994, principals and school facilitators from our first six Comer schools participated in a three-day, two-night Orientation and Training retreat. This retreat was conducted by the three Comer coordinators (the authors), who had attended the two weeks of 101 and 102 training at Yale.

Away from school in a setting with the amenities of a professional meeting, participants began the initial bonding as a work team, learned about the history of school reform in this country, received a thorough overview of SDP's nine components, and began "back-home" planning. They also received a notebook of all training materials and transparencies distributed to participants in the SDP 101 training. A year later, we were pleased to note that during the three-day retreat for the Cycle 2 Comer principals and facilitators, four of the Cycle 1 Comer teacher facilitators assisted. They presented multimedia training and answered questions on the developmental pathways, the SST, the SIT, and the Parent Program.

Following the retreat, the Comer school facilitators were given a list of some immediate steps to guide their work. Thay had time to develop an SDP presence in their buildings to welcome staff, students, and parents, such as banners, balloons, bulletin boards, and receptions. Sherrie developed a question-and-answer handout to distribute to staff and an abbreviated version for parents. The handouts were designed to answer some of their immediate questions about the Comer Process. Each school also made a Comer orientation part of their back-to-school night: an activity for parents to meet the teachers and receive an overview of the curriculum and daily scheduled activities. All three of us attended each one. These activities were important because they brought attention to the beginning of a new initiative and signaled that this would not be business as usual.

Twice-Weekly Comer School Facilitator Training

The content presented at the three-day retreat was the facilitators' first orientation to the SDP. After the retreat, the Comer school facilitators continued to receive "train the trainers" and facilitation training two days per week for the first year of implementation. This training included such topics as the role of the Comer school facilitator, trainer preparation and presentations, giving and receiving feedback, SIT and SSST operations, procedures and tools, organizing the Comer Parent Group, and getting parents involved. Each of us assumed the responsibility of monitoring the implementation of two schools. We attended all trainings and SIT and SSST meetings to assist, coach, and provide direct technical assistance to the Comer school facilitator, principal, and teams. Working with the schools and teams in this way allowed us to coach and give feedback immediately, to establish a service relationship with the schools, and to identify training needs.

Initially, keeping a finger on the pulse of the schools' implementation was the major focus of our twice-weekly meetings. We knew that the Initiative's success depended on our ability to use SDP's problem-solving model easily and flexibly, so we required each Comer school facilitator to keep a weekly log of activities and a journal of his or her reflections. These two documents provided the greatest insights for program modifications.

At their meetings, the school facilitators shared implementation ideas and strategies, and they formed subcommittees on global curriculum and social issues. These subcommittees found ways for staff in the Comer schools to collaborate on writing grants, securing community resources, and creating parent and staff development activities. Currently the facilitators meet every two weeks.

Monthly Principals' Meetings

Our monthly meetings with the Comer principals were established to keep them informed about the status of implementation. Initially, we discussed the facilitators' preparation and the activities in which they would be involving the staff or community. We reviewed district programs that might enhance SDP implementation in each school. We listened to the principals' concerns and together solved problems that were unique to the Initiative. However, we were simply scratching the surface.

From visits to the schools, observation of team meetings, and the facilitators' journal entries, we detected that the principals were not comfortable with all aspects of the Comer Process. Alison interviewed each principal to discover his or her idea of the differences between being a Comer principal and being a traditional principal. She focused on benefits, weaknesses, impact, concerns, and "first steps" to prepare them for the leadership style changes. The collective data revealed the principals' limited knowledge of and experience with collaboration and consensus. Additionally, the collective group of principals wanted support in resolving conflicts that had emerged as a result of increased dialogue and opportunities for genuine participation.

Our first response to the principals' concerns was a weekend retreat. We invited a panel of experienced Comer principals from Cleveland to talk with us and assist us in working through some of the challenges of implementing the Initiative at the school level. Our panel of experts addressed six areas: school power, the misuse of power by the dissenting group of staff, conflict resolution among staff and parents, building and keeping trust, shared decision making, and practical advice. Principals were given a journal and asked to record their thoughts about their emerging role as a collaborative leader. Our monthly meetings following the retreat now served the purpose of training as well as the purpose of sharing information and experiences. As a result, the principals have become a more sociable, cohesive group.

In Year 3, Dr. Beverly Geltner, an associate professor at EMU's Department of Leadership and Counseling designed a professional development seminar for the principals based on what they had said they needed. The monthly information meetings were transformed into dialogue circles about the three books that each principal was reading, which focused on effective communications skills, school change, and leadership development. In conversations about the readings, the principals began to reveal the challenges they faced in their new roles and to learn the new skills they needed.

Parent Facilitator Meetings

Parent facilitators begin their work with a three-day orientation and training. During the first semester, they come to the Comer office for weekly meetings and training, and during the second semester, they come twice per month. Along with Sherrie, Dr. Nora Martin, a professor in EMU's Department of Special Education who attends the weekly meetings and works with the parent facilitators, has developed much of the training, coaching, and resource materials. Some of the topics are: the parent facilitator's role, preparing staff for increased parent participation, increasing the level of parent participation, how to design a parent volunteer program, and how to prepare and deliver presentations.

A highlight of each meeting is the opportunity for each parent facilitator to share with the others the progress that has taken place at her school and to discover the challenges that are common to the position. One such challenge is clarifying the role of parents in the school and improving staffs' acceptance of parents. Parent facilitators have found that some staff members are not comfortable having parents in the building and some see little value in providing social activities at the school for parents. Together with the university professor and the Yale implementation coordinator, the parent facilitators spend time developing strategies to increase understanding of the broad role for parents in the school.

The Comer Kick-Off

The Comer Kick-Off brings together administrators, instructional and non-instructional staff, parents, community, university, and area and central office representatives to introduce the new Comer schools and recognize the schools that have completed one year of implementing the SDP. A keynote speaker reminds the participants of the Initiative's mission and encourages them to keep our focus on children first. Both Drs. Comer and Joyner have delivered keynote addresses for the occasion.

Workshops that focus on various aspects of SDP implementation are also a feature of the Kick-Off program. Some of the favorite workshops are on team building, the developmental pathways, parent involvement, and SIT and SSST operations. Additional sessions present topics related to the Kick-Off's theme, which changes each year.

During the first Kick-Off in October 1994, presenters were recruited from EMU, Yale, and the Detroit Public Schools. The Year 2 and 3 programs featured several of the first year facilitators and team members. One participant summed up the sentiments of the majority in this way: "I really got a lot out of the . . . school workshop. . . . They are a Detroit school just like we are. If they can do so much in two years, so can . . . we. We just need to get with the program."

Site Visits

Site visits to SDP schools in other school districts proved invaluable. A representative group of school staff, parents, and administrators traveled to Cleveland, Ohio; Prince George's County, Maryland; Washington, DC; Chicago, Illinois; Miami, Florida; and Guilford County, North Carolina during the first three years of the Initiative. Our teams observed SPMT and SSST meetings, received samples of forms and documents used by their teams, and talked with staff and parents. More than any other single activity, the site visits moved us toward full implementation, as these candid remarks show:

SST Member: Now, I *see* what our Student Support Team can become. I *see* how my training can benefit all children, if I can work differently. I *see* how an outside agency can help me in serving more children. I *see* how what I thought could never happen in an urban district can be accomplished. Now, I must help others to *see* a bigger picture.

Teacher: This school has gotten so much through grants. I am going to organize a grant writing committee to look for money for our programs. I can think of two or three programs already that could possibly be funded.

Parent Facilitator: Those parents got their own thing goin' on. I saw a lot of parents taking care of their personal business at the school. They could get food, clothes, and a [physical] check-up right at the school. And parents did it all. We can do this. . . .

Administrator: All of the schools in Detroit can benefit from Comer. We can all do this for our kids!

SDP Leadership Training 102 at Yale, and Principals' Academy

Comer school facilitators participated in the SDP Leadership Training 102 at Yale, which focuses on sharpening the facilitation skills needed to coach and guide the process at the building level. They shared some of the things they were doing, got ideas from other schools, and networked with Comer schools from around the country.

Twelve Comer school principals participated in the Yale Principals' Academy with more than 100 other principals from across the country. They told us that the experience interacting with SDP national office staff and other principals gave them affirmation for what they were doing, new ideas, and a greater understanding of the Comer Process.

Reflections at the First Port of Call

The Comer Schools and Families Initiative is a ten-year venture; at this writing we have completed the third year of implementation. The Partnership Agreement spells out transitions at this point: The full-time involvement of the Detroit-based national implementation coordinator will decrease to allow for the part-time involvement of several SDP faculty members. The district coordinator is retiring from the district, and the assistant superintendent who administers the Initiative is also leaving the district to pursue other educational opportunities. So this is a moment to take a reflective look at where we've been and, if need be, make adjustments to the route we will follow to get where we want to be.

From 1994 (the first year of implementation) to 1996, there was marked improvement in student achievement at the six elementary schools that were the first wave of schools in the Comer Schools and Families Initiative. On the Michigan Education Assessment Program (MEAP), the percent of students scoring at the Satisfactory level in Reading increased. The schools had increases of 4%, 10%, 16%, 28%, 30%, and 31%. In Math, one school had a decrease of 14%. The other five schools had increases of 6%, 8%, 20%, 21%, and 44%.

Cycle 2 schools (the second wave of six schools) experienced similar successes: increases of 9% to 33% of students scoring at the Satisfactory level in Reading, and increases of 13% to 59% of students succeeeding in Mathematics.

The Skillman Foundation funded the independent Abt Associates to conduct quantitative and qualitative research from 1994 through 1999. In the second report (Millsap, et al., 1997), Abt Associates write, "One of the most exciting patterns we see in the Comer schools is the extent to which the program is reaching into the core operations and basic relationships and beginning to effect change." They also write, "Recognizing that implementing the Comer model is seen as a five- or six-year process, the Cycle 1 and Cycle 2 schools have made significant progress. The School Improvement Team and Student Support Team are in place, principals are relinquishing some decision making authority, and staff are coping with assuming more responsibility." Moreover, the Abt Associates observe, "After two years of implementation, several patterns emerge from the Cycle 1 schools. Where schools are successful with some aspects of the Comer process, they are typically successful with others. Those that are struggling more (though still at the mid-point on five-point scales) are struggling overall, yet in all schools the staff are optimistic that the Comer process will bring improvements to their school."

Our voyage continues, but we've already gotten our sea legs. All hands are trained and on deck, ready to take careful readings and correct our course as we steam toward our goal of excellent schools supported by the entire community of Detroit.

Reference

Millsap, M. A., Chase, A., Brigham, N., and Beckford, I. (1997). Second year progress report: Evaluation of Detroit's Comer Schools and Families Initiative. Cambridge, MA: Abt Associates, Inc.

CHAPTER 13

A Day I Will Never Forget

Jerrett Claitt

Jerrett. Photograph by Laura Brooks.

Through no fault of his own, Jerrett found himself in a frightening, dangerous crisis. But, in addition to his mother, he had a teacher who had already impressed on him that she trusted him and believed in him, and he chose to confide in and be guided by this powerful ally.

I am writing about a day I will never forget. It was a snowy afternoon on a Friday in January. Our school had a tournament in basketball. It was classes against classes in the ninth grade. I had 12 points, but we still lost. I was happy because I had 12 points.

On my way home with my friend, I encountered something terrible. I was wrongly accused of something I did not do. We were on our way home. My friend was drinking a bottle of juice. While we were crossing a street, a man in his car came speeding towards me. My friend threw the bottle at the car. The man stopped the car and turned it around and tried to hit us with the car.

My friend started to run. The man swerved onto the sidewalk. He got out of the car and grabbed me up. He was stronger than me. A police car came. The man threw me on top of the police car. The police officer got out of the car. He started to frisk me. I was trying to explain to the officer I didn't do it. The man was calling me a little bastard. Then my friend who really threw the bottle came back and told the officer he did it. They frisked him and handcuffed him. Everything was happening so fast. I couldn't really keep my head focused.

The police let the man threaten and hit me while they were frisking me. I feel that the police officers were wrong in the way they went about dealing with the situation. They didn't ask me what happened. They just listened to what the man had to say.

I told my mother and my global studies teacher, Miss Powell, two days later. Miss Powell had said that I can make it in life, and I thought I could trust her with the story, so I told her. I followed her advice.

Sometimes Miss Powell stops the class and makes us all get into a circle: the Circle of Knowledge, she calls it. She asks us, "How can I improve the class and make the work better?" She'll encourage us to do better and do more in school and live our life to the fullest instead of just wasting it.

CHAPTER 14

Making a Personal Commitment

*Vivian V. Loseth, Thomas A. Barclay, Juan I. Alegría,
Della A. Alfred, Rodney L. Brown, Phyllis Shalewa Crowe,
Christine Hides, SuAnn Lawrence, Lisa A. Marth, Barbara Monsor,
and Michelle Adler Morrison*

Photograph by Laura Brooks.

In Chapter 3, we introduced Chicago's SDP schools through the words of parents, teachers, and administrators who are totally committed to their children's and their own growth and development in schools. Now, the facilitators at Youth Guidance introduce themselves—who they are, their successes and struggles, how they keep their spirits up, and where they are headed.

Reflection *by Vivian V. Loseth*

There is nothing more difficult to take in hand, more perilous to conduct, or more uncertain in its success, than to take the lead in the introduction of a new order of things.

Niccolò Machiavelli
The Prince, Chapter 6

Since 1924, Youth Guidance (YG) has taken the lead in introducing a "new order of things." A private social service agency founded in 1924, our mission has been to help disadvantaged inner-city youth become responsible, productive adults. To accomplish this, we provide a variety of mental health, educational enrichment, job development, and social services, both directly and in collaboration with other public and private organizations. Originally, we operated a downtown clinic offering counseling services to troubled teenagers. In 1969, we formed a partnership with the Chicago Public School system. Since then, Youth Guidance has been a school-based agency, with our human and financial resources located in the schools. Youth Guidance directs the implementation of the Comer Process in Chicago.

Bringing the School Development Program to Chicago presented yet another opportunity to take the lead in the introduction of a new order of things. In 1991 we began full implementation of the SDP in four elementary schools in the neighborhood known as the Near West Side. We selected this area because Youth Guidance already had a presence there, and we were known to be effective in our work with children and their families. By 1998, the Youth Guidance Comer Team was facilitating the Comer Process in twenty Chicago elementary schools. The Chicago Team is unique in the SDP: We are the only team centered at a social service agency. In this respect, we may most closely resemble Dr. Comer's original team in New Haven.

We brought the SDP to Chicago at the same time that the city was embarking on a major newly legislated school reform initiative, which introduced Local School Councils. At that time the Chicago Board of Education operated as a segmented hierarchy with an authoritarian management style that fostered isolation, as opposed to collaboration. Within this paradigm, it was common practice for teachers to go into their classrooms and close out the rest of the world, protective of their space, time, students, and their own special interests and needs. Parents and outside groups were not welcome.

It was in this climate that we started our journey of school transformation. With the change in Chicago's school administration and with Paul Vallas at the helm, the district has become more amenable to the various programs initiated to support whole school change. However, we continue to work through barriers that stand in the way of teachers teaching in ways that help students learn.

Our fourteen-member team is multidisciplinary: Facilitators are social workers, educators, psychologists, counseling ministers, and evaluators. Our goal is to create a child-centered school environment that supports the academic and psychological development of all students. Each facilitator spends two days a week in each school coaching, modeling SDP's three guiding principles, and providing staff development and technical assistance. This ensures that all school community stakeholders understand the Comer Process and integrate it into daily school functioning.

In the words of one facilitator, Juan Alegría, "Humanizing education is a noble quest that requires the very best of our minds, hearts, and essence as a global community. Losing one child to violence, neglect, or ignorance detracts from the fullness of all of our lives." Thus, the facilitators endeavor to create communities of hope for all our children. In their voices you will hear their love of children; their passion and commitment; and the skill, patience, tolerance, and warmth with which they carry out their life's work. They are truly the best, committed to nurturing each other on our journey of school transformation.

You Don't Have to Walk Alone *by the Chicago Comer Team*

Among the most powerful aspects of life in an SDP school community is the parent leadership training. This training supports parents' efforts to improve themselves and their families' future, and inspires them to take responsibility for protecting and guiding all children. As Thomas Barclay says, "If I walk along the street and see your kids doing something wrong, I correct them. And I give all of you permission to do the same for my kid."

"We all have to juggle problems," Thomas Barclay said as he juggled yellow balls somewhat unsuccessfully at the second citywide SDP parent leadership training in Chicago. "Here, juggle one of my problems for a while," he said to a parent while throwing a ball to her. Turning to the parents, he announced with a great flourish, "We all have problems. This woman, too, has problems. Let's say her daughter is pregnant." When the woman replied, "She is," Barclay's jaw dropped and all his yellow balls fell to the ground. Recovering quickly, Barclay said, "I don't want to see any smirking here. How many of you have pregnant daughters or young mothers at home?" Slowly and silently, hands were raised throughout the room. The yellow balls forgotten, parents shared with one another how they were struggling to deal with their daughters and the newborns.

The theme of the parent leadership training was "You Don't Have to Walk Alone." Not having to walk alone was the key to a lot of the excitement in the room. One by one, people shared painful events—pregnant daughters, parents unable to help their children because they themselves were on drugs. The participants talked about the need to overcome their negative perceptions of the parents who abuse drugs if they are to help them and their children.

At the parent leadership training, the Comer Team used the expression "Sparkling Moment," as in "Let's create a sparkling moment here." It's a positive, can-do attitude that is forward looking. The expression conveys, "Let's go find creative solutions instead of dwelling on the problems." For example, a parent group was discussing ways to involve more parents. The group of parents said, "Maybe what we can do is buy them bus tokens; maybe we can pick them up; maybe we should go to their houses."

A lot of great ideas are generated at the spring parent leadership trainings, and there is a high energy level. The Comer Team says to the parents, "Write it down, and we will check in September," or "If you are writing it down now that means you are making a commitment to doing it." By saying "write it down," the Comer Team holds not only the parents but also the Team responsible to implement the ideas. Too often, great ideas remain stuck in a folder someplace. It is not until an idea is shared publicly that a sense of obligation is locked in.

The parent leadership trainings are in early spring because, the parents said, "We want to have this before testing begins." They wanted to learn how they could be helpful in the classrooms. When the parents talked about why they volunteer in the schools, a common expression heard over and over again was, "I went into the schools to help my child and to help all the children in the school."

Lany Miller, a grandparent from Chalmers Elementary School, initiated the SDP parent leadership trainings. After she attended the fourth annual retreat for the whole SDP network, she approached us with the idea of holding a conference just for parents. Lany Miller and Rhonda Jones from Jordan Community School harnessed the energy of parents throughout the city to plan the parent leadership training with our support. Lany was very adamant about parents having a piece of every part of it. She did not want us even to go over the menu without the menu committee. She wanted a lot of buy-in.

The topics for the workshops were identified by the parents based on their needs, for example, brainstorming ways to find out how they could help increase the students' test scores. (During workshops, parents come up with ideas and the facilitators help them to crystallize these ideas into plans of action.) In the process of planning the trainings, incredible learning takes place when parents are assigned roles of chairing a meeting or leading a workshop. One workshop was on the topic of school improvement plans. The parents completed a self-reflection survey of best practices of parenting and parent involvement in promoting children's development, especially academic development.

Parents change when they become part of a school. A parent volunteer objected to receiving an appreciation at a Local Council Meeting. She wanted it to be presented at the school in front of the students so that her children could feel proud of her.

In the Discovery Room *by Phyllis Shalewa Crowe*

Children in any school can be "discipline problems." SDP schools, which historically have been in communities struggling with many societal ills, are always seeking additional ways to support troubled students. The Discovery Room is a place in which they can learn and practice using new inner resources that will help them engage in the orderly life of their classroom.

The Discovery Room at Brown Elementary School is a Comer concept. It is a place where children can work out personal issues that prevent them from doing their best in the classroom. Teachers send children to the Discovery Room for a time-out, a forty-minute session, or for an all-day, in-school suspension. While in the Discovery Room, children receive one-on-one consultation, individual instruction, or whatever they need to return to the classroom environment. Sometimes, they just need to hug, to interact with a puppet, or to play a game in order to calm themselves enough to return to a learning mode.

When children enter the Discovery Room, they see all kinds of visuals, posters that are part of a Peer Counseling initiative developed by Youth Guidance personnel. The posters list twelve kinds of behaviors that interfere with academic learning: small feelings (e.g., the child has no confidence or feels he cannot be helpful to others), misuse of others, misuse of self, lack of respect for adult figures, negative influence on others, easily misled by others, aggravates others, lack of self-control, stealing, using alcohol or drugs, lying, and signifying (the child seeks status by talking loudly and negatively about others). The Peer Counseling initiative guides a group of students in collective problem solving. A student's inappropriate behavior is discussed. The first step of the discussion is the identification of what, specifically, is the problem. As a group, they decide how to handle the problem behavior.

Four of us recently visited Nash, a nearby school that has been doing Peer Counseling and the Discovery Room longer than we have. The results there have been very favorable. Suspensions have been reduced, and the children are able to mediate their problems better among themselves—without a lot of adult intervention. Dealing with discipline problems had often taken up to 90% of the administrators' time. Now, the Discovery Room and the Peer Counseling initiative developed by Youth Guidance help the school *prevent* problems. Students are mindful of behaviors that disrupt teaching and learning. Teachers and administrators discover that their freed-up energy enables them to focus on the core work of the school, and students own the responsibility for their behavior.

Rejuvenation *by the Chicago Comer Team*

Interpersonal support is a hallmark of every aspect of SDP. From the littlest child to the highest-ranking administrator, there is no level at which people have to bear their burdens alone.

Each week, on Friday afternoons, the Comer Team gathers at the offices of Youth Guidance to get rejuvenated. We are in twenty different schools, and most of us do not see each other all week long. During our Friday meetings, we share information and solve problems about what is going on in some of the schools. We laugh, cry, and yell. Some of us may have some horror story and need to vent it. "This just happened to me. I just want to share it with you, and I need some feedback from you, and then I'll be ready to go again." A lot of our colleagues have gone through similar experiences, and their support re-energizes us. The process of letting it go—telling somebody about what happened—is a healing process for us. It helps to rekindle the flame we need within us when we go back out there again. On Mondays, we are ready for action in the school communities because we took the time to provide each other with this precious support.

One Friday afternoon in 1997 we opened our rejuvenation process to include a researcher from the Yale Child Study Center, Michael Ben-Avie, who tape recorded our comments. These are the ones he selected as most fully describing our life's work.

SuAnn Lawrence: A school that I worked in last year had fourteen parents die. Many of the parents died from AIDS. That's devastating in a school of only 500 families.

Della Alfred: Children come to school terrified. We are dealing with urban schools that have gangs around them, young parents on crack. In one of the schools, a parent was killed in a drive-by shooting. One teacher said, "I'm not dealing with that—I'm here just to teach these kids. Your crisis intervention team is going from room to room and interrupting my instructional time." I had to share with that teacher, "Your instructional time is not even happening. The children are not with you regardless of how much you teach." We went into this particular classroom and this teacher was appalled to hear what goes on in the community.

Christine Hides: Part of teaching is having a relationship with the child. Often, the world of the child in the public school in Chicago and the world of the teacher are very different. Teachers cannot use their own experiences as a basic building block to teach the children. We help teachers to know about the lives of the children—to know who they are. Generally, when people look at programs they think in terms of purchasing a curriculum. We don't bring something from the outside and put it inside. We take what's inside and make it stronger.

SuAnn Lawrence: In one of our schools, they have a washer and dryer because there are so many children that are not being taken care of properly. In other schools, some of the teachers take the laundry home and do it for the children because their parents are unable to adequately take care of them.

Rodney Brown: If children were computers, then we could just sit them down, program them, and they would spit out the information, and we could go about our way. However, they are human beings, with their own unique developmental issues and needs. Therefore, we should consider the needs of the whole child as we teach them in the school. Also, the developmental needs of the faculty and staff should be taken into account. For example, if I am sick or have some major medical problem, that could influence how well I concentrate on my job. If someone died in my family, that could affect how I am working. As adults, we recognize that we have bad days and good days at work depending on a lot of other things in our lives. The same is true of the students.

Barbara Monsor: The Youth Guidance facilitators' effort to create change in SDP school communities in Chicago has become more impressive and inspiring to me as the years have gone by. It is the special charge of facilitators to challenge resistance and nurture the creativity and energy that come from greater communication and openness. They must guide the almost inevitable exposure of underlying conflicts that are barriers to successful teamwork.

Every bit as impressive to me was to watch individual parents who responded to the challenge to participate by providing leadership, creativity, talent, and support. These parents have gained in personal pride and efficacy as they have shared their abilities on behalf of their children and communities. School staff displayed strengths, talents, and commitment when they felt safe and were challenged to share ideas and to solve problems.

When more people participate, more people take responsibility and help to solve problems. When more people cooperate in reaching group goals, they begin to focus their attention on their tasks as they have never done before. They then may become aware of the barriers created by current teaching and administrative methods and relationships, and they may feel responsible, capable, and free to work together to solve those problems.

I discussed these ideas with Maurice Harvey, principal of Chicago's Jordan Community School (pre-K through 8). Jordan Community School has implemented the Comer Process since 1994 and it has an excellent School Planning and Management Team. He told me, "As an administrator, I had to redirect my thinking. I had to cope with the loss of authority. At the Comer meetings, particularly the meetings of principals organized by the Chicago Comer Team, all the principals talked about the adjustment. Participation in these meetings and workshops, as well as my own reading, has helped me to understand and accept the redefinition of leadership."

The amazing thing to me is that, given time to work, and firm support from above, there is ample evidence that the Comer Process can turn even the most hopeless schools around. The quality of leadership is critical, however. There must be dependable support for the process, but not autocratic direction and decision making from on high. Sometimes all that is needed is the self-assurance and good example of a few persons implementing the Comer Process and searching for better methods, who then begin to get improved results. At first those who are most ready to be persuaded will follow. Gradually those who can, but have resisted trying, will begin to pay attention.

Juan Alegría: When I started here eight months ago, my sense was that this is a great opportunity because we are making education a public matter. My initial image was that I would enter the school and immediately begin to have an impact. Everyone in that building would come to believe that they were involved in education—from the security person

to the person who cleans hallways. Whole communities would be partners in education. They would all realize the genius in every child that
we need to awaken. My first couple of months in trying to have this
impact were terrible disappointments one after the other. People didn't
know what I was talking about when I said that everyone is involved
in education. I had to keep some of those ideas very much inside of
my heart. Over time, I came to understand that people have to replace
the ideas that they have about children with other ideas. This process
is done very slowly.

Della Alfred: When my momentum starts to fade, I call on the Comer Team
to help pull me up.

Michelle Adler Morrison: I think that the worst moment that I faced with one
of my schools was their open rejection. I was told, "We really don't
want Youth Guidance here. We don't want anything to do with this.
There is nothing that you can tell us that is going to convince us." Oh,
I cried a lot; Vivian Loseth cried a lot; we cried together a lot. We had
no idea that it was going to be this hard. We thought that we were coming in with this great process, and we never thought that someone
would not want it. It just seemed unbelievable.

We just knew that there was too much at stake for the school for
us to walk away. The school was in a crisis, and the children were not
getting what they needed. Helping the children and the school was
way more important than being personally rejected. We tried to figure out what to do. I think what happened is that we persevered. We
didn't run away. We spent a great deal of time and energy trying to
develop positive relationships with the people in the schools and the
parents in the community. Today, I'm part of the family there. I think
that they are firm believers in what we are doing.

Lisa Marth: The people at one of my schools weren't overtly telling me to
leave. They were extremely polite. I was practically standing on my
head offering to do whatever they wanted me to do. I was rejected in
every way. No matter what way I did something, it still came up
wrong. It shook my confidence some and so I had to go deep to the
core of who I am—my beliefs, commitment to this work, myself as a
person and as a professional. I couldn't deny that I was a human being going through this experience. Being able to talk with the team
about the reality of what really was going on and what it felt like
helped me to know that they all cared about me. They believed in me.
Sharing the struggle with the team took the focus off of me and onto
the school. Rationally and cognitively, I knew it wasn't about me, but
emotionally it felt like it was about me. At one point I said to Thomas
Barclay, "What did you do putting me in this school?" Thomas said,

"We know you are a fighter."

Two and a half years later, I now understand why Thomas and Vivian put me in that school. The irony had always been that I truly respected what was happening on a day-to-day basis and wanted to contribute to the growth of the staff and parents, thereby impacting the students' lives. Yet the staff and administration's need to keep me at arm's length did not provide an opening for me to share my talents and the resources of the Comer Team. The turning point came on a beautiful spring day. I had on my yard work clothes and my Bulls baseball cap as I was joining students, parents, and staff for the kick-off of the Gardening Program. I'm not sure at what point the opening emerged: Was it while wheel-barreling mulch or digging holes for the park bench? It may have been when I ran to the store to get ice for the school picnic. All I remember was that we were working together. Once I felt the opening, I went for it. I felt the freedom to share my ideas, support, encouragement, and my sense of humor. I had become part of the team.

Over the past year and a half, there has been much growth at the school. There has been an increase in the reading and math scores. The PTA is reorganized and contributing to the school. Staff is collaborating on a regular basis. They are examining student work, using peer coaching to support one another and implement new instructional strategies—with the ultimate goal of having an impact on student learning. The commitment to professional growth and sharing of the talents across grade levels and subject areas seems unending.

It feels good to know I may have had a small hand in creating the space for this growth to occur. I know that for me both personally and professionally, I have grown and will always be thankful for the opportunity to be a part of the team. You may ask what made the difference, and I have to say it falls back to Dr. Comer's statement: "Nothing is more important to success in schools than the quality of relationships between and among students, staff, and parents." Relationships take time to develop. It takes a personal commitment to stay focused on the children while developing relationships. Having been there, I can say that it is not easy. Yet the commitment pays off in the end, with results for children and a sense of accomplishment for staff.

Juan Alegría: My experience was that we were encountering rejection and people not wanting what we had to offer. In the face of that, initially we were trying to be good troopers—encourage people and be real cheerful. My sense after a while was we had to open up to the reality of how hard it was. It was difficult to feel that level of rejection, especially knowing that we were offering a process that could help. In the beginning, people in the schools just didn't want to make the effort. My sense was that we needed to be very consistent—to walk the talk. Lone Rangers are obsolete in this day and age.

At Youth Guidance we needed to create a team. This was the only way to assimilate some of the blows that we were receiving at the individual schools. Administrative issues were consuming our time. We needed to open up on a personal level, trust each other, feel that we were truly a team. Some of the risks that we ask people in schools to take, we, too, had to take, especially risks on a personal level. We had to go through the process ourselves.

Michelle Adler Morrison: When we appeal to teachers, we ask them why they entered the teaching profession. "What were you hoping for," we ask, "to educate just a few of the children in your classes?" They say "No." I think that a lot of the teachers that we see have their own sense of failure. If they are brought into a more nurturing and resourceful community of teachers, they feel more effective. They begin to feel that maybe there is something they can do to influence more of the children. To help them overcome their sense of burnout, we organize networking events. Teachers rejuvenate when they meet people who are really putting themselves on the line to try to see some change. They realize that it is not about personal incompetence—it is about what we collectively can achieve. Sometimes we have all felt that we are not getting anywhere or not progressing fast enough. The more we collectively address all the forces working against us, the more likely it is that we come up with ways to feel hopeful every day.

PART III

Learning, Teaching, and Development in SDP School Communities

Valerie Maholmes

This section of *Child by Child* highlights the work of the School Development Program's newly created Learning, Teaching, and Development unit. The unit was formed in 1997 to help schools and districts make deliberate connections between the collaborative decision-making processes led by adults and the classroom processes experienced by children. The unit's mission is to help schools see teaching and learning as synonymous with child development by creating learner-centered environments that foster critical reflection, analysis, and implementation of research-based teaching strategies.

The goal of the Learning, Teaching, and Development unit is not to offer schools a set of prescriptions or a series of programs, but rather to engage schools in processes for creating an environment in which everyone learns, everyone teaches, and everyone develops. This level of engagement in the Comer Process leads to a change in the attitudes, beliefs, and assumptions that influence educational policy and practice. These new perspectives inform the creation of a balanced and aligned curriculum, as well as a climate supportive of collegiality and sharing of instructional practices that are reflective of students' multiple ways of learning.

Through a series of case studies and vignettes, this section illustrates ways in which child development and educational practice go hand-in-hand. Beginning with a focus on the characteristics of the Comer classroom (Chapter 15) and ending with examples of administrator decision making (Chapter 22), each chapter addresses ways in which educators in schools implementing the Comer Process use the guiding principles and the six developmental pathways as a framework for providing a caring, nurturing environment and high quality educational experiences for all students.

CHAPTER 15

Learning, Teaching, and Development in the Comer Classroom

Valerie Maholmes

Photograph © 1999 by Michael Jacobson-Hardy.

Underlying the Comer Process are the six developmental pathways and the guiding principles of consensus, collaboration, and no-fault. Every day teachers rely on these ideas as they assess curriculum, develop appropriate and enjoyable new material, and create optimistic, energetic, yet peaceful classrooms.

184   CHILD BY CHILD

It's 8:00 a.m. Do You Know Who Your Students Are?

At an early morning faculty meeting, Marlene Guy, principal of the former
Richardson Elementary School in Washington, DC (the school district closed
Richardson in 1996) put this challenge to her staff: "Do you really know
who your students are?" "Where do they live?" "What is their home learning environment like?" " What challenges do they bring to school?" "Do
they need glasses?" "How does each learn best?" These questions sparked
a lively discussion in which teachers acknowledged that they needed to
know more about their students.

Responding to this challenge, teachers reviewed student data and historical records to get information about issues that might have affected their
students' learning. They also used the data to identify students' prior
knowledge and skills and then began the process of defining, aligning, and
assessing their curriculum. At the end of this process, based on what they
knew about their students' overall development, they identified what was
most important to teach.

Ms. Guy put these questions to her staff and they responded the way
they did because SDP school communities are truly "child-centered." Administrators and teachers strive continually to maintain trusting, respectful, responsive learning environments in which students feel safe to share
their thoughts without being singled out or ridiculed. Genuine in their concern, teachers give students honest feedback and handle even the most del-
icate issues with fairness and an eye toward nurturing the whole child.

The Comer Process

The Comer Process does not offer a set of prescriptions or a canned cur-
ricular approach. Instead, each classroom is a small-scale version of the
whole nine-component model. To develop these collaborative, engaging,
well planned, and responsive classrooms, teachers work together to decide
how and what to teach. A thorough knowledge of child development supports them in addressing all the educational needs of each child, and in
creating a positive classroom climate. In addition, a focus on building positive relationships between adults and students keeps expectations and outcomes high for everyone involved in the students' lives.

Six Developmental Pathways

The Comer Process teaches that children grow along six developmental
pathways: physical, cognitive, psychological, language, social, and ethical.
At the heart of *cognitive development* is students' ability to think critically,

grasp concepts, interpret information, and make meaning of their environment. As students' cognitive abilities are nurtured, they progress from performing simple learning tasks that require memorization and rote recall to mastering complex tasks that require problem solving, reflection, and analysis. When children develop these skills they can be successful learners throughout life. As teachers come to know students in this area, they balance rigorous academic learning with attention to the other aspects of development to enhance students' ability to perform these higher-order tasks.

Physical development refers to the biological maturation of the child. It is the most noticeable and tangible aspect of development. However, size, shape, and obvious physical characteristics only partially define development in this area. To varying degrees children develop physical capacities such as eye-hand coordination, dexterity, visual acuity, and auditory perception. These abilities are not always immediately observed, but they strongly influence the way students perform important academic activities such as reading, handwriting, using technology, taking notes during lectures, listening to audio tapes, and carrying out hands-on activities. Teachers in Comer classrooms plan lessons and activities that take into account students' ability to perform physical tasks. Teachers are also aware of how students' general health and well-being affect learning, and they ask for support from the Student and Staff Support Team to ensure that students' physical needs are met.

Language is the economy of classroom interaction. Ideas, thought processes, and feelings are the currency that teachers and students exchange with each other as they express themselves and work to understand each other. Comer classrooms are rich with opportunities for students to speak and write their thoughts. Students also have opportunities to listen to and internalize the "rhythm" of language as they hear a wide variety of stories, poetry, and other readings.

Students' *social development* is enhanced by healthy interpersonal relationships in a wide variety of social settings. Since learning is a social enterprise, students' skills are also enhanced when they have opportunities to work on complex learning tasks through structured group activities. In this way, students learn how to work well with others and to try out their classmates' learning styles and ways of solving problems. They also acquire the skills that will enable them to be comfortable in many different social contexts. In Comer classrooms, social development is viewed as a way to present academic content. Teachers plan learning activities based on their knowledge of students' readiness and ability to engage in social tasks while managing new content. Teachers are careful to design social learning activities to enhance, not replace, learning of important subject matter.

The ability to reason and make conscious decisions to behave in certain ways is the crux of the *ethical* pathway. Development along this pathway progresses from having a basic ability to distinguish between desirable and undesirable behavior to having the ability to understand ethical principles and use those principles to regulate one's own actions (Kohlberg, 1981; Piaget, 1973). In Comer classrooms, teachers use a variety of strategies to promote ethical development ranging from discussing the ethical dilemmas in the literature they read to role playing, reflecting, and self-analyzing. To address discipline issues, Comer teachers rely heavily on classroom management strategies and engaging curriculums. Fair and sensible guidelines for personal conduct and group interaction are consistently adhered to and carried out.

When students believe they can learn and have success at learning, they develop a healthy disposition that promotes their *psychological development*. The opposite is also true. When students believe they can't succeed in school, they often act out as a way to mask their feelings of inadequacy. While SDP school communities set high expectations for student learning, teachers are careful to support self-esteem and a sense of personal ability by setting achievable learning objectives. They provide ample opportunities for every student to succeed in mastering rigorous material. Thus, students develop confidence in their ability to learn to high standards, and they show positive behaviors in class.

While each of these six pathways needs to be nurtured, they also interrelate to "the whole child." It is knowing about the whole child that inspires teachers to expand their repertoire of strategies capitalizing on students' assets rather than focusing on deficits as they create an effective, healthy learning environment.

It's the First Period of the School Day. Can We Talk?

The first thing you notice in Mr. Garner's fourth grade classroom is the organization of the room. Students' desks are clustered to make discussions and collaborations easy. Learning stations border the room to encourage individual and group exploration. An oversized chart hangs on the classroom wall showing the names of the collaborative teams and the designated team leaders for the day's lesson. Students rotate this responsibility so that everyone has the opportunity to lead in one or more of the class activities.

Mr. Garner introduces the morning's topic, and the groups decide how they will complete the assignment. An array of materials, resources, books and technologies are available to help facilitate the students' work. One group decides to write in their journals and then share with each other what they have written. Another group chooses to read aloud passages from the text and handouts, being careful to slow down if a team member needs clarification or to stop if a member has to momentarily leave the group. A third group is doing a hands-on activity. They are locating on the class map the geographic regions highlighted in the texts and will have a discussion on the folklore of the peoples in that region. Each student appears to be intently engaged in the learning activities that he has agreed to carry out and is respectful of other group members. Mr. Garner moves quietly about the room, listening to discussions, providing technical assistance, and coaching where necessary.

Before the time is up, Mr. Garner calls the team leaders together to share their experiences during the group activity and to explore ways that the students could, perhaps, do things differently next time. The meeting is brief, but each leader has an opportunity to speak. Mr. Garner then gives the leaders a set of questions for their teams to answer. In performing this final task, students demonstrate what they have learned and share their diverse perspectives on the morning's topic. After every team shares, Mr. Garner moves on to the next planned unit of study.

In this classroom, Mr. Garner has established a community of learners in which children's ideas and thoughts were valued and in which everyone played a significant role in the learning process. He modeled high expectations for the students in both academic learning and classroom citizenship. The students, in turn, had high expectations for themselves and for each other. They met with enthusiasm the learning challenges presented to them.

The class meeting format Mr. Garner used is based on Glaser's research (1969) delineating three class-meeting prototypes: educational-diagnostic, social problem solving, and open-ended. Each of these meeting types uses free-flowing discussions to get students' opinions on curriculum content, social behavior, or issues in the students' lives. Mr. Garner designed his social problem-solving process based on his knowledge of his students' development. He chose to use small groups so that students would feel comfortable sharing their concerns. By providing this forum, students became stakeholders in classroom interactions and outcomes.

Building on the foundations of development and relationships, teachers in Comer classrooms create an environment in which students are active learners and decision makers. Students need opportunities for self-directed learning and for constructing knowledge in ways that are meaningful to them. In doing so, students take responsibility for their actions and develop the habits of mind that foster a life-long love of learning.

At the start of the class period, teachers in Comer classrooms clearly describe to students the learning objectives for the day and the processes for pursuing these objectives. Students are invited to suggest how they will carry out the various learning tasks. Students also make suggestions regarding classroom rules and share their views on how certain discipline issues could be addressed. Thus, students contribute to the management of the classroom and to the group spirit that develops when teammates make decisions together.

Comer teachers also are facilitators of learning, giving students the opportunity to lead certain class activities. Students take pride in their individual work and also in the fact that they have contributed to an engaging and productive learning environment.

The Guiding Principles: The New Golden Rule for Classroom Interaction

In Mrs. Holloway's fourth grade classroom students work on collaborative projects, doing research, and seeking new knowledge on the Internet. They also have had a long-term writing project. At the beginning of the school year, they were asked to create a character. As the year progressed, they had to build a cohesive story around their character, taking into account lessons they had learned from specific units taught in class. On the day I visited, students shared their stories, and I had an opportunity to observe the guiding principles of SDP school communities—consensus, collaboration, and no-fault—in action.

The process for sharing involved the storyteller's providing a thorough description of his or her character's attributes, the chronology of the character's development, and central themes in the story. After the sharing, the teacher checked for understanding of the essential ideas in the stories by having the class reflect on what they had heard and then formulate questions for the storyteller. The storyteller's answers had to include a reasonable rationale for themes in the story, significant incidents, and particular actions the character took.

A student volunteered to be the first one to share her work. The class listened attentively as she divulged the elements of her story. When she had finished, the teacher asked the students to take a few moments to think about what they had heard, write down their questions, and then wait to be called on by the storyteller. A few moments passed, and then several children raised their hands and waved excitedly in anticipation of being called upon. The storyteller invited a student to ask the first question: "How could your character drive a car to get away from the monster if his leg was broken?" The storyteller hesitated to think for a moment and then attempted to respond. Mrs. Holloway observed the student having difficulty, so she facilitated a discussion to clarify the inconsistencies. During this process, the teacher was careful to model no-fault as she encouraged the students to rephrase their questions and to explore the concepts more deeply. One student shouted to the storyteller: "That's stupid! That doesn't make any sense!" The teacher responded calmly: "What you are really saying is that you don't understand the point the storyteller is making. Is that correct?" "What would be a better way to voice your concerns to the storyteller?" "Perhaps you could restate that in a way that helps the storyteller understand what you are asking."

Once the questions and answers had been heard, the teacher guided the students in reaching consensus that they had explored the topics as deeply as they could and that it was time to move on to the next story. When all the designated stories had been told for the class period, the teacher gave the students time to work individually, adjust their stories, and flesh out new ideas for their characters. Later they were to work in teams to share the new developments with their teammates.

In this example, the teacher used the guiding principles to both establish and maintain a safe environment for communicating, risk taking, and learning essential skills such as listening, reflecting, and formulating questions.

The guiding principles in SDP school communities are consensus, collaboration, and no-fault. They promote positive interactions among those who work together to make decisions on behalf of children. Through *consensus* decision making as opposed to voting, winner-loser behavior is dismantled. All participants are allowed the opportunity to have their concerns voiced and respected. Through *collaboration*, people from diverse segments of the school community work in teams to address the critical issues in the school. They ensure that decisions and policies take into account the perspectives of the various representatives of the school community. The concept of *no-fault* allows team members to get at the heart of issues without blaming each other or paralyzing the decision-making process with finger pointing and other negative interactions. Together these principles create a positive climate that permeates every facet of the school community. Teachers model the guiding principles so that the classroom environment emanates this tone as well.

The guiding principles help foster an atmosphere of trust and mutual respect in the classroom. Using these principles, teachers and students establish guidelines for classroom interactions as well as boundaries for discussing sensitive issues. Teachers encourage students to use descriptive rather than judgmental language as they work together on class projects. In doing so, teachers create a positive and emotionally safe environment for students to engage in collaborative work. In addition, students learn to respect diversity of ideas and styles of learning. They develop listening skills and confidence in giving and receiving feedback as they practice the fundamentals of consensus building. Opportunities to experience the Comer guiding principles in classrooms enable students to internalize the qualities and become adept at the skills that are the hallmarks of our democratic society.

The teacher's success in using this strategy of applying the three guiding principles in the classroom was based on the relationships she had established during the year and on the knowledge she had of the children's level of development and readiness to perform such tasks. Mrs. Holloway had experimented with different ways to model the guiding principles. Through reflection, revision, and refocusing she was able to create an innovative strategy for integrating the principles with academic learning tasks. As the year progressed, Mrs. Holloway continued to adjust her strategies to match the students' evolving skills and abilities.

It's 3:00 p.m. How Well Did Your Students Do Today?

At the end of a school day, every teacher asks these questions: "How well did my children do today?" "Were my teaching strategies effective?" "What could I do differently to make sure I reach every student in my classroom?" The Comer Process relies heavily on the principles of action research for assessing and modifying educational practices. The Comprehensive School Plan and the data used to construct the plan are at the heart of the schoolwide assessment and modification process. Similarly, teachers' instructional plans, students' work, and supplemental data are at the heart of decisions about teaching strategies, student learning and development.

In the Comer classroom, teachers develop instructional plans based on data they have about their students. Learning and development goals are established that take into account students' levels of readiness and preparedness for challenging academic work. To keep a finger on the pulse of students' progress, teachers refer to the Comprehensive School Plan, which contains the goals and benchmarks of what students should know and be able to do. As they review these data, teachers reflect on their own practice to determine how effective it has been and whether they need to make adjustments to accomplish the goals stated in the plan.

Homework

Personal journals, class writing assignments, and performance on tests show whether students are mastering important content. In addition, observations of the way students approach their work help teachers determine whether students are grasping critical concepts. Thoughtfully constructed homework assignments also provide useful sources of data for teachers about how students learn independently and how they seek help. Some students show incredible creativity and resourcefulness when they are given broad outlines for coming up with ways to represent their knowledge and understanding, while other students need scaffolding and support to complete their assignments.

Homework assignments are equally important in helping teachers understand the way parents and families are engaged in a student's learning. Since parent involvement is a critical element of the Comer Process, homework is an area in which parents and teachers can become teammates.

A parent of a sixth grade student once shared her frustration about her child's homework assignments: "I don't understand these homework assignments. Whatever happened to work sheets? My child doesn't have enough work to do, so I make up my own worksheets and have my child complete them. I check them, and I drill him on the worksheets every day." Much to the teacher's dismay, the child rarely brought completed assignments to school and didn't show that he understood the content. When the teacher asked him about this, he said that his mom helped him with his homework.

In an informative meeting, the teacher discerned that the parent was trying to recreate her own childhood homework experiences. She was also attempting to find some common academic ground upon which she and her child could maintain a relationship as her child approached adolescence. Perhaps the teacher's most important observation was that the child was under a great deal of psychological stress because he had to choose between two important authority figures—the parent and the teacher. The challenge for the teacher was to acknowledge in a positive way the child's efforts without casting a shadow on the parent or diminishing the child's self-concept by making him feel singled out for not doing the "right" homework.

With this information in hand, the teacher brought the issue to the Student and Staff Support Team to further define the problem and devise a solution. The team examined the information, worked with the teacher, and developed strategies that helped her successfully approach this sensitive issue with the parent and at the same time support the student's learning. As a result of these interactions, the teacher realized she needed to create new channels of communication with other parents. She called upon the parent volunteer in her classroom to inform other parents about the classroom activities and upcoming homework assignments. With support from the teacher, the parent volunteer conducted a series of roundtable discussions to talk about the various strategies that would be used during the course of the year and ways in which parents could support their child's learning at home. Thus, the teacher was able to clarify priorities and expectations, and she laid the groundwork for learning to continue at home. She also opened the door to meaningful classroom participation for parents. Teachers in other classrooms joined in these roundtable discussions, and eventually this process became a tradition for all the sixth grade teachers.

Conclusion

Ever since its beginnings, the Comer Process in the classroom has reflected a fundamental shift in how education is viewed and carried out. The process focuses teachers' attention on children's development and on the way positive relationships support learning. Teachers collaborate in an energetic culture of critical reflection, analysis, and action, and they rely on research to perfect the way they teach. Through these efforts, teachers know their students well and create lessons that stimulate their students' many ways of knowing. Teachers enable students to become self-aware and reflective and to recognize their current strengths and weaknesses. They help students build a healthy self-concept for learning and a strong sense of efficacy as they achieve high academic goals.

What is a Comer classroom? In the Comer classroom, the teacher and the students draw on the three guiding principles—consensus, collaboration, and no-fault—when they interact with one another. The guiding principles help teachers when designing classroom learning activities. The Comer classroom is a place where children learn, grow, and develop. It is a place where every child is given the nurture and support of caring adults. It is a place where every child can succeed.

How the student relates to the teacher, how the teacher views the potential of the student, and the expectancy they both bring to the interaction are all guided by the three principles, which act as a signpost that says for the teacher: "Pay attention—the students I am about to interact with are persons, each with their own rich life story, capable of learning, in need of my love and the help I can offer them—and I am here in order to promote their development and education." The three guiding principles positively influence the students when they act as a signpost for them that says: "Pay attention: I am about to interact with a teacher or classmate. I want to make sure that my behavior enables me to have a place in this group. In this place, I can succeed."

References

Glaser, W. (1969) *Schools without failure.* New York: Harper and Row.

Kohlberg, L. (1981). *The philosophy of moral development: Moral stages and the idea of justice.* New York: Harper and Row.

Piaget, J. (1973). *The moral judgment of children.* New York: Free Press.

CHAPTER 16

The Developmental Pathways
Study Group

David A. Squires, J. Patrick Howley, and Richard K. Gahr

Photograph by Laura Brooks.

*Even seasoned teachers benefit from guidance that expands their understanding of their
students. Knowing what's really happening in children's lives can make all the difference
in helping them to take their next developmental steps. In an on-going study group on
child development, teachers deepen their ability to perceive and support the children in
their care.*

The Developmental Pathways Study Group is a response to the ongoing question of how to help educators think about children's development with both their heads and their hearts. The process helps adults to strengthen their knowledge of child and adolescent development using Comer's six developmental pathways as a framework. The study group is made up of ten to twelve teachers, administrators, parents, school nurses, guidance counselors, and community or parent volunteers, and meets every two to three weeks during September through May. Through carefully designed experiences that deepen their understanding of child development and Comer's developmental pathways, group members learn how to apply this knowledge to classroom practice and school policy.

Each member of the group selects one child to study in depth for one academic year, learns how to observe the child, and records his or her observations in a journal.

Members use direct observation; conversations with the child, family members, and others who know the child; visits to the home or neighborhood; school records; and samples of the child's creative efforts. As study group members read the information to the group, they gain deeper insights into what children actually think about and do, how they see things, and how children's developmental agendas and their life's work influence their behavior (Prescott, 1957). The study group process has been used in teacher education programs and parent groups and with others who work with children. Over the past four years, the authors have adapted, refined, and field tested the study group and integrated the study group process into the School Development Program. It now incorporates the developmental pathways and the principles of no-fault problem solving, collaboration, and consensus. The following assumptions underlie the study group process and give it deeper meaning:

- There are reasons why children behave as they do.
- The causes of children's behavior are multiple, complex, and interrelated.
- A child is a whole.
- Each child is unique.
- Every child is inherently valuable.
- Democratic processes (collaboration, consensus, and no-fault) are the best means we have for respecting and valuing individuals and for providing the opportunities for each to arrive at optimum self-realization.

We have facilitated such study groups, and in this chapter we describe the process using our own knowledge and experience, teachers' journals, interviews, and comments made at group meetings. Instead of presenting the information academically, we wanted to bring the process alive for you, as it is experienced by a teacher—since teachers make up the majority of each group. We hesitated, however, to disturb the privacy of any one individual by seeking to print a journal account. We are telling you about the *process* through the eyes of a fictitious group member who is a blend of the many participants we have met over the years. Because our narrator is a fictitious person, we asked three outside readers with more than 75 years of combined experience leading child study groups (and training others to become leaders of such groups) to review the chapter. These readers agree that our composite journal echoes the many participants' writings that they have read in their years of training. They felt, as we do, we had fulfilled our intent: to present an accurate rendering of participants' experiences in the study group process. For readers interested in an academic presentation of the study group process, we recommend Daniel Prescott's *The Child in the Educative Process* (1957), which is based on his more than 25 years of experience with child study groups at the University of Chicago and the University of Maryland.

The chapter traces our narrator from her initial interest and the beginning sessions, offering her reactions midway through, and her reflections on the experience at the end of the first year.

Initial Interest and Beginning Sessions

I joined the Developmental Pathways Study Group because it was different. The usual in-service opportunities from the school district were one-shot affairs, which—although I had participated—I was getting a little tired of. When my principal approached me and said they were looking for a few people from the faculty to participate in this group and that it would meet once every two weeks for the school year, that was a draw. It was a drawback, too, because of the time commitment. I talked with Anne, my colleague who teaches fifth grade, and she said she'd like to go, too.

I know from the reports of the School Planning and Management Team that they were interested in piloting this because it directly addressed the developmental pathways. I have been concerned that our school is too test driven and content oriented without giving enough attention to helping our students develop as good people, which was one of the reasons I got into teaching in the first place. The pathways were addressed in the Comprehensive School Plan, and the SPMT identified a group leader, J. Patrick ("Pat") Howley. The district had agreed to grant us in-service credits for our participation. As you can see, we knew this was coming down the pike and that there was enough interest to warrant the long start-up and training time involved.

About ten of us signed up. We met in the classroom that was assigned to Pat Howley; he was the group leader. There were six teachers, a parent, the principal, the nurse, and the school psychologist. As it turned out we had representatives from the three teams: the SPMT, the Parent Team, and the Student and Staff Support Team. Although we all knew each other, we introduced ourselves and also told why we were interested in the Developmental Pathways Study Group. One teacher in the group had just a year of experience, but the rest of us had been around awhile. I was surprised that many of the group were looking for a deeper understanding of child development and the developmental pathways. They seemed convinced that this couldn't be done in a one-shot workshop. Many also mentioned the difficulty of committing so much time across the year. Almost immediately, we began writing in the notebooks that we had brought with us. Pat asked us to reflect on two questions: What would you like this group to be for you? What would you like this group to be for the school community? We read our responses to each other. What impressed me most from what people had written and the discussion that followed was how much we were all looking and hoping for more community in our lives.

Pat reviewed the group's purpose: to study a child's life and to learn how having a stronger developmental perspective would help us in our relationships with children and in our approach to teaching. Obviously, the first thing we had to do was choose a child for study. After some discussion, we agreed (by consensus, of course) on the following list:

- We should be drawn to a child, choosing a child who has a particular "tug" on our hearts.
- The group of children as a whole should represent a "normal" range of children the school serves.
- There should be a likelihood that the child will be in this school for the year.
- The child should not necessarily be a problem child.

Originally, I had thought of Doug, a problem child in my classroom. Pat, the group leader, however, said that we weren't here to "psychoanalyze" any of the children—after all we weren't psychologists. Our purpose was to learn about child development through studying an "average" child. After thinking about this, it really made sense. What I wanted to learn about and needed to know about were students in my class who were "average" and, therefore, may have slipped through the cracks. If I could understand them better, I would probably be better able to deal with the Dougs of the world. Then Jordan came to mind.

In a notebook, we wrote down the names of a few children and then described in a few sentences why we might be drawn to them. We then read these to the group and people asked questions that helped some make a choice. Everyone agreed to come to the next meeting with a firm choice.

Here's what I wrote about Jordan in my journal, "Jordan is quiet, most times. He has a winning grin and really tries hard most of the time. He has a particular spark that I don't think many people see that every once in a while shines. That spark is what attracts me to him."

Pat then discussed with us our Code of Ethics for the group. As we are learning about the lives of children, it is necessary for the group to maintain confidentiality. This means that our conversations would stay in the group and not be discussed outside of the group, even with spouses. We also talked about the need to tell parents and the students about what we would be doing. When talking with parents, Pat said to emphasize that we would study their children to further understand principles of child development through one of the community's children. Naturally, in the group we will also practice the School Development Program principles of collaboration, consensus, and no-fault. We discussed ways that the group would help maintain the Code of Ethics and different strategies for informing parents and children of our interest.

Pat then introduced four questions that would guide our study this year:

1. What is this child trying to do in his or her life?
2. What is this child up against?
3. What does the child have in his or her favor?
4. At this point in time, do I see any way that I could provide support for this child's growth and development?

When I thought about Jordan and these questions, I realized that I didn't really "know" very much about Jordan, at least very much about him in the questions' terms. What I ended up doing was putting those four questions on a file card and slipping it in the notebook's pocket so whenever I wrote in my journal, the questions would always be in front of me. Pat said we would continue to use these questions after people collected information in their journals, and we would read the journals to the group. The questions would help each individual focus on the child he or she had chosen.

Next we talked about all the sources of information about the child: conversations with the child; school records; conversations with family members, classmates, and teachers; visits to the home or neighborhood;

sporting events the child might participate in; classroom observation; and of course, work or creative efforts of the child, like a story, a picture, or a project. This seemed like a lot to do.

We collect this information in our journal, which we keep in our note-book. Our purpose in the journal is to write accurate, nonjudgmental an-ecdotes about what we see. On the right-hand side of the journal we write our objective, anecdotal descriptions of what we see and hear from the child or from others. On the left-hand side we write our own personal responses to what we find out, our own opinions, and some of the ideas the group might have when we read the journal at one the of sessions.

That sounded easy. But it turned out to be difficult to write objectively. I remember that I wrote in my journal on the right side of the page, "Jor-dan was having a bad day." The group helped me see that that was my judgment or opinion and really belonged on the left side of the journal. The group helped me clarify what I saw by asking, "How did you know Jordan was having a bad day?" I replied, "He didn't talk to anyone, which was not usual. He sat on the hill at recess while everyone else played kick ball. And when I asked him what was the matter, he just looked at his feet and didn't say anything." The group agreed that those descriptions were much more objective and should go on the right side of the journal.

As I wrote about Jordan I thought about the four questions on the card. In my journal I remember writing about what I thought Jordan was up against. I really didn't know. It became a mystery, a puzzle that I was try-ing to figure out.

After the first session, we spent time in each meeting with a few peo-ple reading the journals, both the right and left sides. Then the group would respond. At first, the group was learning how to describe children "objec-tively" and so there was discussion about what should be on each side of the page. As we got better at doing that, we concentrated more on trying to understand what was happening in that child's life. Pat was a good fa-cilitator, as he wasn't trying to "lay" something on us; rather, he responded to each of us and tried to help us take the next steps so we could get to know our children better. Pat continued to go back to the four questions, but emphasized the one about how can we help the development of the child now.

Group members also grew more knowledgeable. They started offer-ing fewer of their opinions and started to ask more questions to get the per-son who was reading their journal to take the next steps in his or her thinking. Pat emphasized that the role of the group was to help each par-ticipant grow, and that we grow when we are asked to deepen our own thinking.

I remember that the group asked me questions about Jordan's bad day like: Did this occur often? Was this part of a pattern? Were there other times when these behaviors were in evidence? Had I noticed anything that happened in school? What did I know about what was going on at home or with his group of friends? What next steps made sense for me? How did I feel about the way I responded to Jordan? These questions helped me probe more deeply and led me to other sources of information. But their cumulative effect was to help me see that I am the person who *can* generate the answers. I am the person who will help to unfold, with Jordan, his life's story.

The other thing I understood was that, even after a few weeks of focusing on Jordan, I really didn't have a lot of objective information about him. I did have a lot of judgments about Jordan, perceptions about Jordan that really relied on very little objective data. How quickly I jump to judgment, not only with him, but with many of my students.

The other thing I struggled with was the actual process of writing. There was a lot that I observed that I didn't, for one reason or another, actually write down. This made my journal a little "thin." Others had the same difficulty. We spent some time in the group in the first few sessions discussing how to get more time to do the writing we knew we should be doing. We were sorely aware of the realities of our over-committed lives, but we also understood that our commitment to each other and to our children was on the line.

Midway

After a few months, each of us had some information about our child, we had listened as others read their accounts of their children, and we had learned to separate our objective information from our conclusions and judgments. I felt like I was getting to know Jordan and the other nine children being studied by the group as well.

Pat brought in articles that informed some of the issues that we were discussing from our journals. I remember discussing an article called "The Mental Health of Students: Nobody Minds? Nobody Cares?" (Purkey & Aspy, 1988). I was amazed to read that there is research to indicate that:

1. Schools that facilitate affective development also facilitate cognitive development.
2. "Inviting" practices are related to positive outcomes.
3. Students learn more when they see themselves as able, valuable, and responsible.

4. Students learn more when they choose to learn.
5. People are the most important component of schools.

Purkey and Aspy argue that these five axioms for school achievement are most important because a myth has developed that education has to be either humane or effective, but that it is impossible to do both. I became a teacher *because* I wanted to do both! It was great to feel the support of hard research about something that I had always felt in my heart. Pat had a real knack for choosing articles that responded to issues in our children's lives. The articles helped me think more deeply about my mission as a teacher and strengthened my commitment to developing the whole child.

As we continued our observations and writing, we began to notice recurring patterns of behavior. For example, when Jordan was upset, he would usually withdraw from the group and from me for awhile. Pat pointed out that these behavior patterns are clues to the child's life, to what the child is currently working on in his or her development. From that example and from other observations I had made, I thought that Jordan was trying to understand how to deal with conflict. Other children were trying to learn about making "friends" with other students, or dealing with issues of responsibility in homework, classwork, and on the playground. All those details that we wrote in our journals started to make more sense as they were woven into recurring patterns.

From a teacher's point of view, I found it surprising that the children's developmental work generally had little to do with what we were studying in math, science, or social studies. Indeed, what appeared to be most important in a child's life was not necessarily the agenda that we, as teachers, had for them at school. When Jordan withdrew, he didn't need another math assignment to pull him out. I began to see the world of the classroom and the world of the student as two very different places.

We discussed this in the group, as others felt the same way. At first, I felt helpless. If Jordan has his own developmental agenda, then, of course, other students in the class did, too. And what I was doing in the classroom, all that content, didn't match well with what they were dealing with. I felt I was trying to show a movie at the beach at noon. It would be difficult for kids to see the movie (the content of lessons) when the sun (their developmental agendas) was so strong and bright.

Through our discussions I found that my initial reaction was a little strong. However, the issue was still there. Over a number of months I found myself searching for and trying different ways to make my classroom and my teaching more attuned to students' needs. The group helped as they were struggling with the same thing. We discussed: a weekly class meeting on Monday mornings in which we would talk about what had happened over the weekend and what we were going to do during the week; listening more "intensely" to students and techniques to accomplish that; tying content in reading more closely with some of the developmental needs of the class; having more open-ended discussions about story characters' feelings; and setting up guidelines for listening and responding in the classroom so students would feel safe in sharing more. Our guidance counselor was a great resource. She came in and modeled how to do class meetings. Most in the group started to view the group members as a resource that could be used to help each one of us. This was a new feeling and way of using each other that I had not experienced before.

Along with our learning how to discern patterns in our children's lives, we also practiced making "multiple hypotheses" about the patterns. Pat indicated that there are many reasons why we do things; if we quickly settle on assuming just one reason for our child's behavior, we may miss something of significance. To do this, we examined one recurring pattern that we wanted to understand better and then invented many reasons for the patterns. At first I could just think of one or two hypotheses. But this was a group activity, so they helped me stretch. Once the hypotheses were generated, Pat would always ask, "Is there any information to support the hypotheses in the journal?" That would take us back to the written observations once again.

This way of thinking took me more than a few sessions to understand and accept. I had been used to coming to judgment quickly because my judgments seemed logical; I had no need to look further; there was too much else to be done. So this did not build on my strengths. But now I was focusing on Jordan. As the group added to my few hypotheses, I saw that some, not all, really helped me understand Jordan in a different way. I also saw that my *quick* way of being was shutting off avenues of understanding that might help me assist Jordan to take his next steps.

When listening to others generate multiple hypotheses, I knew that a few times I saw the patterns differently. When I shared my perceptions, particularly when I related them back to the child's story, they became powerful new ways to think about a child. This helps me to see that my ideas about children can be more effective if I take time to "think before I leap." The important thing is not to come to a judgment, but to come to a better understanding of a child. I learned that suspending judgment and thinking through multiple hypotheses is a key for me to understand a child better.

As this is a group process, it became clear as we repeated our search for multiple hypotheses that none of us had "the answer." The group collaborated in a way that helped us to see the multiple answers inherent in the journal of the child's story. I understand the process of collaboration differently as a result. Before, I understood collaboration to be a process where everyone got to say his or her piece. Collaboration insured that everyone was heard. But our group's collaboration felt different. The process gave testimony that collaboration was "hearing" others' reflections with respect. Collaboration went from passive (being heard) to active (hearing). And hearing means listening. Listening means understanding that I don't have all of the hypotheses, that someone else has one that will help me be more powerful in the lives of children. I had never before understood collaboration as a process that could help *me* do better. It had always been, "just make sure everyone is involved." Through this new way of thinking about collaboration, I came to rely and trust the group more and let go of quickly jumping to conclusions.

Pat Howley continued to bring in articles. The articles focused on developmental theories, which was a great review of much of the stuff I had "learned" in graduate school many years ago. But this learning was different because the theories weren't just ideas to be memorized. Now we applied them to the individual children in the group. Piaget, Erikson, Havinghurst, Comer, all had proposed theories we examined, always with the question, "How does the theory develop our own insights about the children we are studying?" I was connected to these ideas in a way I hadn't experienced before.

Once we had a few months of group work completed, Pat introduced us to classifying the observations in our journal by Comer's six developmental pathways: the physical, language, psychological, social, ethical, and cognitive. We categorized all of the entries in our journal according to the pathways. We discovered that not all pathways had equal amounts of information from our journal. For example, my journal had very little about Jordan's ethical and physical development, although there was lots of information on his psychological and language development. I started to concentrate more on the areas I had ignored.

As our year of study was now almost over, I read the whole journal through again and listed all the *facts* I had observed about Jordan according to the six developmental pathways. As I reflected upon this information, I returned to the four questions that I kept on my card:

1. What is this child trying to do in his or her life?
2. What is this child up against?
3. What does the child have in his or her favor?
4. At this point in time, do I see any way that I could provide support for this child's growth and development?

Organizing the data in this way gave me some refreshing new insights. It also suggested new ways to work with Jordan, and new areas that I might examine when collecting additional data.

The other thing I must mention is my changing relationship with Jordan during this time of November through February. As I became more focused on Jordan and gathering and categorizing all the information, I really got to like him. There was a bond there that I had not felt with many of my students recently. I knew him in so many different ways than I had gotten to know most students, and that knowledge helped build an understanding and an acceptance. Before, I would have been irritated at his continual withdrawal; now I understood some of the reasons for the withdrawal and many more of the issues he was trying to deal with. He really was a spunky kid wrestling with difficult problems, seeking solutions in the best way he knew how.

One of the members of our group, the school psychologist, told us that in his third meeting with James, the boy he had chosen, James opened up much more. It had not occurred to us to meet directly with our children and have conversations with them. As a result, an unplanned but very important discussion about talking with children continued for quite some time. Our school psychologist was surprised. He just took it for granted that we would spend time talking with the children. He shared with us how he had learned to sit quietly and just be a friend to children. In this way he could invite conversation by asking open-ended questions like, "James, will you please tell me more about the project you are working on?" and "What do you like best about your quiet reading time?" We began to see that by hearing James talk about his own experience of the school activities, our school psychologist was truly entering James's world and seeing what it was like for him. The school psychologist suggested that nonjudgmental, respectful questioning and just being with the children might bring us powerful insights about them.

The bond that was created between Jordan and me that I mentioned earlier happened primarily because I began to meet with him on a more regular basis and hear more about what life is like for him both inside and outside of school.

The Group Wraps Up

During the group's last two months we wrote a summary of our journal. By this time we had examined a few areas of the child's life in depth; we had data from the journal along all the developmental pathways, and we had tested our multiple hypotheses against the journal's information and with the group members. Our final summary was structured around the four questions.

Over the last few sessions, in addition to reading our final summaries to each other, we also considered a variation on the last question: How can the school as a whole support children's growth and development? In our studies of individual children we found many similarities. For example, the child's developmental agenda was often quite different from the teacher's agenda or curriculum for the child. While the child was trying to figure out his or her role within a circle of friends and in relationship with family, the school was requiring work in content areas. Often it felt like the energy that the children used on "their" agenda really left little room for the school agenda. There were ways that I had changed my classroom schedule and teaching emphasis during the year. Others had made similar changes. This led us to thinking about how to address this on a schoolwide level.

We knew that not everyone in the school would be interested in a year of the developmental pathways study group. We knew that the Student and Staff Support Team played a role in helping to develop the overall school climate. We also knew we had to do something to continue our learning together for the next year. By this time we had really bonded.

We generated a list of fifteen ideas that could help the school become more "developmentally sensitive" to the developmental pathways of students. To create the list we used the same process we used in studying our individual students. We gathered information, noted patterns, developed multiple hypotheses, classified our understandings according to the developmental pathways, and then rechecked the data gathered. A light bulb went on—we were beginning to apply the process we learned to other aspects of the school.

But we knew that these fifteen ideas needed to be shared with others in the school. We used the School Development Program structures to help us do this. The nurse and the guidance counselor, already a part of the SSST, took the fifteen ideas to the SSST for their consideration. The principal and a couple of teachers, already part of the SPMT, took the ideas to the SPMT. And the parent member, with the support of a few of the teachers, took the fifteen ideas to the Parent Team. As the Comprehensive School Plan for the next school year was being developed at that time, most of the ideas were incorporated into the plan. The idea that I was most excited about was that the group was going to stay together and become a subcommittee on learning and development to help with the implementation of the ideas included in the Comprehensive School Plan. I really feel that this group has a solid grounding in a developmental perspective and will help to make the school more child-centered.

In the last few meetings we also reflected on our own learnings and shared some of the changes we had experienced during our year together. Here are a few of the things that were most important for me.

I was amazed at what I learned from my colleagues as they shared their observations and perspectives. In our group, it was sometimes easier to see what colleagues had overlooked in their observations and questions. However, I came to realize that I, too, had a narrow perspective and that all of us were helping each other to expand our vision and see much more. Indeed, I now view things from two perspectives, my own and that of my students. Those two perspectives help me talk to myself about my students, first as a teacher, then as someone who deeply understands from a student's viewpoint. I can hold both perspectives at once, even though they usually tell me different things.

I grew to know, to understand, to accept, and to love Jordan. Indeed, the knowledge and understanding came from the journal-writing process in which I tried to figure out who Jordan was and what his life was like for him. I climbed out of my shoes and tried to walk a mile in his. Acceptance came increasingly as I was able to suspend my own jumps to judgment and try to figure out the multiple and complex reasons for his behavior. The more I just tried to understand, the greater my acceptance. The more I understood the contexts of Jordan's family and friendships, the more I understood what he was up against and his tenacity in trying to deal with very complex situations. The initial spark that drew me to Jordan in the first place was this tenacity, tempered with graciousness and a usually unflagging spirit. That grew from admiration to love. I knew the joy and pain he was going through, and I loved him for the spirit in which he was able to grow.

I was also able to see this process take place with others in the group. We had a wonderful group of children we studied. Although each child brought out his or her own individual issues, most of our work and concern was with generic developmental issues. It helped me to get out of just thinking about my grade level and take a more expansive look at what children are struggling with and accomplishing across age groups. This helped to "center" me more on child development and to see it within the context and progression of how all children develop and grow.

Reflections

In retrospect, the group had a profound effect on how I view my role as teacher. It reinforced and strengthened my view of the importance of a developmental perspective. And in strengthening that perspective I am less content driven and more concerned with the developmental needs of my students. I choose the content more carefully because I am thinking of how I can help students take the next step in their development *through* the content I am teaching. Consequently, I have switched my reading selections to those that explore developmental tasks my students are dealing with. I spend more time in group work and in helping children understand groups, roles, and how to be effective in a group. We talk more about hopes and dreams. We are better able to discuss our feelings. I am more aware of how friendship and family influence what a child is working on. We have talked a lot about how to approach problems in a structured way. I have started to use more conflict resolution strategies as one way to make social problem solving more structured. I now know that students take a lot of time working through developmental issues; I am more patient with this process. But mostly I am aware of how different the child's agenda is from the school's agenda. My job is to select content and processes for my class that will meet children's developmental needs as well as provide good subject area instruction.

My understanding of the three principles of the School Development Program—collaboration, consensus, and no-fault—has been reinforced and expanded through the group. Taking on a developmental perspective means I apply no-fault problem solving to my students. They have developmental tasks they are struggling with. My job is not to judge but to help them take the next steps. I have been successful in doing this with Jordan. I can do a better job in the future.

I also take a more no-fault approach to myself. Rather than beat myself up for all those things I wanted to get to and didn't, I ask myself if I've worked hard, worked smart, worked developmentally. This has allowed me to let go of some unreasonable expectations that drove a wedge between me and really seeing, hearing, and understanding children. The group has provided a working laboratory for collaboration and consensus decision-making processes. Over and over, I found that the group could help me see things in a new way, focus on important issues, and clarify my own thinking and direction. Collaboration was no longer just getting everyone involved, but truly the best way to help make *the best* decisions. I trust this more now.

Not only has the group had an impact on my professional role; I have changed a lot personally. I give myself the gift of more time and energy spent reflecting, developing multiple hypotheses, allowing myself not to close too quickly. My world isn't as neat and orderly as it once was, but the variety sparks vitality. I found in asking the four questions of Jordan's life, I also had to ask them of my own. "What am I trying to do in my life? What am I up against? What do I have in my favor? Is there a better way to support my own learning and development?"

The study group certainly helped me take the next steps in my own understanding of my role as teacher. But I also took a look at my role as parent, as spouse, as the daughter of aging parents. Jordan's struggles and my struggles are not too different. Indeed, examining Jordan's life allowed me to also re-examine my growing-up, my parents and our struggles, my friends. I have let go of some things that had disturbed me for years. Finally, I saw in Jordan a little bit of who I was. And my love for him strengthened my love for me. Not that all these personal things were the focus of the group; they weren't. But that did happen for me as I became more involved in the process.

Earlier in our meetings, Pat Howley had shared this thought: Perhaps as we, the teachers, changed and developed, our students, in turn, would also change and develop. At first, I didn't understand how that would be so important but later this thought became a very powerful insight for me. I came into this study group so that I could help one child to grow. What I came to see was how much I was changed by participating and what a difference I could make for all the children in my classroom. I feel I'm now more understanding of all children, their developmental needs, and their frames of reference. I also see that my outward behavior has changed: I listen much more to children, and I encourage them to listen to one another. I ask more questions of myself and of my colleagues. I inquire more frequently to understand another's point of view—a child, a parent, or a colleague. I've learned to integrate the six pathways into my learning activities because I understand how they all are interdependent in helping a child to achieve and develop. And most of all, I feel a surprising sense of renewal both as a teacher and in my personal life.

Acknowledgment

This chapter is dedicated to the memory of Julia Weber Gordon who pioneered the Child Development Program in New Jersey. She was a child advocate, an artist, and the author of the classic book, *My Country School Diary*. The book tells of her four-year experience teaching in a one-room school house in an isolated mountain neighborhood. It was translated into four languages, and showed how children can live with and teach each other as preparation for becoming active, participating citizens in our democracy.

References

Prescott, D. (1957). *The child in the educative process.* New York: McGraw-Hill.
Purkey, W.W., and Aspy, D.N. (1988). Mental health of students: Nobody minds? Nobody cares? *Person-Centered Review, 3,* 1 (February).

CHAPTER 17

And We're Both in the Same Class

Liznell Carter and Makhosazana Ndlovu

Liznell (far right), Makho (second from right), and other students visiting Yale.
Photograph by Laura Brooks.

The notion that different people can mean different things while using the same words sparked a conversation about motivating students by "pushing" them. Liznell preferred to be pushed against so that she could rebound. In contrast, Makho preferred to be pushed forward, both as a prod and as a support. Their interchange gave them a glimpse into a hidden but essential aspect of effective classrooms: Teachers have to become curious enough to learn each student's personal style.

Makho Ndlovu: I want a teacher to tell me the truth. I don't want a teacher to lie to me if I'm not doing that good. I wouldn't want a teacher to tell me that I'm a good student when I'm really not just in order to get my self-esteem up.

If students are not operating at their full potential, I would sit them down and let them know. I'd say, "What you are doing right now is terrible. I don't know what you have been doing, but you've got to improve because this does not make sense. You're blocking yourself from working when you say, 'I can't do it' or 'I'm trying as hard as I can, but I really can't do it.' I don't want to hear 'I can't' because you can do anything. Keep pushing, and you'll get to where you want. If you have a 20, and you want to get to 90, you can't get there immediately. You have to get a 30, then you get a 40, then you get a 50, and then maybe you'll get up to a 90." What works for me is to aim a little higher each time.

Liznell Carter: When somebody says to me, "You know what, Liznell? You're not going to make it anyway. You're always going to be that type of person that gets to the door and knocks, but nobody is ever going to let you in," I go, "Really? Oh, is that so? Well watch me!"

Sometimes it's good to aim high, and always be up there: "I see it, and I've just got to get it." Once I make it to the top, I want to stay there. That's where the adventure comes in: Holding on to your place at the top.

Sometimes people have this thing: "I've got to be at the top. I've got to be at the top." And when they're not there, they just give up and they let themselves drop. That's when the teacher has to give them space to drop. Because if they were always the overachiever type of person and you give them a place to drop, then they'll be able to see themselves, and they'll notice that something definitely is wrong, and they'll say, "Is this me? No, this is not me! I've got to make it to the top before I lose my place."

I want the teacher to give me a chance to see what I'm doing wrong. If the teacher notices that I'm just giving up, then the teacher should talk to me. Not push me the way I liked it before when I was on top, but to push me back up. The teacher can say to me, "I told you once before that you couldn't do it, and you proved me wrong. I said, 'No, you can't,' and you said, 'Oh, yes I can!' Now do it again."

Makho Ndlovu: That's not the way I'd do it. A student needs somebody to push it out and let it be known that it is there. The student just has to work on getting it out.

If the student is trying and not getting it, you have to switch to something else. What I would do as the teacher is to tell the student,

"Looking at your grades, I don't think that you're going to get to the top just by cramming it all in your head and hoping to get a higher grade." And what I need to do as a student is to work step by step and get as much as I can get. Don't force it in, but also don't be passive about it.

Liznell and Makho's Suggestions for Teachers Who Want to Get Better Results from Their Students

- When you're away from a student and are considering new things to try with him or her, picture the student in your mind's eye.
- To a student who is doing well, ask:
  What am I doing that is working for you?
  What am I doing that doesn't work well for you?
- Also, to a student who is not doing well, ask:
  What am I doing that is working for you?
  What am I doing that doesn't work well for you?
- The way that you present yourself to the children day to day makes more of an impression than you think.
- Every year you should be refreshed and learn new methods.
- Make sure that your students can depend on you and also that they become more and more independent.
- Move yourself, your attention, and your materials around so that everybody feels that every chair is in the front of the room.
- Encourage the students to open up to you about their process.
- Ask your class for ideas to make the class more interesting.

CHAPTER 18

A Balanced Curriculum

Standards and Assessments for High Performance

David A. Squires and Angelique Arrington

Photograph © 1999 by Michael Jacobson-Hardy.

In Chapter 1, senior educators speak about the urgent need for accountability. Here, two SDP implementation coordinators describe a balanced curriculum process that responds both to the developmental needs of children and to city, state, and national standards. For schools and districts that have successfully implemented this process, the impact on student reading test scores has been uniformly positive (See Ben-Avie, this volume, p. 4, and Squires, 1998a).

Here's the scenario: The School Development Program has helped your school over the past several years. Your teams are in place. Parents are more active in school activities. The climate of the school is changing for the better. Collaboration and consensus are the rule rather than the exception. What's next? What's most important?

The next step is to examine the school's curriculum, instruction, and assessment. What are your students learning in reading and language arts, math, science, and social studies? Will the curriculum help further the students' development and improve their scores on national and state tests? Does your school have a way to monitor and evaluate its curriculum and instruction through a means other than standardized tests?

The School Development Program has a process to help schools and districts balance and align their curriculum with national, state, and local standards as well as with the six pathways of development: physical, cognitive, psychological, language, social, and ethical pathways.

If education is to improve, schools and districts must develop the capacity to describe, balance, align, and assess their curriculum. Programs, like superintendents, may come and go, but a carefully developed and balanced curriculum, unlike add-on programs, provides the structure so that current results can shape future improvement.

As the process of curriculum development begins, it is important to differentiate curriculum from other elements of the educational process:

Textbooks are not a curriculum. There's too much information for teachers to cover, let alone for students to learn. Teachers choose what's important for them without knowing how their decisions impact students as they progress through the grades. When there is no guarantee of student mastery, this year's teacher is faced with a hodgepodge as last year's students are mixed into new classes. Review now consumes the first quarter, leaving fewer instructional days for the current year's content. With less time, teachers choose to teach fewer of the grade level expectations. Students aren't prepared adequately for next year. The cycle is repeated.

State and national standards are not a curriculum. Rather they describe in general the appropriate content, but do not present a way to manage the decisions districts and schools need to make in order to create the scope and sequence of the instructional program.

Standardized and state tests are not a curriculum. The fearsome pressure teachers and administrators feel to perform well contracts the curriculum to a pinhole, a restricted funnel for the development and education of children.

How Do We Balance the Curriculum?

If textbooks, standardized tests, state standards, or add-on programs alone shoulder the load of focusing schools, the results will not meet public expectations. Only a balanced curriculum process can be a skeleton to support the tendons and muscles of powerful instruction that balances the needs of children with the demands of society.

The balanced curriculum process helps schools put child development at the center of curriculum development by building professional relationships through collaboration and consensus. The process increases management capacity to refine a school or district curriculum while maintaining accountability and commitment. The balanced curriculum process provides the tools and processes to structure the school's or district's work to identify the most important content that will support students' development and performance.

The process involves three steps: defining the curriculum, aligning and balancing the curriculum, and assessing the curriculum. This can be done at either the school or district level.

At the school level, the principal and grade-level or subject-matter representatives attend a series of four workshops in which the steps to a balanced curriculum are explained and simulations help school or district teams anticipate problems and possibilities they will encounter when the school team implements the program back at the site. District curriculum, assessment, or staff development personnel are included in the workshops and do follow-up work at the sites. The four workshops follow a standard format and are supported by manuals customized to include the appropriate standards and assessments for the site.

Session 1

- Activity 1: Introduce the balanced curriculum process
- Activity 2: Provide an overview and rationale for the balanced curriculum process
- Activity 3: Define components of a good program in the subject area
- Activity 4: Outline unit titles and specify length of teaching time for each unit

Session 2

- Activity 5: Read and process national standards in the content areas
- Activity 6: Incorporate the developmental pathways
- Activity 7: Generate activity-based objectives and descriptions for each unit

Session 3

- Activity 8: Align and revise unit objectives to the state assessment system
- Activity 9: Align and revise unit objectives to the standardized test objectives
- Activity 10: Validate alignment and balance (internal and/or external validation)

Session 4

- Activity 11: Develop assessments with formats aligned to standardized tests
- Activity 12: Develop rubrics and performance assessments aligned to the unit's content
- Activity 13: Forge agreements about using unit assessments to improve program
- Activity 14: Develop ways to use results from unit assessments and standardized tests to improve the program
- Activity 15: Plan for continued implementation.

To develop a districtwide instead of a school-specific curriculum, unit descriptions and activities are generated monthly or by some other relatively short period of time. Then district administrators and building representatives participate in sessions in which the district curriculum is balanced and aligned, internal or external validation takes place, plans for assessment are made, and implementation and monitoring issues are discussed.

Let's listen as two teachers—Anne, who teaches third grade, and Ed, who teaches sixth grade—and their principal, Deloris, discuss the balanced curriculum process in math that was implemented in their school over the last two years. These three characters are fictitious—they are a blend of principals and teachers who have worked to create balanced curricula from all over the country. I have created this dialogue to personalize the balanced curriculum process and show the professional changes in the ways teachers and principals view their roles (Squires, 1998b).

Why a "Balanced" Curriculum?

Deloris: I was initially interested in the balanced curriculum process because I knew—just knew—that our teachers and students could do better on the tests given by the district and the state. Just because our students come from a poor neighborhood doesn't mean they perform poorly. But we did have a way to go.

Ed: A balanced curriculum that we defined as a school made planning for teaching easier. I knew that if our grade level could get together and all decide on a common curriculum, then we could divide up the planning and we wouldn't have to plan and assess all the units individually, as we had been doing before. Plus our students would then receive a consistent program in every class at the same grade level.

Anne: My initial interest came because I was not sure what should be emphasized. There are so many competing priorities. The text, which I mainly followed, didn't really have enough practice in it for many of the topics I was supposed to cover. The standardized tests we take emphasize other topics. Then our district is suggesting we teach the topics in a certain order. And I had read some articles about the new standards proposed by professional organizations of math or reading and language arts teachers. The articles suggested emphasizing more the process of coming to solutions, rather than just the solutions themselves. Of course, some of our vocal parents wanted "The Basics." Others wanted lots of enrichment. I saw the balanced curriculum process as a way to make informed decisions so the curriculum would be focused to meet the developmental needs of my children.

Deloris: As a school administrator I saw the balanced curriculum process providing a way to avoid the duplication across the grade levels that I saw while observing classes.

Anne: That's true. Before, I spent a lot of time reviewing at the beginning of the third grade because I wasn't sure what content the students had mastered in second grade. Different second grade teachers appeared to emphasize different things. So when they configured the classes for third grade, I had to spend time figuring out where the students were.

Ed: I've found the same thing. I now know what has been emphasized in fifth grade and that students really know that content. Now I spend much less time on review and much more time on sixth grade content. My students come out ahead.

Defining the Curriculum

The past and the future combine when defining the curriculum. Defining the curriculum means teachers look backward and discuss their past practices to define the best of what, collectively, is already being done. Teachers also discuss what makes up a good subject-area program. The outcome of these discussions results in an entire faculty understanding their own standards.

Ed: We began the balanced curriculum process by talking about what we thought made up a good math program as a way to define standards for ourselves. I was surprised at how many ideas I had about teaching math; it was interesting to see that others thought the same way.

Deloris: This was another way that we started "where we were." As a faculty we reached a consensus about what we thought made up a good math program. These were our standards that we developed ourselves. We could then take a look at each unit and see if the unit met our own standards. This helped me to understand what the staff understood about the characteristics of a good math program. Naturally, I saw some opportunities for future staff development work.

Ed: Just to piggy back on that comment: I felt that a good math program should involve hands-on problem solving experiences that were similar to math problems they will encounter outside school. Well, when I actually looked at my own instruction, and particularly my unit tests, I found I did not have very many of those "real world" problems. Our grade level is working on improving in this area.

Deloris: This is an example of how we are aligning our units to our standards. We begin with what we are doing and what we know—no reinventing the wheel.

The curriculum consists of units taught sequentially. Each unit has a title and a specified amount of time; for example, a geometry unit may take two weeks. As faculty publicly share their work, scope and sequence issues surface and become resolved. Then, 2–5 important activities are agreed on by teachers at the same level or course. Everyone agrees to complete these activities, although different teachers will approach them differently depending on their class. For each activity, the group agrees on brief statements about what most children will be able to accomplish by the unit's end. These are called "activity-based unit objectives." Once defined in this way, each unit is a professional promise that most students will complete the work successfully.

Deloris: The next activity in the balanced curriculum process is for each grade level to define its unit titles and the approximate beginning and end dates for each unit. After all the grade levels completed the unit titles, we posted the results in the teachers' lounge. That was a real eye opener for me. We saw that addition and subtraction was taught at each grade level through grade 6 and that out of the seven grade levels in our school, a total of a year's worth of K-6 instruction was devoted to addition and subtraction. There was a lot of overlap between grades.

Ed: I couldn't believe that all that time was spent and I still had a lot of kids in sixth grade struggling over subtraction.

Anne: The pattern was clear. We were so busy trying to get through the textbook that students just didn't have enough time to really understand and learn some of these concepts. Because students didn't master the content, it was repeated at the next grade level. We could get more time by making promises about what we thought kids could learn, not what we as teachers could cover.

Ed: The conflict of mastery over coverage was one that was resolved by talking about our promises to the next grade level. We would only promise what we thought most students could learn.

Deloris: The idea of teachers at one grade level making promises about what most students would learn is one of the most powerful ideas in the balanced curriculum process. I remember sitting with the fifth grade teachers when they were discussing what they could promise to sixth grade about fractions. One teacher didn't think a promise about fractions could be made for most students, so she wanted to concentrate on division of whole numbers. Another teacher said he thought fractions were important but never covered them because time ran out at the end of the year. A third teacher said she had covered fractions but didn't really feel that enough time had been spent so students would remember the material over the summer. So, even though fractions was a textbook chapter, the grade level reached consensus not to promise an introduction to fractions, so they could spend more time on multiplication, division, and problem solving.

Ed: As a sixth grade teacher, this really helped. I now know that my main goal is to help students understand fractions and decimals in order to solve problems. So I constructed most units for fractions or decimals. I no longer feel resentful that students don't come to me with an introduction to fractions. I'm just happy that they really know how to solve problems using the four basic operations, but especially multiplication and division. I know the fifth grade teachers really have tried to keep their promise to me.

Anne: Discussing our promises at third grade really helped me clarify what was most important. But it also gave us a new way to "be" with each other. Before the balanced curriculum process, we almost never discussed what we were teaching. We assumed that since everyone had the same materials, more or less, that the same content and concepts were covered. Once we started discussing our units as promises, we found we were together on some things but not on others. Now we have a united front.

Ed: After everyone posted their unit titles in the teachers' lounge, we met and "did deals." Our "deal" with the fifth grade was that they would make sure kids knew multiplication and division. Now our sixth grade team had enough time to really come through on our promise to the seventh grade that kids would understand fractions and decimals.

Anne: I liked "doing deals." I tend to divide the year up into months, and I know what I am doing, in a general way, during each month. As a grade level, we found we agreed on the general unit topics, and we "did deals" to iron out our differences. However, I did give up one of my favorite units on geometry and making snow flakes because other things were more important and needed time. After "doing deals," which insured an appropriate scope and sequence, we developed one or two major activities for each unit and described these using activity-based unit objectives.

Ed: Coming to consensus on just 1–5 activities again helped us focus on what was most important for students. I tend to think and plan my teaching through activities, so this was a natural process for me. Teachers on our grade level had a great time brainstorming a list of possible activities. Then we chose the best ones.

Anne: Although agreeing on one or two activities for everyone was important, it was even more important that I had the freedom to teach the rest of the unit in a way that fit my students' needs and my own teaching style. So the process defined the most important activities in the curriculum, but we could arrive at those activities in different ways. We could also cover other related areas if we had time.

Ed: Once we had described the activities, then we attached educational objectives to the activities. For example, we wanted students to understand the concept of area (the educational objective), and we decided that students would practice estimating the areas and then confirming that estimate by placing graph paper over the object and counting the squares (the activity). So the activity-based unit objective read, "We will find the area of many objects by estimating the number of graph paper squares, then use graph paper to cover the objects and confirm our predictions."

Anne: Describing the activity and attaching the educational objectives to the activity allowed us to communicate well within and between grade levels about what our promises were all about. Before, we told each other we were concentrating on problem solving, without telling what the major activities were that students would accomplish. Now for each unit we know what the major activities are that all students will be doing. Our promises are now specific.

Deloris: The activity-based unit objectives have really helped each grade level understand what all kids should be able to do in order for the teachers to keep their promises. For example, the second grade team reviewed the activity-based unit objectives of the first grade team. They were impressed. Based on the review, they returned and made some of their activities a little more difficult. They told me that if most first graders were able to complete that activity, then the second grade teachers could challenge them a little more than they had thought was possible at first.

Ed: Having everyone on the grade level complete the same one or two activities in each unit allows us to get together and look at our students' work and talk with each other about how to further improve the quality of student work next year.

Balancing and Aligning the Curriculum

Balancing and aligning the curriculum also means looking to the future to improve on the past. To do this, teachers need to understand national and state standards that define current best practice and important content. Faculty see the congruence between their standards and those from outside sources. Then they modify the curriculum so the future is better than the past.

After the curriculum is defined, the curriculum is aligned to self-defined standards, national standards, the developmental pathways, state and standardized tests, and texts and other curriculum documents. Once faculty are introduced to state and national standards and assessment specifications from standardized tests, the defined curriculum is aligned to standards and assessments. To do this, a grid is used: The unit activities are listed in the left-hand column, and the standards, standardized tests, developmental pathways are column heads across the top. Teachers mark an X where there is alignment—where the vocabulary or ideas used in the standards is reflected in the activity-based unit objective.

Balance is important. Have certain standards been over- or underemphasized with too many or too few activities? The grid provides faculty with a way to ask and answer those questions.

Deloris: So each grade level has defined 10–15 units in math. Each unit has a range of 1–5 activities that are described and linked to educational objectives. We defined our own standards for a good math program. Now we get into the alignment process.

Ed: I really liked the faculty meetings in which we got to dig into the national standards proposed by the National Council of Teachers of Mathematics (NCTM). Those standards helped me to orient my own math teaching much more toward problem solving, reasoning, and communication skills, rather than emphasizing the memorization of algorithms.

I found that most of my activity-based unit objectives contained problem solving, so I was able to show good alignment with problem solving sections of the grid in the NCTM standards and also on the problem solving section of the standardized test.

Anne: There's really a lot to align the curriculum to: national standards, state frameworks, our own standards, developmental appropriateness of the curriculum, the state test, our district standardized tests, and the instructional material, including text books, that we use to teach.

Ed: When we did our grid, we found that there was little alignment between the "Communications" standard of the NCTM and our activity-based unit objectives. Not many of our math activities really required students to communicate how they solved or thought about problems. Our curriculum was out of balance. I remember that we decided that we would incorporate at least one major writing assignment in each math unit. Once we decided on the activity, we rewrote our activity-based unit objectives and "realigned" by placing new checks in our alignment chart. We now had a better balance in the curriculum. And, of course, this will also help us in our reading and language arts programs as well.

Anne: At the third grade level, we found out that the state test emphasized using graphs to solve problems. Yet we had not included any activity-based unit objectives that dealt with graphing, although we thought we would cover it tangentially in a few units. Again, our curriculum was out of balance. So, we went back and revised the activity-based unit objectives to make sure students had a couple of important projects that included graphing and problem solving. When we completed that process, we had validated the curriculum from our internal perspective.

Ed: Taking a look at how our math activities aligned with the developmental pathways reinforced where we needed to pay more attention. We included more activities with manipulatives and addressed the physical pathway. Manipulatives also address the cognitive pathway (when students use manipulatives to show their understanding) and the social pathway (when manipulatives are part of group work).

Deloris: Then the grade level took their revised activity-based unit objectives from the grid and filled out a unit record sheet on which they recorded which areas each activity-based unit objective was aligned to. It seems amazing, but the result of all this work actually fits into

one three-ring binder that I have on my desk. Each grade level consists of 10–15 sheets; each sheet represents a unit. This book records
the staff's promises to each other and—what is more important—to
the students and their parents.

Ed: Now for the first time ever in my teaching career I am confident that I
am teaching and students are learning, not just covering, all the important concepts in math. I don't have to worry or feel guilty about
not doing the best job for students.

Deloris: And we have managed in the space of one year to get agreement
within and between grade levels about what is most important for our
students to learn in math. We now have a balanced and aligned curriculum that has been validated by the school district's teachers.

Next, we invited some teachers and administrators from the Association of Supervision and Curriculum Development to be our "external" validators. They took a look at the grids, validated that we had
successfully aligned the activities to the standards and the standardized
tests, and then made comments about areas in which they thought we
were still out of balance with too much or not enough emphasis given
to various areas. Parents were also pleased that other professionals had
examined our curriculum in detail and judged it satisfactory, although
we did continue the revision process based on their comments.

Assessing the Curriculum

Each unit is assessed in two different ways:

1. A performance assessment is designed to assess students' conceptual understanding of each activity; and
2. A format assessment gives students practice on the format and concepts aligned with standardized and/or state tests.

As a whole, the balanced and aligned curriculum represents a "bet" that
student performance on both types of unit assessments will predict results
on standardized assessments. We would expect high unit assessments to result in high standardized performance because teachers develop units
where most students will succeed; the unit assessment shows if the promise has been kept, and the unit assessments are aligned with standardized
assessments. Where this is not the case, teachers and administrators can
examine and fix the problem.

Deloris: Assessment is like a bet: We're betting that if students do well on
the 1–5 activities we describe in each unit, then they should do well

on the end-of-year assessment and/or the standardized assessment. We want a predictable curriculum with no surprises or disappointments.

Ed: What we had to do was decide as a grade-level how to "grade" or assess those activities. I was relieved that we didn't have to invent a whole new assessment process, since the assessments emerged from the activity-based unit objectives.

Anne: Our grade-level conversations around how to assess the activities really pushed us to think about all the issues I learned about performance assessment in my masters' program. The activities are performances. We are designing instruction, and we are promising the next grade-level that students will be able to satisfactorily complete these activities or performances. Our grade-level conversations pushed us to define for ourselves, in ways that everyone could agree on, what was a satisfactory performance.

Ed: Fortunately, we have had some staff development on rubrics, which became a useful tool for defining different levels of satisfactory and unsatisfactory performance on the unit's activities.

Anne: And we learned that while each of us had our ideas about satisfactory performance, when we sat down to combine our ideas, we usually finished with ideas that were stronger than the initial, individual ones.

Deloris: Using student work to refine rubrics really pushed teachers to become more specific about satisfactory performance. I think sharing their intuitions helped them refine and raise their own expectations.

Anne: Because we now had similar expectations and conducted the same assessments, certain columns in our grade books were the same for everyone in the grade level.

Ed: Let's not forget the other aspect of assessment. While satisfactory performance of the activities made sure students could demonstrate an understanding of the content, we also needed to make sure that there was "format alignment" in which students practiced answering questions on the unit's content in the standardized or state test format. We used the grid again, to identify which areas from the standardized assessments were covered in our units. Then we checked the testing company's resource book to see how the format of the standardized test was described.

Deloris: I am proud of this faculty because they have collaborated on having one content and one format assessment for each unit. They use the assessment as a way to discuss both student work and their own teaching approaches and strategies. Now that most of the assessments have been developed, they can re-use the assessments next year, thereby saving time usually used in creating new assessments.

Anne: I was chair of the committee that designed how we would collect the information from the unit tests to see if we had won our bet: that satisfactory performance on the unit assessment would mean good scores on the standardized test. We had representatives from each grade level and the principal on the committee. At first, teachers were suspicious of how this information would be used, particularly if it would affect their evaluations.

Deloris: I assured them that it wouldn't. I tried to be clear that we wanted to use this information to identify our strengths and needs and to see if we won the bet. But there was still some resistance. We discussed the issues fully at the School Planning and Management Team meeting.

Anne: Finally, the committee recommended to the SPMT that teachers would turn in student results to their grade-level chair, who would keep the results confidential. Then the chairs would report to the principal's secretary that teachers had completed the unit.

Deloris: In this way, I knew we would have the information on file while teachers were reassured that it would not be used in an evaluation. However, I did have enough information to know whether teachers were falling too far behind and wouldn't be able to help students understand important concepts that were promised to the next grade level. This allowed me to problem-solve with a few teachers on how to meet their promises to the next grade level when they got behind.

Ed: When we got our standardized scores back at year's end, we examined the item analysis and made a list of areas we did well in and areas where we needed improvement. Then we took out the grids that recorded the alignment. The grids showed us which activities were keyed to the tested areas. The standardized assessment confirmed the curriculum activities in which we tested well, while showing which activities needed to be strengthened. To do this, we knew the areas where we tested well and found the associated aligned unit activity. The data confirmed these units were doing the job. Then we examined the tested areas where we didn't do well, found the aligned units and activities on the grid, and went into problem-solving mode.

Anne: Were the activities difficult enough? Was the assessment really aligned? Had we spent enough time on the unit? Did we need to build in review of the concept more frequently during the year? Did we need to build this into other unit activities? Did we need to rethink and revise the unit assessment?

Deloris: Fortunately, we built in time for each grade level to spend two days during the summer completing this activity. Then, at a fall faculty meeting, we shared our work and discussed implications for the changes between grade levels. At the beginning of the year, everyone knew what promises we would make to the next grade level for the coming year, and the faculty received the published curriculum.

Anne: Looking back, what seems to be an overwhelming task has really helped me improve how I think about what I teach. Now things seem much more logical and connected.

Ed: I don't worry about whether the emphasis I am placing is right and appropriate. I know it's the best our grade level knows how to do. Better yet, we know how to fix it when the program doesn't meet our expectations.

Deloris: We also need to complement the district administration for helping to bring this focus to our school. As you remember, they came after each step just to make sure we were on the right track and to learn what they needed to know about implementing this process in the schools that begin it. I feel that the structures and processes of the School Development Program directly address curriculum and child development issues in the school.

References

Class Management Guide: CAT5. (1993). Monterey, CA: CTB MacMillan/McGraw-Hill.

Cohen, S.A. (1987). Instructional Alignment: Searching for a Magic Bullet. *Educational Researcher* (Nov), pp. 16–19.

English, F.W. (1992). *Deciding What to Teach and Test: Developing, Aligning and Auditing the Curriculum.* Thousand Oaks, CA: Corwin.

National Council of Teachers of English and the International Reading Association. (1996). *Standards for the English-Language Arts.* Urbana, IL: National Council of Teachers of English.

Squires, D.A. (1998a). A Balanced Curriculum Process: Results So Far. New Haven: Yale Child Study Center.

Squires, D.A. (1998b). Toward a Balanced Curriculum: Aligning Standards, Curriculum, and Assessments. *ERS Spectrum: Journal of School Research and Information, 16,* (3), pp. 17–24.

Squires, D.A., & Joyner, E. (1996). Time and Alignment: Potent Tools for Improving Achievement. In: *Rallying the Whole Village: The Comer Process for Reforming Education.* Comer, J.P., Haynes, N.M., Joyner, J.T., and Ben-Avie, M. New York: Teachers College Press.

Squires, D.A., & Kranyik, R.D. (1995). The Comer Program: Changing School Culture. *Educational Leadership, 53*(4), pp. 29–32.

Wishnick, T.K. (1989). Relative Effects on Achievement Scores of SES, Gender, Teachers Effect and Instructional Alignment: A Study of Alignment's Power in Mastery Learning. Unpublished doctoral dissertation, University of San Francisco.

CHAPTER 19

Getting the Most from Students

Effort and the Student-Teacher Relationship

Fay E. Brown and Darren W. Woodruff

Photograph © 1999 by Michael Jacobson-Hardy.

Many students, parents, and teachers believe that children fail because they lack ability. SDP's successes have repeatedly proved that belief to be false. As two Yale-based researchers report, by creating positive relationships SDP teachers help students sustain their efforts at developmentally appropriate tasks. Thus the children learn not only their class work and the value of persistence, but also a justifiable faith in their own potential.

At the end of a full day spent observing students and teachers in an urban high school located in the northeast as part of a school climate evaluation, we were encouraged by the principal to look in on a math teacher's after-school tutoring session. We walked over to Mr. King's classroom expecting to find a group of serious-minded students hard at work over their algebra and trigonometry textbooks. To our surprise, the climate in the classroom was quite different. The students, who had come on their own initiative, were in fact preparing for algebra, but at the same time they were relaxing and interacting with their teacher and each other in a comfortable setting. The radio was playing, and Mr. King greeted students by name as he passed around glasses of apple juice. The environment that afternoon was one of casual, pleasant social interaction. Students enthusiastically shared their thoughts on the events of the day, and Mr. King *listened* to them, talking and commenting on their observations, all the while filling up the chalkboard with math problems. He was clearly involved in their lives and interested in their issues, problems, and questions about school and other events. After about 15 minutes, the students made a smooth transition into tackling their math problems and asking questions on the day's homework. Their effort and focus on the academic tasks seemed to be facilitated, and perhaps made possible, by the engaging and supportive social climate that Mr. King had created.

The power of this interaction between the students and their teacher is in the teacher's use of his social skills with students as a *bridge* into the academic subject matter. The productive time spent on the building of math skills seemed to be a natural extension of the positive relationships and interactions already established with the teacher. The girls and boys in the classroom came from diverse backgrounds, but they responded in a similarly positive fashion to genuine adult interest and respect.

James P. Comer, the founder and chair of the School Development Program (SDP), emphasizes the importance of the social context in teaching and learning. He told us that nothing is more important to success in schools than the quality of relationships among students, staff and parents. Additionally, he notes that "where there is a good climate of relationships, there is academic achievement, and you can accomplish the business of socializing kids and making gains at the same time. One need not interfere with the other" (Comer, cited in the National Center for Effective Schools Research and Development, 1989, p. 43).

The Power of Persistence

In the elementary school setting, we see the importance of relationships coupled with the student's willingness to expend effort in accomplishing learning tasks. Observing some third graders in the SDP's Essentials of Literacy Reading Room, we see initial differences in the students' willingness to try and in the outcomes of such differential effort. "I will not give up until I find something," said David as he earnestly flipped through the magazine pages, searching for examples of objects or foods that start with the letter J. He flipped and flipped and then suddenly he exclaimed, "Yes! I knew that if I just kept looking I would find something. Here is a picture of a jaguar." He was so excited to see the fruit of his efforts. "Good job," we told him, "we are proud of you. You said you wouldn't give up, and certainly your persistence paid off."

Another student, Darrell, behaved differently. He was asked to copy some words from one page to another, and his response was, "I can't do that." When asked why, he said, "It's too hard." When we asked him what was so hard about it, he explained that he just did not know how to write the words. We encouraged him to try, and even with our reassurance, he hesitated awhile before he made an attempt. It is interesting that once he decided to try, he found out that it was not very difficult at all.

Of all the children in the Reading Room, we choose to focus on David and Darrell because they provide such contrasts. We had several questions as we pondered these incidents. For example, would Darrell have behaved in such a *helpless* manner if he were working on David's task? Likewise, would David have behaved in such a *persistent* manner if he were working on Darrell's task? Or, was the difference in the boys' behavior the result of something else? The truth is that we became concerned about Darrell and were reminded of the fact that, too often, many students are extremely quick to give up in the face of difficulty without first trying. For many students, the willingness to expend effort in accomplishing a task, particularly a somewhat challenging one, is nonexistent or almost impossible to bring about in the classroom. The question for the teacher then becomes: Why?

For many students, the school setting has been inadequate in providing the kinds of stimuli and relationships that can nurture untapped academic potential or generate a genuine interest in learning. *Getting the most* from all students is not an impossible task. In addition to academic development, success in school encompasses the strength and form of the relationships—the bonds—established between students and teachers. A student who is nurtured, encouraged, and drawn into the life of the school will likely perceive school as a place where consistent effort, positive interactions, and ultimate success are possible, rewarding, and even desirable outcomes. All students are capable of having a highly successful school experience if their teachers foster the expectation that they can succeed at the things children their age should be able to do. It is also important that students be encouraged to develop and maintain perceptions and attributions that are positive and self-valuing.

Encouraging Effort in Children

Researchers have found that the ideas students have about their own inner qualities often influence them to succeed or fail in school. Weiner (1979, 1985) states that students tend to think that their academic performance has four causes—ability, effort, task difficulty, and luck—and that they consider ability and effort to influence their performance the most. Weiner (1979) noted that "outcomes frequently depend upon what we can do [ability] and how hard we try [effort] to do it" (p. 5). In other words, if we believe we can accomplish a given task successfully, we are more likely to expend the necessary effort.

Weiner says that ability is stable, internal, and uncontrollable, whereas effort is unstable, internal, and controllable. When students think of their success as the result of their own ability or effort, they feel proud, competent, and confident. In contrast, when students think of their failures as internal, particularly due to lack of ability, they can feel guilty, ashamed, and resigned to failure. These feelings of competence, pride, and shame, Weiner says, are directly associated with the students' sense of self-esteem, and will have the effect of either helping or blocking achievement. It is also important to note that students' ideas about their ability and effort actually motivate their behavior. If a student who has had several failure experiences in school thinks that those failures are caused by his own lack of ability, he will probably expect failure in similar situations in the future. "After all," the student says inside, "my ability can't change," and he feels incompetent and may not even try. On the other hand, if a student has had failures in the past, and has decided that he simply didn't do enough, he will not necessarily expect to fail in the future. "After all," the student says inside, "it's up to me how much I work," and he will potentially change his level of effort to succeed, whether by self-motivation or through support and encouragement from knowledgeable teachers and classmates.

In looking at the differences between David's and Darrell's behavior in the Reading Room, one may argue that David's persistence at his task may have been the result of his positive ideas about effort and his willingness to try. On the other hand, Darrell's lack of effort may have resulted from his negative ideas about his ability, probably a result of previous failures. Darrell did not attempt his writing task and then ask for help or give up after first trying; instead, his immediate response was to give up, stating, "I can't, because it is too hard." Our impression of Darrell is that he has experienced many failures and has learned to become "helpless."

In this particular class, Darrell is currently receiving some individual attention aimed at changing those helpless behaviors. The Reading Room, which is built on the operating principles of the School Development Program, utilizes strong student-teacher relationships and instruction across six developmental pathways to promote positive, holistic development. In addition to developing cognitive skills, the SDP puts a strong emphasis on the physical, social, ethical, language, and psychological development of children. This "Comerized" approach to teaching and learning has resulted in classrooms where students like Darrell experience a greater sense of support and are encouraged to expend effort to achieve success with academic tasks.

Students' Perceptions: Learning and School Success

Students have a great need to perceive themselves as being able and competent, and their sense of self-worth is closely tied to their feelings of competence (Covington, 1984). It is, therefore, very important for children to be encouraged from an early age to develop a sense of confidence and competence that they can draw upon as students and as productive members of society.

The importance of this perception of competence and confidence is highlighted when one considers the possible outcomes of the reverse perceptions held by some students. We learn from the work of Abramson, Seligman, and Teasdale (1978) and Dweck (1986) that if a student has several failure experiences and perceives a sense of inadequacy or powerlessness to change those experiences in the future, he or she can become a victim of the "learned helplessness" syndrome. In other words, the student feels that what he or she does has little or nothing to do with the outcome. Furthermore, this feeling of helplessness can have the devastating consequence of being generalized to other situations, in and out of school.

To change the behaviors and perceptions of helplessness, other researchers (e.g., Diener & Dweck, 1980; Schunk & Cox, 1986) have used retraining techniques with a number of students. In this procedure, helpless students were trained to take responsibility for their failures and to attribute them to insufficient effort instead of lack of ability. Following the training, students showed increased persistence on academic tasks and learned to view failure not as insurmountable, but as a cue to employ different, more effective strategies to succeed. In other words, they learned to try and they learned *what* to try.

This lesson of learning to try and learning what to try is one that we advocate that all students need to internalize. They need to learn to believe in themselves. Like the *Little Engine That Could* in the children's story by Watty Piper, which believed it could and demonstrated that indeed it could, many children need help in building that sense of confidence and even more help in believing that much can be accomplished as a result of focused, goal-directed, sustained work.

It is important to note, however, that students should not be expected to change the learned helplessness syndrome by themselves, just as they did not create it themselves. Academic achievement is a result of the student's perceptions and behaviors *intertwined* with teacher perceptions and behaviors related to their vision of the student's capability. Teacher behavior, much of which is based on beliefs regarding students, can have a direct impact on student performance. Furthermore, when the interaction between teachers and students is positive and at a high level, as with Mr. King, student outcomes are generally positive. When, however, there is a disconnect in the student-teacher relationship, achievement may be compromised.

Teachers must focus their attention on preventing learned helplessness, and instead, help students to develop "learned *helpfulness*" behaviors that can optimize classroom experiences and are transferable to situations outside of the classroom. In Comer schools, where the emphasis is on developing the whole child, the positive climate that teachers are encouraged to create in the classroom helps to build student confidence and to prevent the occurrence of learned helplessness behaviors.

Teachers' Perceptions of Students and of Self

Mrs. Warren is a teacher in an urban middle school. In May, she attended one of the SDP training sessions, and we had the privilege of hearing her perspective on teaching her students:

> I do everything I have to in order to get my students to learn. Some of them don't understand how important it is to get a good education, so it's my job to help them to understand. You see, I believe that all my students are capable of learning, so I will try to reach out to them in every way I can. Sometimes that means that I have to go to some of their homes to make sure that they show up for school. Some students don't understand hard work, so I teach them the importance of hard work, and they see how hard I work.

The literature on teaching and learning shows that the *vision* a teacher has for students—the internal sense of confidence and expectation regarding their success or failure—can often become a self-fulfilling prophecy. The perceptions and beliefs that a teacher holds regarding student potential, ability, and social status can function as a "mediator" of teaching behavior in the classroom (Ashton, et al., 1983). These teacher attitudes and beliefs can be overt or subconscious. Consequently, it is critically important for teachers to be properly trained and equipped to project a "vision of excellence" for their students (Demon-Berger, 1986).

In a similar vein, Hilliard (1991), in his work on learning, asserts that there are "seeds of genius in all of our children." He offers a parallel designation of "genius teachers" to describe the ability of effective teachers in maintaining over time a positive vision for their students and in utilizing that vision to inform their classroom practices and student relationships. Effective teachers use their positive beliefs in student success as a launching pad for creating strategies for teaching in a relevant, interesting, and understandable manner.

When teachers believe that their students can succeed, their actions in the classroom reflect that belief and the students *respond*. As stated by Ryan and Cooper (1995), "students of whom much is expected will conform to that expectation, and students of whom little is expected will match that expectation" (p. 384). It is critical for the success of our children that the complexity of teaching in today's schools not erode positive teacher visions for student success, but that teachers be given opportunities and resources to develop the skills they need. The School Development Program strongly advocates this teacher support by making staff development one of the three key operations that schools need to function effectively. After all, there are many teachers who are dedicated, committed, and willing to teach in ways that will enable students to learn—if only they are provided with the support and staff development that they need. Teachers need the same quality and consistency of support that we advocate for our children. In this way, they will be better prepared to further the development of their students.

Bandura (1977) defines teachers' confidence in their ability to reach students as high teacher "efficacy." If a teacher's confidence is low, then the behaviors and techniques necessary for successful teaching and learning will likely not occur. Conversely, high efficacy teachers possess sufficient confidence in their teaching to take on challenging students and help guide them towards success. Teachers clearly need a broad level of support for developing and maintaining high efficacy in reaching all their students. Without high efficacy, teachers often regress into lower levels of classroom effort. The tendency then is to focus on the easily reached "high-achieving" students rather than on "low-achievers," and to become resistant to experiences that might change their perceptions of those students from negative to positive (Good, 1984). The viewpoint of many low-efficacy teachers is that their students are "unreachable" anyway, and that they can therefore deny any sense of responsibility for poor student outcomes. But to get the most out of all students, teachers have a moral responsibility to be committed, to be active learners, and to demonstrate to students the importance of sustained effort in achieving success.

The Teacher-Student Relationship

Within the SDP model, positive relationships are at the heart of the learning process. In Mr. King's after-school sessions, a *shared focus*—success with math—exists with Mr. King and his students. They demonstrated a level of mutual understanding and acceptance that in turn facilitated academic growth. This critical sense of *connectedness* that we observe in effective classrooms is what we call "same page behavior" (SPB). SPB describes the kinds of positive, complimentary teacher-student behaviors and interactions that lead to successful teaching and learning. Teachers are more effective at their teaching and students can more easily learn when SPB has been firmly established and is consistently practiced in the classroom. When students perceive their teachers as warm and caring, their behaviors and classroom performance will likely reflect this perception (Rogoff, 1990).

Again, we recognize that there are many teachers who epitomize great teaching. We are grateful for and applaud the efforts of these teachers, but are reminded daily that the educational system is a microcosm of the larger society, wherein some people are elevated to success, while a significant number of people are relegated to failure. Many of these failures begin in the classroom, which sometimes makes it appear that the idea of same-page behavior is only a dream; but we believe that this dream can come true. The persistent and successful work of many faithful, committed teachers demonstrates that fact. We worry, however, about those who perhaps were once committed and dedicated but who, for various reasons, are now sitting by passively in countless classrooms, watching their students fail.

On a daily basis, many students encounter life situations that present serious challenges and often seem insurmountable; thus, it will not take much for many of them to give up on school and academic learning. Since for such students getting an education is often not a priority, teachers must be willing, like Mrs. Warren, to help them see the relevance of staying in school and, like Mr. King, to be creative. Teachers and students need to be working together as an enthusiastic, energetic team, toward a shared vision of student success. When teachers and students are on a *different* page, successful learning and development is undermined, and the result can be frustration, and ultimately, failure for both teachers and students.

Concluding Thoughts

In order to teach all children effectively, a foundation of positive relationships between teachers, students, and their parents must be established as a starting point for promoting student success. Furthermore, it is important that the relationships in schools be underscored by the three guiding principles that are fundamental to the School Development Program: collaboration, consensus, and no-fault.

The act of collaboration between teachers and students with the aim of accomplishing a shared goal is a form of same-page behavior and is necessary for successful outcomes with many of our children. In addition, teachers and students must come to consensus that, at all times, the classroom must be a positive environment that is conducive to focused and sustained effort, positive interactions, respect, intellectual stimulation, and overall learning, growth, and development.

Additionally, there can be no compromise on the principle of no-fault. Students cannot be blamed for what they do not know—especially when it is evident that they are trying. Often, students in the same school come from a variety of backgrounds—some impoverished—and do not behave as middle-class culture demands that they should. Consequently, they are often subtly blamed for their position in life in the sense that little is expected from them and therefore little is demanded. We cannot blame our students for not knowing and still expect to get the most out of them. We cannot maintain a deficit perspective of our students and expect to get the most out of them. We cannot provide a substandard environment for students and expect to get the most out of them.

Teachers must be infectious in their desire and commitment to the effort of teaching and using their classroom practices to develop the whole child. We recognize that teaching is "hard work," but with the right vision, skills, and support, it can be done. Indeed, teaching can be gratifying and effective—it is being done effectively every day by many committed individuals. But everyone in the profession needs a high level of commitment. We all need to be on the same page with our students—a page that outlines success. As one teacher said recently, "Teaching is the hardest work I have ever done in my life—but it is also extremely rewarding."

In presenting examples of good classroom climate such as Mr. King's math lab, we are not arguing that every classroom must be permeated by social exchanges in order for children to learn. However, as we see with the SDP model, emphasis should not be placed on developing students' cognitive abilities alone; there must be a simultaneous focus on the physical, social, ethical, psychological, and linguistic aspects of their development. In other words, educators must endeavor to promote students' holistic development. In accomplishing this noble task, we recognize that there are and will be some hurdles to overcome. Our work in schools has helped us to develop the following recommendations for teachers.

Let your students know you believe in them and that you are there to assist them to become the best that they can be. While it is admirable to be sensitive and understanding, it is also important to be demanding. Provide needed help to students that will be instrumental to their learning. Promote a culture of great effort and goal-directed, sustained work in the classroom.

Be prepared to work "double time" to help many students catch up to where they need to be in order to be successful. "Double time" does not necessarily indicate double the amount of time, but rather a greater commitment to advance students' learning and development. Dedication and commitment are not frills or simply buzz words in the educational arena; they are essential attributes for any individual who wishes to be an effective teacher.

Know your students well and bond with them to prevent counterproductive behaviors. Help students to evaluate academic failures in terms of effort or lack thereof, rather than lack of ability. When students fail despite great effort, help them identify other strategies and direct them to other people who can help them. As the SDP's Ed Joyner told us, "Engage with your students in a conspiracy for success."

Be tenacious and consistent in working with parents and others in the school community to promote students' holistic development. Teachers cannot bring about student success by themselves; they need the help, support, and involvement of parents and the entire school community. Parent organizations and teacher/staff meetings may be used as avenues for increasing parent involvement in classroom activities and in the life of the school. Teachers can assist parents in learning more about the strengths and learning styles of their children so that they will be better able to reinforce their children's learning at home. School policies and practices can be structured to emphasize and reward maximum staff and student effort and higher expectations for success.

Just imagine what it would be like if the climate in all classrooms were so open and supportive that students didn't think twice about saying to the teacher, "I don't understand. Could you please explain it again?" or "I need some help with the assignment. I have some questions." And just imagine what it would be like if teachers didn't think twice about asking the same questions of each other and their principals. Just imagine the positive outcomes for students, for teachers, for parents, and for the overall school community. Getting the most from all students—in terms of their motivation, engagement, and effort in the classroom—starts with a strong teacher-student connection. Same-page teacher-student behaviors, parent involvement with student learning, and school policies and practices that reinforce and reward high academic effort are all part of the formula for developing stronger schools and well-rounded students.

References

Abramson, L. Y., Seligman, M. E., and Teasdale, J. D. (1978). Learned helplessness: A theory-based subtype of depression. *Psychological Review, 96,* 358–372.

Ashton, P.T., Webb, R. B., and Doda, N. (1983). A study of teachers' sense of efficacy. Report to the National Institute of Education, Eric Document 231833.

Bandura, A. (1977). Self-efficacy: Toward a unifying theory of behavior change. *Psychological Review, 84,* 191–215.

Covington, M. V. (1984). The motive for self-worth. In R. E. Ames and C. Ames (Eds.), *Research on motivation in education.* Vol. 1 (pp. 77–133). New York: Academic Press.

Demon-Berger, D. (1986). *Effective teaching: Observations from research.* Arlington, VA. American Association of School Administrators.

Diener, C. I., and Dweck, C. S. (1980). An analysis of learned helplessness: II. The processing of success. *Journal of Personality and Social Psychology, 36,* 451–462.

Dweck, C. S. (1986). Motivational process affecting learning. *American Psychologist, 41,* 1040–1048.

Good, T.L. (1984). Research on teacher expectations. Eric Document 249587, 151–164.

Hilliard, A.G. (1991). Do we have the will to educate all children? *Educational Leadership, 49,* 1, 31–36.

National Center for Effective Schools Research and Development. (1989). *A conversation between James Comer and Ronald Edmonds.* Dubuque, Iowa: Kendall/Hunt Publishing.

Rogoff, B. (1990). *Apprenticeship in thinking: Cognitive development in social context.* Oxford: Oxford University Press.

Ryan, K., and Cooper, J. M. (1995). *Those who can, teach.* 7th ed. Boston: Houghton Mifflin Company.

Schunk, D.H., and Cox, P. D. (1986). Strategy training and attributional feedback with learning disabled students. *Journal of Educational Psychology, 78,* 201–209.

Weiner, B. (1985). An attributional theory of achievement motivation and emotion. *Psychological Review, 92,* 548–573.

Weiner, B. (1979). A theory of motivation for some classroom experiences. *Journal of Educational Psychology, 71,* 3–25.

CHAPTER 20

At First, I Aspired to Be a
Garbage Man

Kenan Smith, Geoffrey Jones, Omar Morris, and Michael Ben-Avie

Geoffrey. Photograph by Laura Brooks.

*Do you know a student whose sights are set too low? Are you interested in finding out
how you can support students to continue their successes? In the chapter that follows,
two young reporters on student life discuss options, opportunities, and programs with a
counselor and a university researcher.*

Kenan Smith: At first, I aspired to be a garbage man. But my guidance counselor convinced me that I was selling myself short.

I thought about going into the sanitation department because I heard the benefits were good and also the pay. I changed my mind because there's a program in my school named the Institute for Student Achievement and it helped me to understand that I should further my education and go to college.

Geoffrey Jones: In ninth and tenth grade, I really didn't want to go to college. I was just planning on getting good grades in high school. Then, when everyone in the classroom, the whole school, and my guidance counselors started talking about college, I said to myself, "Why don't I go to college?"

Michael Ben-Avie: Kenan, Geoffrey—Consider interviewing your counselor from the Institute for Student Achievement. Ask him, "What did you see in me?"

Omar Morris: I am the College and Career Coordinator for the Benjamin Banneker STAR and COMET Program, part of the Institute for Student Achievement (ISA). COMET stands for Children of Many Educational Talents and it is the junior high school component. STAR stands for Success Through Academic Readiness and it is the high school component.

The Institute for Student Achievement (formerly known as the Institute for Community Development) is the creation and vision of Gerard and Lilo Leeds, the founders of CMP Publications, which is a computer publications company in Long Island. The program consists of three basic components: academic enrichment, counseling, and college and career development and preparation. Our personal goal is to make sure that every single student graduates. Dr. Lester Young, the superintendent of Community School District Thirteen, asked for the Institute for Student Achievement to come into Benjamin Banneker. He is "hands-on" here. He sat down with Dr. Lavinia T. Dickerson, co-executive director of ISA, and they worked out what the school needed.

Kenan Smith: What did you see in me?

Omar Morris: At Benjamin Banneker, we do not have any bad students. We just have students who are not educated as to what the opportunities are. We never told you, Kenan, not to be a garbage man. We said, "Do you know what opportunities are out there? Do you know what options are out there?" Kenan, you have always been good in school. You have always been a very bright student and very respectful. These two qualities alone make a counselor look at a student and say, "This student has the ability to do a lot better if only he or she were to be educated about opportunities and options."

Geoffrey Jones: Last year, we met every day. I learned what college has to offer you later on in your life. Also, how to present yourself on an interview, apply for financial aid, fill out college applications, support yourself, look presentable for a job.

Omar Morris: Geoffrey, to some of the students who do not want to go to college, we say, "If you don't want to go to college, that's fine." However, we also add, "What happens in June, when you're walking down the aisle, and now you want to go to college but you didn't apply?" You would have no option then. We encourage students to fill out college applications. We say, "If you are accepted that does not mean you have to go. You make the decision. When June comes, and you do decide you want to go to college, then you have the option." One of the more successful events that took place was the tour to some historically Black colleges. Prior to the tour, only about 25 out of 50 students wanted to go to college. When we returned from the college tour, 49 wanted to apply to college and one to a trade school.

Michael Ben-Avie: How does the Institute for Student Achievement relate to the Comer Process?

Omar Morris: We have so many programs in the school. The problem is that we have not yet been able to coordinate all the different parts. Everyone was afraid to take that extra step because they were afraid of taking the fault. The Comer Process insists on a no-fault stance to problem solving along with consensus and collaboration. From the Comer training that we have had, everyone is now giving their input. No person feels like the lowest person on the totem pole; the principal is sitting at the table along with the parents. They are discussing the children, who are the main focus. With the Comer Process, the school will be able to reach its full potential.

CHAPTER 21

Development

Prerequisite for Learning

Joanne Corbin

Photograph by Laura Brooks.

Simply caring about children is not enough. We must focus our attention on children's development, and structure all our efforts to encourage that development. SDP's director of operations explains how this focus can clarify curriculum and administrative agendas, transforming any school into a more creative, more exciting, and safer place in which to learn and grow.

Have you ever walked into a school and immediately felt the school to be
a positive place, a place where you would have wanted to be a student?
Staff and students greet each other warmly. There is a sense of order, and
as a visitor you are greeted by a staff member or parent and guided to the
main office, which is clearly marked. Everyone has a sense of purpose and
is doing his or her work with pride and commitment. The school is clean
and appears well maintained; students' work is thoughtfully displayed
along the hallways. Compare this scene to one in which there is a sense of
confusion in the building and the mood is very low. No one is paying any
attention to you as a visitor. The school is not well maintained, and the hallways are decorated with advertisements. The interactions between staff
and students are painful to observe: Adults talk in loud voices at children
or talk negatively about children in public places. There is a world of difference between these two schools.

The climate described in the first school does not happen by accident.
It emerges because the adults in the school develop a common set of beliefs and expectations about the children in the school and the work that occurs in the school. The climate of the second school *does* develop by
accident. In that school, negative habits have a chance to take root because
there are no common beliefs about children, about working with children,
and about the work itself. Understanding how children develop and what
they need from adults is important in every school if children are to succeed.
The sound relationships that grow from this understanding are one part of
good school climate.

The School Development Program supports healthy child development by constantly remembering the pathways through which children
learn and grow: the physical, cognitive, psychological, language, social,
and ethical pathways. When school communities participate in our leadership academies and truly understand that these pathways are essential
to education, they automatically develop a child-centered perspective. This
chapter examines what it means to have this child-centered perspective,
and shows how it can make a difference in schools.

The Child-Centered Perspective

The School Development Program teaches administrators, staff, teachers,
and parents the importance of understanding how children develop, and
it teaches the adults how their relationships can support or weaken children's development. Often when educators participating in our leadership
academies first hear the phrase "child-centered perspective," their initial response is, "If we did not believe that children are important, we would not

be in education!" However, a child-centered perspective means much more than simply believing and saying that children are important.

Pretend that it is a sunny day and you need to wear sunglasses to shade your eyes. Do you choose the blue-tinted sunglasses, the green-tinted sunglasses, or the brown-tinted ones? They are all sunglasses; however, the tint of the lens may make a big difference in the visual image you see. Keep this in mind as you think about a child-centered perspective or lens. Let's take the example of a budget crisis affecting a school. The administration may choose a cost-benefit perspective or lens. Viewing the situation through a "money lens," people may "see clearly" that they need to cut the programs that cost the most but serve the fewest students or that do not directly raise grades. (Mandated programs would not be included in this process.) This may make good economic sense. The actions resulting from looking through the "money lens" may be that the arts and extracurricular programs are eliminated. But looking through the lens of child and adolescent development may lead to a different understanding. Despite cost-benefit analyses, administrators may consider the importance of arts and extracurricular events in developing the whole child. (For example, music classes can help students understand abstract mathematical concepts.) The budget dilemma still remains; however, instead of cutting programs, administrators may program the school day more creatively or may join with the community to find new ways to maintain the programs.

It is important to think about schools from various perspectives; but when other priorities dominate, children's development suffers. Decision making within schools, therefore, must consider the children first. When we support the development of the whole child, we build the foundation for academic achievement (Comer, 1980; Goleman, 1995).

Child Development as a Lens

It is not always easy to become familiar with how children develop and to understand what this means in the school context. An example provided by Lorraine Flood, the CoZi coordinator in Norfolk, Virginia (see Chapter 6) emphasizes this point. Flood describes a kindergarten teacher's skepticism about the effectiveness of the prekindergarten program in her school:

> Her initial comment was, "I don't see how these kids learn anything with all this playing going on." She was eventually convinced by her friend, another preschool teacher, to request assignment to a pre-K class. Three years later this teacher is convinced that the preschool program is more than wonderful, and is capable of helping three- and four-year-olds get ready for school. She moved

back to kindergarten with the children who had been in her prekindergarten class. Not only did she bring the preschoolers into kindergarten, but she also brought a new attitude based on the developmental approach. Her classroom is set up to support active learning activities and to stimulate young minds. The teacher reports that many of her children are ready for what she calls first grade work.

So often adults view children's playing as unproductive. This is far from the case. Giving children the chance to play allows them to understand the relationship between objects and themselves and between other people and themselves. It also gives them the chance to increase their communication skills, interaction skills, conflict management skills, and problem-solving skills. The next time you watch a group of children playing in day care or on the playground, try to figure out which pathways they are developing. Children's play is the best work there is: focused, skill-oriented, and continually growing more complex.

It is acceptable for there to be lots of toys in preschool, but there are fewer and fewer toys in kindergarten and first grade. Nonetheless, children at these ages may still need the support of play materials to express themselves and solve problems. The teacher Flood described continued some preschool activities in her classroom because she had a better understanding of how toys and household objects could be used to encourage learning.

Let's look at another example through two different lenses: the management lens and the child-centered lens. One morning I walked into a middle school. As I walked down the main hallway, I heard male students yelling and saw students hurrying away from a place I couldn't see. I became cautious as I approached. Turning the corner, I saw an adolescent boy lying on the ground, holding his stomach and wincing in pain. One male teacher was beginning to attend to him. Another teacher was telling another student to bring the school nurse. Other teachers, men and women, were yelling at the students to disperse. The nurse examined the student and slowly got him out of the hallway. During my visit, I heard nothing more about this incident. This was particularly striking because I was there to participate in a meeting about the school's ways of supporting students.

The situation provides an opportunity to think about the lens through which we choose to develop a response. A school may choose to handle this in a management fashion: dispersing the onlookers, making sure the student receives the necessary medical attention, and dealing with the disciplinary issues. This typical response occurs when administrators are concerned only about the management of the school. When they are also concerned about developing children, their responses will be more meaningful.

A school with a child-centered perspective will handle this situation differently. Keeping onlooking students away is important and can be done with firm and controlled voices. Attending to the student's medical condition and physical safety are necessary, and attending to the climate of the school is next. When a student sees or hears about something bad happening to another student, she worries that a similar thing could happen to her. The adults in the building must develop a method of creating a feeling of safety for all of the students in the school. When teachers briefly tell students that the incident is being handled and that they can go on to their next class, they offer some acknowledgment of the situation and reassure students that the adults are taking care of it. When there is no mention of the event, as in the case I witnessed, there is no validation of what was witnessed. Thus there is no way to address the issue with the other students and calm their anxiety. For each incident, a staff member should be in charge of determining the reason for the fight and attempting to resolve the situation. When staff make it very clear to students what the consequences of their behavior will be, they help the students to develop self-control and help prevent similar situations.

In summary, there are several elements to a child-centered perspective. Adopting this lens helps us remember that:

All children are active participants in their own lives and should be valued as active agents. New research about how children develop has revealed that it is healthy to let children have a more active role in daily activities and make choices (within reason). Of course, this should be done with supervision and guidance from adults.

All children are in the middle of developmental tasks, continually increasing their physical, cognitive, psychological, language, social, and ethical skills. Children do not just learn a skill or become successful at a task; there is much effort and trial as anyone learns something new. Even after learning a skill, there will be failures until the task or skill is mastered.

All children are stimulated by activities aimed at their developmental understanding. Adolescents can engage in discussions regarding ethical decision making with a level of understanding that involves taking multiple perspectives, empathy, debate, and problem resolution. Expecting or encouraging the same level of decision-making from younger elementary school age children is demanding too much for their cognitive developmental level.

Child Development and Contextual Understanding

Our understanding of any situation and our ability to develop solutions are also influenced by how tight our focus is: Are we zeroing in on each issue by itself, or are we viewing each issue within the wider scope of the whole school? Was the fight mentioned earlier the only conflict in the school all year? Is there a pattern of fighting everyday? Different situations require different interventions.

Maintaining a Safe Environment

Addressing the aspects of school climate that can inhibit violent or out-of-control behavior is the first step in developing a school that is child-centered. To decrease negative talk and harmful behaviors, many schools are developing schoolwide programs such as conflict resolution programs and codes of behavior. And when students participate in creating these programs, they are more likely to support them than to resist them. The following story describes how a school transformed its expectations around negative behaviors (Savo, 1995). Before the Peace program, the school experienced frequent student fights and the principal spent most of her time handling discipline issues.

The Clinton Grove Elementary School in Prince George's County, Maryland, has created a Peace Program that increases personal responsibility in maintaining a safe and orderly learning environment. It is not enough for the adults in the building to be the only ones working to establish and maintain this environment; every student learns to resolve problems peacefully, either by walking away or ignoring inappropriate behavior and/or comments, through discussion and conflict resolution with impartial conflict managers, or by getting an adult to help them.

The principal begins the school year by discussing the Peace Program with each class. Within the first week, each class creates a "peace banner" to hang in the hallway outside its room. Because each day is a new opportunity, each day the school flies a blue "peace flag" with a white dove under the U.S. flag in front of the school. A message outside the school announces the total number of peaceful days to that point in the school year. The numbers change daily, but they freeze on days when the peace flag is taken down.

The students who have broken the peace are photographed while they take the flag down, and the photos are kept confidential in the principal's office. When parents are called in, they make a commitment to work on alternatives with the students at home. Classroom banners hang as long as each child shows respect for other children and for adults. A week's worth of peace results in a Friday afternoon announcement and a blue peace ribbon to add to the class banner. Each quarter ends with classroom parties for classes with the most blue ribbons.

Because Clinton Grove wants to continue building peace and respect for others into the fiber of daily life, they have added a "positive language" component to the Peace Program. Their successful, inexpensive program has united the entire school community and is being used by other schools as well. Fifth and sixth grade students in two school systems are in the G.O.L.D. (Generating Outstanding Leadership Development) program. They have developed a project called Project U.S. (United for Safety), which is based on Clinton Grove's Peace Program and which has interested other principals.

As overall school climate improves, there are positive consequences for such specific issues as peer conflicts, physical fighting, parent involvement, and student and staff morale. Positive consequences promote appropriate responses and decision making rather than punishment. In an excellent school climate, there is consensus among the adults in the school about what student behaviors to expect and how to reinforce positive behaviors, which alternatives to provide when there are problematic behaviors, and how to foster personal responsibility in the students.

Teaching Essential Lessons through Daily Life Experiences

Clinton Grove's program is also effective because it addresses the many areas of development that are important for children, not just the academic area. It uses peer modeling and support to improve social interactions; it builds students' emotional skills by training them in alternative behaviors for resolving conflicts. The program enhances students' language abilities by supporting their efforts to explain themselves, rather than triggering their frustration and old habits of fighting. Programs are more likely to be effective when they take into consideration the six developmental pathways through which children develop.

Extending the "No-Fault" Concept to Children

In addition to keeping the focus on children, a developmental perspective extends to the children SDP's concept of "no-fault." Considering a child's stage across the developmental pathways allows the adults to consider alternative reasons for his or her behavior, rather than immediately jumping to conclusions. When the adults are able to suspend their judgment and think about the larger contexts—the school as a whole and each child's growth over time—they begin to consider alternative strategies. Additionally, focusing on the six pathways enables the school to address large group or global school issues concerning children. An example of a global school issue is children's anxiety about moving up from elementary school to middle school, from middle to high school and from high school to college and the work force. Looking at the situations from a developmental perspective allows the school to develop support strategies before problems develop and escalate.

The benefits of a developmental perspective are numerous and overlapping. In schools, this perspective:

- focuses the adults' attention on the children
- extends the concept of no-fault to the relationship with and between children
- provides a framework for adults to think about children's behavior in a larger context
- enables adults to develop alternative strategies that promote health and positive self-esteem in children
- helps focus on the global issues of school, leading towards preventive interventions

Positive and Consistent Relationships

Children can't learn and grow in a vacuum. They must have positive relationships and consistent interactions with competent adults in a safe environment. These relationships must include mutual genuineness, respect, unconditional positive regard, and trust. Of course, it is the adults who must model these qualities for the children.

Creating the Relationships

Teachers and principals must take the time to get to know each and every student. They must learn their hobbies, their likes and dislikes, their patterns and responses in certain situations. The teaching and nonteaching staff must focus on building genuine relationships with students. Many teachers will call a student's parent during the first week of school to introduce themselves and give the parent relevant information about school. Although this very first, positive contact is with the parent, the student knows about it and gets the message that this teacher cares about him or her. Another way to develop positive and genuine relationships is to have the teaching and nonteaching staff participate in advisor/advisee groups with students.

Respect

Respect is a key ingredient of any meaningful relationship. Children must feel that they are valued, just as they are, just for being. Children need to know that what they do and what they say is valued. When their words and behaviors need correction, it should be done in a way that helps them develop internal mechanisms for control and gives them alternative positive responses. Such measures to correct troubling behavior send a very supportive message to the student, one that is not disrespectful and punitive but that enhances self-esteem.

One aspect of developing a meaningful relationship with children involves letting them know that their culture, religion, family, and background are valued. Implicit or explicit messages that devalue these core characteristics have no place in the school environment. A second important aspect of building relationships is unconditional positive regard. This means maintaining an attitude of "no-fault" when interacting with children and establishing high expectations for them, even when their behavior is distressing. These elements are the foundation for trust between school staff and students. It is important for students to know they can rely on the adults in the school in any situation.

Physical and Emotional Safety

Students can fully attend to and engage in the learning process only when they are physically and emotionally safe. Students rely on adults to protect them from harm through fire drills or other emergency procedures. And they also rely on adults to monitor the interactions that occur in school so that they can feel safe and comfortable. Humor, sarcasm, and teasing can be appropriate in school, but when a child restricts his or her activities or feels intimidated as a result, a breach of emotional safety has occurred. Many times school personnel are themselves fearful but are unable to discuss their concerns openly. On the other hand, we have found that when teachers feel safe they can provide a school climate that enables students to feel safe.

Consistency

Most people take comfort in knowing that some things in their daily lives will be the same. For example, typically, their homes and jobs do not change daily. Children's environments can be viewed in the same way. Knowing that the teachers and principal will be the same from day to day and from year to year provides stability. Expectations about homework or behavior and responses to situations should be consistent. Feelings of security are increased when events in life are predictable.

Applying the Pathways

There are many things educators know about child and adolescent development, but we tend to know them in isolation. We do not take the time to think about developmental theory and school contexts simultaneously, and to develop integrated plans. Indeed, the time to think reflectively on our actions is missing in most of our everyday lives. But we must make the time if we are going to make a difference in the education of children. It often appears as if there is an invisible wall between our knowledge about child and adolescent development and the school context, including school policies, school programs, relationships and overall school climate.

So how can we break down this barrier? Several examples may be helpful. In one elementary school, teachers were distressed because students were not doing their homework. The typical school response of detention or notes to the parents was not working. The six developmental pathways provided a framework for reflecting on the reasons for this situation. Teachers considered the possibilities that some students did not have the appropriate physical space at home to do homework and that students preferred to socialize and play. The question then became how the school could support children in doing homework while keeping their developmental needs in mind. The staff identified a number of strategies. For example, some assignments allowed students to work together, which supported their social interaction needs. The staff also identified a room at the community recreation center that was available for those children who lacked an appropriate space to work at home.

Schools have limited time and resources. When an assessment is completed, staff should identify only the two or three most important contributions to any issue and develop strategies for these. In this example the ethical pathway was not considered to contribute to the issue. In many situations some pathways may not be applicable. A framework like this may be used for developing strategies for a range of schoolwide and individual student issues. Many educators who have used this framework report that it is important to identify the strengths of a situation across the pathways, and not only to assess the difficulties.

It is clear that when schools think about children from a developmental perspective the options for responding to situations multiply. Rather than responding with routine and ineffective strategies such as detentions, schools can create new approaches that may be more successful in changing individual behaviors.

The pathways also encourage educators and parents to notice and understand how children's needs change over time. A clear example is coed

physical education classes for middle and high school students. Coed physical education classes in elementary schools are the norm. By adolescence,
many girls do poorly in P.E. class because they feel uncomfortable when
interacting with boys. The lack of privacy and insufficient time to shower
and change are often cited as barriers. During puberty, when both girls and
boys are adapting to these changes, adults' lack of awareness adds to the
stress of this developmental period. Although most school personnel are
aware of the changes during puberty, applying this knowledge to daily
events and school practices is the challenge. Adults should ask the question,
"How can we make sure that P.E. classes address the developmental needs
of young people?" Addressing the administrative issues, scheduling issues,
or staff concerns should be secondary. Discussions among the school staff
and parents about their underlying beliefs regarding children's development are helpful in arriving at a common set of beliefs, practices, and programs within the school.

Developing individual identity is the major task of high school students. During this time, they are concerned with their relationships with
others, the world, and their future direction. Young adults crave experiences that allow them to try out skills, identify their unique strengths and
learn new things. The adults in students' lives—parents and teachers and
mentors—must encourage them about what they might do or become,
rather than limiting their hopes for the future. There are far too many stories of high school students being counseled out of a particular college or
an academic track because of a particular test score or the misperceptions
of key adult advisors. Many students have dropped out of school or have
not been challenged to integrate the educational process with their life
course. Many adolescents have had a hard time connecting the lessons of
the classroom to their daily experiences and their thoughts about what their
future life will be. Schools that build authentic, "real-world" learning experiences into the curriculum are effective because they tap into young
adults' desires to be active creators of their future.

How SDP Integrates the Six Pathways into School Life

Translating child development knowledge into school policies and practices requires consistent attention. Within the School Development Program, it is usually the Student and Staff Support Team (formerly known as
the Mental Health Team) that takes the lead in this area.

The Student and Staff Support Team

The Student and Staff Support Team (SSST) may include the school social worker, guidance counselor, psychologist, nurse, and an administrator. The SSST collaborates with the Parent Team and the School Planning and Management Team, helping them apply child development knowledge to school practices and policies.

Even though many districts have reduced or cut the budgets for such student services, it is important that schools identify those persons who have knowledge and experience in children's health, psychoemotional well-being, and cognitive abilities to participate on the SSST. This includes reaching out to community-based organizations that are willing and able to participate on the SSST and/or provide services to students.

SSSTs address issues relating to an individual student or group of students along the six developmental pathways. Examples used earlier in this chapter (the fight in the hallway or students not completing their homework) are appropriate for an SSST discussion. These teams identify areas of strength and weakness on each of the pathways for each student and develop strategies for addressing the problem area. A form is usually developed that has the six pathways down one side with space to write next to each pathway. Making sure that each pathway is assessed allows the staff to support the child holistically and include all relevant information in the development of a strategy.

The School Planning and Management Team

The School Planning and Management Team (SPMT) insures that the programs brought into the school and the activities developed within the school are planned with knowledge about child development. The SPMT has a special strength in its representativeness. School staff, parents and other stakeholders in the school can bring to the table their knowledge of child development. This team may also want to take a look at the various programs and activities operating in the school and assess which of the pathways are being addressed through each activity. Because children need to *develop* holistically, it is important to make sure there are activities and programs that *build* children holistically.

This also means assessing whether programs are meeting the developmental needs of the children at every age. For example, an elementary school may have student mentoring programs in which fourth graders mentor second graders. Because these matches tend to occur at the higher grades, the kindergarten and first grade children may not be involved.

Schools must review the entire school program, see where the gaps are and where the need is, and develop supportive programming. The Peace Program described earlier is another example of the kind of schoolwide programming an SPMT might develop to meet the needs of the students. Children and adolescents must have the opportunity within their educational program to develop the social skills, communication skills, self-management skills, and problem-solving skills that will enable them to successfully handle life beyond school.

The Comprehensive School Plan

The Comprehensive School Plan provides an opportunity to integrate the developmental pathways into classrooms. The Comprehensive School Plan is generally developed by the curriculum subcommittee of the SPMT and includes academic, social development, and public relations goals.

For example, an SDP school community took a reading objective from a school plan ("Reading will be taught from a child-centered perspective incorporating discussion, writing and integration with content in other subjects") and charted the application of the pathways. (The objective will, of course, vary depending upon the outcomes for each grade.) The first column listed the pathways. The other columns described strategies to support reading for different grades. Consider the action plan that was developed for the tenth grade:

- *Physical:* Interest in reading materials which provide information about lifestyles and life choices
- *Cognitive:* Can increase abstract thinking skills by using materials which focus on hypothesizing
- *Language:* Provide a variety of avenues to express ideas of written material (visual arts, song, performances)
- *Psychological:* Increase interest and motivation, allow for self-selection of some materials
- *Social:* Provide guidance in collaborative work to lessen criticism
- *Ethical:* Provide opportunities for adolescents to discuss ethical questions from the materials; debates

In this example every box is completed; in reality, there are instances when a pathway may not be applicable to a particular objective. When adults think about a reading objective in this manner, they help students make the connection between what they are doing in school and what is going on in their lives. This is what turns students into life-long learners and responsible citizens.

An Action Plan for Staff Development

Incorporating the developmental pathways into the school context takes concerted and consistent effort. School staff may need to have a review of the various theories of child development. Many staff members have had one course in child development. Others may have had related courses some time ago. Therefore, an action plan is needed.

The first step is to arrange a program or workshop in which a well-qualified local person reviews child and adolescent development for your school. A local person can help build district capacity to implement and sustain the program over the long run.

The next step is to have staff members assess their beliefs and viewpoints about children, particularly in light of the theories they reviewed in the step above. Many of us confuse our personal experience and beliefs about child development with good practice and knowledge about children, and it can be difficult to change belief patterns. Through discussion, decide as a staff which theories support the beliefs and expectations about children your school wishes to promote. This is an important step in developing a common perspective about how to interact with and best support children. With this agreement, individual adults in the school can receive clear and consistent messages about their work and interactions with children. This also provides a standard of behavior to which individuals can be held accountable.

Once a consistent understanding about children is developed, *then school programs, activities, classroom lessons, and so forth, can be developed and aligned with the school's and the community's belief systems.*

As these are steps that will benefit every adult in the school building, nonteaching staff and parents can and should be involved in these activities. In this way, every adult who comes in contact with any child can support his or her development across all the pathways.

Conclusion

There are many challenges in taking these steps, such as finding the time to do this kind of integration; changing individuals' beliefs about children, adolescents, and about school; and learning new skills. However, unless these or similar approaches are taken, the other priorities in a school system somehow have a way of being attended to first. Students' developmental needs *must* drive the questions that are asked and the programs that are developed. Then the administrative personnel, policy and procedural tasks—admittedly, big challenges—follow as a logical sequence of useful steps toward a clearly envisioned, brighter future for all of us in schools.

References

Comer, J.P., Haynes, N.M., Joyner, E.T., and Ben-Avie, M., (1996). *Rallying the Whole Village: The Comer Process for Reforming Education.* New York: Teachers College Press.

Comer, J.P. (1980). *School Power: Implications of an Intervention Project.* New York: The Free Press.

Goleman, D.(1995). *Emotional Intelligence.* New York: Bantam Books.

Savo, C. (1995). Let There Be Peace At School. *SDP Newsline,* vol. 4., no 2.

CHAPTER 22

When We All Work Together, Everything Is Possible

Jerry D. Weast, Lillie M. Jones, Larry Allred, Mike Booher,
Elizabeth Bridges, Pauline Brown, Doris T. Davis, James Fuller,
Jeanette Gann, Mary Hoyle, J. Patrick Howley,
Sharon A. Johnson, Tina Johnson, John Lauritzen, Charles Morris,
Donna Morrison, Walter Matthew Pritchett, Jr., Vernice Thomas,
Richard Tuck, Leigh Tysor-Holt, and Gwendolyn Willis

Photograph by Laura Brooks.

When superintendents want to create a culture of collaboration that involves the whole community, how can they turn that vision into daily practice? The Comer Process insists that the education of the young is a collaborative investment of the whole community and a shared responsibility. Community members begin to go beyond themselves to focus on the greater good and tackle a bit of the whole. They become "stakeholders" whose "stake" is in the life success of every student.

Child by Child: The Comer Process for Change in Education. Copyright © 1999 by Teachers College, Columbia University. All rights reserved. ISBN 0-8077-3868-9 (pbk.), ISBN 0-8077-3869-7 (cloth). Prior to photocopying items for classroom use, please contact the Copyright Clearance Center, Customer Service, 222 Rosewood Dr., Danvers, MA 01923, USA, telephone 508-750-8400.

A Culture of Collaboration *by Jerry D. Weast, Lillie M. Jones, and J. Patrick Howley*

Everyone says that collaboration is a good idea, so why does SDP invest so much time and effort training people in this guiding principle? The reason is that, in our fragmented educational system, people don't actually know how to work together as a team because they haven't had opportunities to learn through trial and error. Elementary, middle, and high school principals rarely even talk with one another, let alone plan together for the long term. At each school district's central office, staff members usually are too busy to take the time to build a team and change their work routines. All too often we expect schools working by themselves to solve national and societal problems. We expect schools to transform themselves into human development centers without the support of the school district central office, the school board, community agencies, leaders in the community, and people in the business world. Sometimes school communities try to change but are thwarted in their efforts because of lack of support.

In this chapter, the Comer Action Team of Guilford County Schools in North Carolina describes the high-functioning culture of collaboration they have nurtured, in order to improve the lives of all the children in the school system. But first, a little background will help place this district in context.

The Guilford County Story

Guilford County has come a long way since 1960, when it became prominent as the birthplace of the student sit-in movement for desegregation. In recent years, both *SchoolMatch* and *Money Magazine* have cited Guilford County Schools (GCS) as one of the top systems in the nation. The first school system on the Information Highway with two-way interactive video, GCS received a top award from the National School Boards Association in 1995 for technology innovations. That same year, the district received the Golden Key Award, North Carolina's top honor for parent involvement. In March 1997, Superintendent Jerry D. Weast was invited to a major meeting of Japan's Electronic Industry Association held in Tokyo, to make a presentation about GCS's workforce preparedness programs and technology.

These accomplishments seem incredible when one considers that GCS is relatively young as school systems go, the result of a merger in 1993 of three formerly independent school systems—Greensboro, High Point, and Guilford County. The merger was a response to rising costs and educational inequities: enrollments were declining, the tax base was eroding and shifting, minority and low-income students were concentrated in the

Greensboro and High Point city systems, yet school facilities in those two systems were underutilized (white students left the two city school systems to attend either private school or the former county school system), while some in the county system were becoming overcrowded. In addition, the three separate systems competed for funding from one local source, the Guilford County government.

Today, GCS is one of the 60 largest districts in the nation and is the third largest in North Carolina, with 61,089 students. One of the results of the merger is that the district now has a unique SDP feature: a Comer Action Team. Usually SDP school districts appoint a Comer facilitator who has many responsibilities such as planning, providing training in each of the schools, making school visits to observe and coach, and trouble shooting. In the Guilford County School System (GCS), with 45 SDP school communities and growing, these responsibilities could not fall on any one person. The Comer Action Team includes the directors of professional growth and training/innovative programs, special programs, and community intervention; the supervisor for grants and special projects; the supervisors of social workers and alternative programs/dropout prevention; and the substance abuse lead teacher. Team members hail from elementary school, secondary school, and administrative backgrounds; their mix of talents, interests, and abilities fosters a holistic approach to problem solving. As a team, they offer technical assistance to SDP schools.

The Comer Action Team will now take you on a "site visit" to the district, where you can hear directly from people who work day by day in implementing the Comer Process. First, you will visit with Superintendent Weast, as he shows the life experiences that shaped his philosophy of education. In 1997, Jerry Weast was named State Superintendent of the Year by the North Carolina School Boards Association.

Collaboration Enhances Organization *by Jerry D. Weast*

My dad raises sweet corn and soybeans in Kansas. He recently turned 79 years of age. He's still plowing the ground whether he needs to or not, planting those crops, and that year he had 49 bushels of wheat per acre. Because he has had poor crops of corn in the past, his goal was to raise 100 bushels of corn per acre. I said to him, "How are you doing that?" He said, "Oh, I'm 79." I said, "What's that got to do with it?" He said, "I probably only have five or six crops left to raise that 100 bushels of corn. I have to do a few things different if I'm going to make it." That sobered me up real quick.

Educators! Consider your age and how many crops you have left—

that's the number of years you're going to work. How much time do you have left? How are you going to organize your time and your talent to effect change at your school or in your district? We are talking about spreading the vision and bringing equity to children. How many of you feel like you've got time under control and it doesn't matter? How many of you think you've got enough time? With only so many years left, you have to be strategic in your actions and remain focused on children. In Guilford County, we're going at warp speed because we're organized.

When I became superintendent, I took a look at the county. We had about 300 different, well-meaning programs out there, but we were providing a diffused environment for sometimes the most fragile children. I needed a program to focus the community and to empower the site-based decision makers who are in the schools—the teachers, principals, parents, and even some students. We built around the Comer Process because it's research-based, it's been around since 1968, it's driven by somebody who didn't start out in education but showed a lot of caring for children, and it worked with the children I wanted it to work with—children we historically did not expect much of, children affected by poverty.

In Guilford County, we were able to get rid of 90 percent of what we had been doing! We first chose a few things to do very well, and we made sure that those few things meshed well with each other. Now, standing on that firm foundation, we can do so much more in all our schools—from preschool all the way through preparing our high school students for college and jobs. And a significant part of that foundation is collaboration. Let me give you an example.

Our county spreads over 650 square miles. We did not have the people or the money to screen all young children for developmental delays. We turned to others for help. Through collaborations, we are now screening over 1,000 three- and four-year-old children. We say to mothers, "If you think that your child is developmentally delayed, come to us." Over a thousand people come out of wherever they live, and bring their children to get checked because they're worried. We're not like the stock market where you have to worry every day and find out what you have done by reading the paper the day after. We can predict and start building a program for those children. Ninety percent of the children who will show up in our first grades or kindergartens are already in our communities. Only about 10 percent are moving in and out, even in a high-growth district like ours.

We found out that between 1,100 to 1,500 children are developmentally delayed as much as 18 to 20 months. That's between 1.9 percent and 2.5 percent of all our children. Can you imagine yourself as a kindergarten teacher and you've got somebody reading and somebody who has never seen a book sitting beside each other? We started a program for four-year-olds about three and a half years ago. We found children who on a developmental scale of 100 points scored 0, 1, 2, 3 and who needed to be at 50 or above to be developmentally ready for kindergarten. Can you allow yourself to do anything even a *day* late? The answer is, if you develop a proper program and put in the proper interventions, then you can have children coming out of those programs for four-year-olds scoring 60, 70, 80 points on the average as a group, as we did. In 1994–1995, the average gain of the preschool students was 39 percentile points. In 1995–1996, the developmental growth of 400 preschool students averaged 59 percentile points from a pre-score of 21 to a post-score of 80. If you want to make some changes in your districts, that's where you should start.

There is a difference between loving a child and having high expectations for a child. Many teachers tell me, "Oh, I love the children, Jerry." I say, "Well, if you love them so much, give them the skills." Students unable to read have been graduating for years. They have been "pushed up." In GCS, we do not wait until the children are in fourth grade to see whether they are independent readers, transitional readers, or nonreaders. We are checking every single one of our 5,168 second graders. We know that we can teach every single child to read. We do so by organizing our schools and asking parents and community members to collaborate with us.

We found as a district that middle school is the level at which we went back to holding hands and having low expectations for children. Why? Crowd control. We were working to keep the students busy. Teachers had signed nonaggression pacts: "Don't hassle me; I won't hassle you." At the high school level, we found out that there were three tracks in high schools. Three tracks! The first group consisted of the students who would naturally thrive. They were the compliant ones: They learned the codes, they knew what it was all about, and they were organized the way we wanted them to be organized. Everybody else was divided into two other groups: The ones with potential and the ones that we thought didn't have potential. Nowadays, we nurture the potential of all the students and our students succeed in school.

My wife has a 1966 Mustang. In 1966, if you had a wrench, a pair of pliers, and some bailing wire, and if you could hear and see and feel, you could work on that car. Today we have a 1995 Explorer. It has more technology than the Apollo 11 spacecraft. The cars in 1993 were about 60 percent high tech. The cars now are about 85 percent high tech, computer driven. The Buick out there has 256 ways that the windshield wiper works depending on the amount of raindrops hitting the window. Are you going to let a wrench and a pair of pliers and some bailing wire work on that car? No. You need someone with special skills.

How many of you have teenagers who want to work for six or seven dollars an hour? Do you know what they're competing with in other parts of the world? Nine and ten cents an hour. Do you have anybody in your family wanting to work for nine or ten cents an hour, less than $1,000 a year? So, what do we have to be in America? Highly productive. How are you going to do that? You're going to organize your high schools, your middle schools, and your elementary schools to accomplish rigor for all.

Every action we take to help get these children out into the world has to be far more effective than ever before, and therefore every action has to be based on a rock-solid foundation. In our district, the foundation of our entire organization is the Comer Process. Everybody on my senior staff made a commitment to implement the Comer Process for five years regardless of how difficult it was to do because we have made a commitment to leave nothing to chance as we thrust our entire school system toward success.

Collaborating with Businesses *by the Comer Action Team*

Thinking about who would make good stakeholding partners, many schools wonder how to start collaborating with businesses. Our experiences in Guilford County suggest that the point of entry is the local Chamber of Commerce.

On July 1, 1993, Superintendent Weast called for increased student achievement and workforce preparedness. Four years later, on March 6, 1997, Weast was invited to Tokyo to tell a major meeting of Japan's Electronic Industry Association about GCS's technology—particularly interactive classrooms with full-motion video, full-spectrum audio, and integrated connectivity—interactive voice—and workforce preparedness programs. GCS's college and workforce preparedness programs are notable in that they are a collaboration of the Chambers of Commerce of Greensboro City and High Point City. In his presentation, Weast showed how GCS is preparing students to meet the challenges they will face in the workforce of the twenty-first century. His presentation outlined four major contributions to life-long learning: home, community (region and state), business, and technology.

Weast's invitation to represent North Carolina in Japan is remarkable considering that as recently as 1993 industrial leaders in the area expressed their frustration that the graduates of the schools were not qualified to meet the technological workplace. Yet by November 1996, *The Wall Street Journal* could run a front-page article on Guilford County workforce preparedness programs that highlighted the three key ideas of the College Tech Prep Programs forged between Weast and Don Cameron, President of Guilford Technical Community College: "turf-free" alliance, collaboration, and high expectations for all students. One component of College Tech Prep Programs is guidance. All ninth through twelfth grade students are required to design career development plans with the support of GCS Guidance Services.

Multiple Points of Involvement

Two early workforce preparedness initiatives, one led by Dow Corning and the other led by a consortium of metals manufacturing companies, have served as models that are now being replicated in seven major industries in the county: banking and financial services, electrical construction, automotive, medium- and heavy-duty vehicles, metals manufacturing, chemical and process manufacturing, and HVAC (air conditioning and refrigeration). *Competitive Advantage* (1997), a folder describing Guilford County Workforce Preparedness designed by the Greensboro Area Chamber of Commerce Economic Development Department, describes the ways in which businesses are involved with the school district:

- Businesses employ student apprentices in a structured on-the-job training program. Apprenticeships are registered by the North Carolina Department of Education.
- Businesses employ students who attend class and meet specified learning objectives.
- Businesses provide unpaid work for students who attend class and meet specified learning objectives.
- Businesses allow students to observe in the workplace for a half-day to a week. This is known as job-shadowing.
- Businesses provide:
    - tuition and fees to the school, college, or student
    - guest speakers and presentations to the schools and colleges
    - field trips for students and teachers
    - Return-to-Industry internships for teachers and counselors
    - professional development for teachers and counselors
    - consultation on curriculum content
    - specialized equipment

Business People as Volunteers

Industrial leaders arrange seminars at which teachers talk directly with industry people about what preparation students need in order to work in that industry. When Ed Kelly, human resource manager of Dow Corning, learned about what the school district was doing to prepare students for college and technical school, he realized that the equipment and the curriculum were not adequate. He volunteered himself and others from Dow Corning to help develop more up-to-date curriculum materials. Dow Corning provided funds to equip a high school lab at a preprofessional level. Then Dow Corning and staff members at Dow Corning contributed their own staff time to the teachers to help prepare them to teach the curriculum properly. Teachers received technical training and guided tours of industries. Students began participating in apprenticeships.

Collaboration means that you have cooperation and the flexibility that comes with shared learning. All the participants in the collaboration learn about each other's needs. Until he retired in January 1997, John Lauritzen was vice president of AT&T at the Greensboro, NC facility and an officer of the Chamber of Commerce. As an officer, he was actively involved in the decision to consolidate the three school districts, in the citizen's advisory board (which aided in the selection of the current superintendent, Jerry Weast), and in several school system activities, including Guilford County Schools' apprenticeship program with Guilford Technical Community College and North Carolina A&T State University. He told us that his initial interest in education stemmed from the fact that AT&T recruits locally and from outside the area. In his words, "When people from outside the area are considering a local community, one of the first things that they ask about is the strength of the public school system. The schools here did not have the reputation that was required to recruit people into the area."

According to the Director of Community Relations for Guilford County Schools, in 1997, 74,000 tutors, mentors, PTA members, Lunch Buddies, and businesses partners volunteered 195,000 hours in our schools. In the next section of this chapter, John Lauritzen reports on his own extraordinary experience as a Lunch Buddy.

My Lunch Buddy and Me *by John Lauritzen*

Until I retired in January 1997, I was vice president of AT&T at the Greensboro, NC facility. I was also an officer on the Chamber of Commerce. In 1992, I heard so much excitement about people becoming lunch buddies. I decided the next year that I'd get involved as a lunch buddy myself and I did, in 1993.

To become a lunch buddy, I filled out an application indicating that I was willing to volunteer. I wrote on the form that I didn't have a preference whether my lunch buddy would be a girl or boy. Someone from the school district contacted me, thanked me for being willing to volunteer as a lunch buddy, and invited me to a briefing session at one of the schools, which I attended. It was at that briefing session that I was introduced to one of the assistant principals at Frazier Elementary School. I also got a little card with the name of my lunch buddy, a boy in the third grade.

I called the principal and said that I would like to find out the name of the child's teacher and asked if there was anything I should know before I came to school. He arranged to have the teacher call me back. She described the child to me. Basically she said that he was a kid that had behavioral problems. She thought he was intelligent, but he seemed to be a kind of a clown in school and had ADD. Another problem was that his mother couldn't give him all the attention he needed: His father had left the family; he had a brother and sister, one of whom was retarded, and they required a lot of the mother's attention. She thought it would be useful to have somebody else involved in his life. I went over to the school and met the teacher one evening. She stayed late, and I just spent a little bit of time with her talking about what her expectations were toward me. I was fully employed. I didn't have a lot of time to get involved, and I wanted to know if I was expected to do anything beyond the lunch hour. She told me that I could spend time in school having lunch and that was really all that was expected. "You'll be amazed," she said, "at what can happen as a result of that."

I ate the school lunch, which I paid for. I sat at the little tables in my suit and tie. We didn't have a private table. As a matter of fact, this was the beauty of it, as it turned out. He would actually escort me to his regular table, where there were six or seven classmates, and I sat at that table. By the way, I'm six-foot-five-inches tall, so it was interesting! The very first week, he didn't say anything. He was totally intimidated. He would answer a question with either a yes or no. Actually the words he used were "yup" and "nope," and that was about it. I'd get a shrug out of him. So I called the teacher after that and asked if this was just too much for him. She said, "No, just keep coming." Over the next several weeks, he actually got to be very talkative at the table. From sitting at the table with the students, I got a strong impression of their perception of their school and community. We talked about all kinds of things—ethics, birthday parties at which they wanted to exclude certain kids or include certain kids. We had a discussion about why they wanted to do that. I said to the students, "You don't want to hurt kids feelings, do you?" I learned a lot about my community by listening to these kids.

I talked frequently to people in my own cafeteria and, of course, with people who reported to me about being a lunch buddy and about the value

I was getting out of participating in the program. I spoke in town at the Rotary Club, the Kiwanis Club, and places like that to try to get other people involved because I thought it was such a rewarding process and I felt that I got as much out of it as the kids did.

Now, what does a third grader know about me? Vice-presidents don't really mean anything to third graders. In fact, I had to sell myself to these children. I was dealing with people who didn't really care what my corporate position was.

I started to do other activities with my lunch buddy. When he was in fifth grade, I took him to see basketball games, ice-skating, and drag racing. And one of the people at work actually had a dragster in a racing event. I put my lunch buddy in the dragster and let him steer it while we pushed it. (Of course, he couldn't be in it during the drag racing event.) I just thought he'd get really excited about it. We talked to him about the mathematics that is involved in putting together a racing machine—that you need to have a good education and there is a lot of engineering in it.

On the way home that night, I asked him what he was going to be when he grew up, and I thought that he was going to tell me he was going to be a drag racer. Instead, he told me that he was going to be a drug dealer.

I said, "What?"

He said, "I like to get things like race cars and dress nicely. In my neighborhood if you want those kinds of things, you gotta sell drugs."

Well, I almost died. I thought I was going to wreck my car. I just said, "There have to be other options. We should talk about that sometime." I really was stunned. I went home and thought about it. I thought about the people at work who were people that looked like him. I said to myself, "What I really ought to do is see if I can bring him to lunch where I work, rather than me going to his school." I talked to his mother and to the teacher, and they both thought that was a good idea.

I brought him to where I worked at AT&T. I made sure that we sat at a table with all kinds of people including several African-Americans. There were African-Americans who were managers and people involved in computers and other aspects of business, and after the lunch I had him go to each of their offices so that he could see the people and talk to them. They had pictures of their kids and computers in their private offices. When I took him home, I asked, "What did you think of that?" He said, "I didn't know we could do those kinds of things."

Around Christmas time, his mother wrote me a note that was just the most touching thing. She said that what my lunch buddy wanted to do when he grew up was be a manager at AT&T.

Collaborating with the Community *by the Comer Action Team*

Creating a culture of collaboration can foster amazing success, both in the school and in the surrounding community. When first-time principal Doris Davis came to Washington Elementary School in 1993, she found a science and technology magnet school in name only. Teachers were aware that their students needed help, but were unaware of the rich resources waiting to be tapped in their families and in the community. As Davis reports in the following account, Washington is now at the heart of a partnership that has brought local organizations, big business, and higher education into the school. Davis' extraordinary leadership in reaching out to the community can provide a model for other administrators who want to tap wider resources for the benefit of their students, families, and faculty. In 1997, Doris Davis was honored with a Patrick Daly Memorial Award for Excellence in Educational Leadership.

Where Does Community Begin and How Far Does It Extend?
by Doris T. Davis

After I had been principal of Washington for a few weeks, I realized that the teachers knew very little about the community and that almost none of them had actually been into the housing community to visit their children and to see their homes. (In 1997, out of 305 students, 264 lived in public housing, 25 in a homeless shelter, 12 in a home for battered women, and 4 in motels.)

I talked with the residence manager at the housing community, Ray Warren Homes. I asked her when would be a good time for our whole staff to walk over and hand out flyers inviting the residents to an open house at the school. To my staff I said, "We need to know where our children live. We need to become familiar with the community." One morning during a teacher work day, we gathered at the school. We walked through the neighborhood. The children were in the yards, and the parents were there to wave and say hello. Our parents were glad to see us.

Teachers had so many misconceptions about a housing project community. For example, they were surprised to see flowers there. However, they were right in knowing that many of the children from Ray Warren have medical needs and that many are going through a lot of turmoil. We have children in our school who are from homes where they do not always get the support that they need. But Ray Warren is also a community that is close-knit. Parents talk to each other. They care about their children.

The walk really opened an avenue for our teachers and our parents to see that we have the same interests—we have to come together for the children. I said to my staff, "If Ray Warren Homes did not exist, we would not be here. When we made a commitment to become teachers, we made a commitment to teach all children. We take children wherever they are and we help them to grow. We have a responsibility as professionals to do whatever it takes to help children to become successful. We have to set high expectations for children and teach them and care for them, and they will do very well."

Today, teachers and parents meet regularly. Teachers pair up to make home visits. If a parent prefers to meet at the school and not at the home, we meet at the school. Many of our parents do not have telephones. The teacher will send a note home saying, "May I come over on Wednesday at 4:00 or would you like to meet me at the library on Wednesday at 4:00?" The library is around the corner from the school, and parents who are uncomfortable entering the school meet with teachers there. We have also used a church for meetings. The school initiated contact with the Salvation Army Boys and Girls Club that's located in the housing community. If a student is having trouble with school work, the teacher will ask permission from the parent to collaborate with the people at the Boys and Girls Club. Together they will map out strategies that might work at school. Either the after-school person or the classroom teacher might realize something about the child that the other does not know because the child behaves differently in a different setting. Maybe at the Salvation Army Boys and Girls Club they want the child to sit down and do his homework. We know from the school that the child does best when he is sitting on the floor or that he needs to do chunks of homework at a time. The teacher will say, "If he has ten problems, let him do five, take a little break, and then do the other five." Sometimes, sharing even small bits of information can help the child to be successful.

We also collaborate with the University of North Carolina at Greensboro (UNCG) and Bennett College. The psychology department at UNCG provides us with doctoral students to work with children and their families when the children meet the Department of Social Service's criteria for Attention Deficit Hyperactivity Disorder (ADHD). The doctoral students suggest strategies on how to work most effectively with ADHD children. Bennett College is a private, four-year liberal arts institution for women. The college welcomes and includes women of all ethnic backgrounds, but historically, most Bennett students have been African-American. Twelve to fifteen preservice teachers intern at our school each semester, tutoring children individually and in groups and assisting in classrooms.

The school is becoming the hub of the community. Parents realize that so many positive things can happen at the school that are good for their children and for their families. We have been able to get glasses and medication for children. We have helped families make contact with the health department and the department of social services. We have helped them fill out forms to become eligible for services. We have had job fairs for the parents, and we have brought in people from the Employment Security Commission to help them learn how to go on a job interview—what to say and how to say it.

The school is in the process of establishing the Washington School Community Wellness Center for children, parents, and residents in the surrounding neighborhood. The advisory council includes representatives from Proctor & Gamble, United Healthcare, Blue Cross Blue Shield, Wrangler, Guilford County Schools, community and parent volunteers, parent educators, and members of our school's staff as well as the dean of the School of Nursing at North Carolina A&T State University, the director of health services at the University of North Carolina-Greensboro, the director of the Nutrition Management Center, and the executive director of the Wellness Council of North Carolina. The Center aims to enhance the quality of the Washington School community by finding new ways to provide social support, to help people get comprehensive health information and services, and to offer and support opportunities for healthy lifestyle changes. The center will also be able to do diabetes and blood pressure screening.

When a mother is aware of her health and when her health needs are being met, she is able to be a better parent. She can feel good physically and feel good about herself and, therefore, give more to her children and be more a part of what is happening in the school. When children know their parents are part of the school, they want to do well. They want to show off in a positive way. So they tend to do better.

Students at Washington have demonstrated steady performance gains on the North Carolina End-of-Grade Testing Program, particularly in mathematics. The performance of fourth grade students on the state-mandated writing assessment has risen markedly since it was introduced in 1993. In that year, only 16.7 percent of fourth graders at Washington scored at or above the 2.5 proficiency level, compared to a district average of 21 percent. Four years later, 66 percent of the Washington fourth graders were performing at that standard, surpassing the district average of 60 percent and the state-wide average of 52 percent.

Collaborating at the Board and District Level

The success of schools depends also on the culture of collaboration that people create at the board and district level. Walter M. Pritchett, Jr., a prod-

uct of the very schools he now oversees and with five grandchildren in the
school system, describes in this section how the school board's commitment to the Comer Process is at the root of the success in all its schools. A
member of Washington Elementary School's class of 1956, Pritchett is the
only school board member in the country who is also a fully qualified SDP
facilitator.

Getting Everyone on Board by *Walter Matthew Pritchett, Jr.*

When eleven people come together to form a school board, everyone has
different interests. You have the business interest, the Black interest, the
wealthy interest. You have the interest of one type of learning versus another type of learning. School board members have had different experiences with the PTAs. Some board members like to deal directly with
teachers; other board members are very student-centered. It's very important, as far as I am concerned, that we sometimes sit in each other's chairs.

In Guilford County, collaboration among us grew very slowly. I'd like
to think that I have done a fairly decent job as a single board member working with a very diverse group in helping to build that collaboration. Most
of what I have learned and most of what I have applied to my work as a
school board member has been as a result of my training at the School Development Program's professional development academy. Once the school
board began to understand the Comer Process, it began to function as a
community, even in the face of a public outcry.

We live in a very conservative part of the country. Dr. Comer talks
about six developmental pathways that we have to work with to promote
children's balanced development, including what used to be called the
"moral pathway." When we started talking about the six developmental
pathways and morals being taught to children, it actually sparked protest
in the community because people felt that we were talking about things
that they should be teaching at home. I think that they did not understand
at the time that we were not talking about religious values. We were talking about getting into the very simple values everybody should learn, such
as respect for one another, respect for property, and trying to do the best that
you can.

Some parents were so concerned that they actually demonstrated at
school board meetings. The school board addressed the parents' concerns
by meeting continually with them, bringing out more information, and
inviting more people to get involved in the process. We explained that we
were not trying to separate the children from the values that their parents
were teaching them. Learning good values at home only enhances what

we are trying to do. We also explained that the six developmental pathways are the way we assess our student population so that we can know how to improve the curriculum.

The school board took a very positive and high-road approach. From my perspective, I felt that the more information I gave school board members about Dr. Comer's ideas, the better they could explain to their constituents what this was all about. Whether people were coming at the school system, coming at the school board members, or coming to the school with their complaints, we were covering all bases with proper and factual information that would allow them to make better assessments. And over time it worked out very well.

Recently the name "moral pathway" was changed to "ethical pathway" to avoid this confusion between religious moral values and conduct based on ethics. People today in the country are concerned about public education. They want to know if our schools are preparing the students to become responsible citizens, good employees, and ethical human beings. They want to know if the graduates of our schools will take pride in their work, care about others, and contribute to the society.

Another fine example of our school board's collaboration occurred when we looked at a school in which a lot of parents did not seem positive about their children's development in schools. When the teachers became aware of information that was gleaned from looking at the children's developmental pathways, they were in a better position to make changes in their teaching styles. Principals and staff members did the looking, teachers did the gleaning, principals broached the subject, and the principals along with the Comer Action Team members coordinated the staff development necessary to promote change.

A lot of our teachers had been looking at things strictly from a scientific-theoretical base, and when we were able to give them clear evidence of what was necessary to help children, they made changes fairly easily. The children, for example, arrived at the school without having breakfast or a good night's sleep. Parents did not read with them or listen to them read. They did not help them study when they got home. Home was not inviting to the students after they got out of school. When we used the developmental pathways to show some of the ills that came out of that, we were able to help teachers who had never experienced anything like that to make the necessary adjustments. It appears that most of our teachers have the training. In some cases, they've just lost their way. We help them to reach back into themselves and pull out the necessary changes that can make a real difference.

As a school board, we had to move from thinking from the top down to site-based decision making. In the top-down type of management program, all decisions are made at the school district's central office—all the elementary schools are cut by one cookie cutter, and all the middle schools are cut by another. Now, in 1998, three years after the Guilford County Schools adopted the Comer Process, we no longer make the child fit the school's culture. Instead, we make the culture sensitive to where the child is starting from and what he or she needs to grow and develop well. Students now have more options open to them as a result of site-based decision making, and schools have far more independence to look at their students as individuals.

As we have begun collaborating well together, we have been able to draw in parents, churches, businesses, and for-profit and nonprofit organizations. The way we have reached out has been by showing that we are very frugal spenders of the county taxpayers' money and by raising academic standards and the students' test scores. We have demonstrated that we are deserving of more money and more resources to do even better. In these three years, we have really built a strong reputation around the country and have been able to encourage people, like the Bryan Foundation and the Cemala Foundation, to donate all sorts of resources to the school system.

In 1996, the school board adopted a resolution renewing its commitment to implementing and expanding the Comer Process. The resolution solidified a child-centered approach across the district. Once the school board started thinking and acting from a child-centered perspective, it changed our whole outlook on the calendar, equity funding, accountability. The equity funding that we put in place is a good example of what happened when we changed to a child-centered way of looking at issues.

A year after the merger of the three school districts into the unified Guilford County Schools, the school board dealt with the needs of some of the poor communities. Initially, school board members from more affluent neighborhoods felt that their particular areas would lose out if the school system were to shift money to High Impacted schools. "High Impacted" schools have low academic achievement, a high percentage of students on either free or reduced-priced lunches, and high numbers of students for whom English is a second or other language.

Once we as a school board adopted the Comer Process, school board members realized that all of their individual interests in particular areas of the school system could fit together. After the shift in mindset, it was almost unanimous that we would take a risk, shift money, and meet the needs of schools that were either socially or economically deprived. We feel strongly about different areas, but we have all come together with our concerns and built what I consider to be a very, very strong school system. As Jerry Weast (1997) wrote:

Four years after the merger, we can let the statistics speak for themselves: Students have improved in the core subjects of reading, writing, and math; our dropout rate has fallen to the lowest level among large districts in the state; student performance on the SAT has increased for the past three years; and local costs per child have dropped 4.5 percent over the period while teacher salaries have risen 18.5 percent and spending on classroom supplies, materials, and technology and staff development set record levels. (p. 38)

Collaboration: A Team Approach to Improving Schools
by the Comer Action Team

We are still in the process of exploring what it takes to collaborate. Although the School Planning and Management Team governs the school, the principal is still the legal authority. Hence all the members of all the teams have to collaborate well to ensure that principals are not paralyzed when they have to fulfill their legal responsibilities. Furthermore, when teams work well together toward goals they have developed together, the meaning of collaboration becomes more expansive.

In Guilford County, we now see that SDP is not merely an educational innovation. The Comer Process at the heart of SDP insists that we embrace community as a way of embodying our highest hopes for all our children. For example, to meet the needs of fragile children—students placed at-risk—Welborn Middle School focuses the collaborative energies of its business partner, Sara Lee Stock Company, as well as energies within the school: peer tutoring, guidance groups, and mentors. Sara Lee Stock company provides paper, pencils, erasers, and notebooks to all students and T-shirts for honor roll students. Company employees volunteer their time as tutors and in the Lunch Buddy program. Among the school staff, "Teachers are working out problems together rather than taking fragmented approaches," said Principal Jeff German.

Peeler Open Elementary School, a magnet school in Greensboro, adopted SDP in 1994, according to principal Martha Hudson, "because a lot of the SDP philosophy meshed with what we were already doing." Having seen SDP in action, Hudson states, "It works because it creates a sense that all the resources within and outside the school are being brought together in the service of children." For example, the AT&T Pioneers, an organization of retirees, painted a giant map of the United States on a slab of concrete adjacent to the school's playground and donated teaching materials to enhance geography skills.

David Huneycutt, the principal of Peck Elementary School, notes, "There is a very close relationship between our Parent Team and our PTA."

In the early morning hours of Friday, March 22, 1996, vandals ransacked Peck, leaving some rooms in near-ruin. Windows were broken, doors unhinged, fire extinguishers set off, paint splashed, soft drinks spilled into television monitors, computers smashed, and drawers emptied. Milk, juice, and ice cream were splattered through the cafeteria, but the media center was hardest hit. Bookcases were overturned, lights and windows broken out, and profane graffiti sprayed on windows and walls. This was the worst case of vandalism in the school system's history.

The senseless destruction triggered an outpouring of support from Peck's SDP family. A neighborhood church half a block away provided a haven for 400 displaced students while school maintenance crews assessed the damage and began repairs. Working shoulder-to-shoulder with teachers on Saturday, a small army of volunteers got the school back in shape for students by Monday. Among the volunteers were Peck parents and PTA members from other area schools. Local businesses pitched in, providing doughnuts, sandwiches, and other refreshments for the workers. After the school received a check from the school system's insurance company, the principal replaced computers, supplies, and other equipment.

If the vandalism was the low point of the 1995–1996 academic year at Peck, then receiving a $280,000 Cemala Foundation grant was definitely the high point. The grant funds a model community school project that complements SDP goals. A collaborative partnership between the Cemala Foundation, Guilford County Schools, and the Glenwood neighborhood, this demonstration project provides a preschool class for four-year-olds, an extended school day, and direct medical and counseling services for families, which is provided in part by a parent liaison.

"Even before we received the grant, we had opened our school as a site for community activities," said principal Huneycutt. A local community organization meets at Peck even though few of its 100 mainly elderly members have children at the school. Soccer and T-ball teams practice on Peck's field. The YMCA uses Peck's ball field and conducts other after-school and weekend activities on the grounds. "The SDP," notes Huneycutt, "has given the community a way to interact more effectively with the school."

"Together we can make a difference" is the motto at Sedalia Elementary School, a community school located in a rural industrial area in eastern Guilford County. At Sedalia, principal Lane Anderson III encourages collaboration among the students—and not competition. Principal Anderson explains to us the school's approach: When students compete against one another for grades, they lose sight of the value of learning itself and also can take their failures personally and feel alienated. Instead, schools should motivate each student to strive for his or her personal best, in order to experience both the value of persistence and the pride of succeeding. In such a school climate, not only does failure come only when one stops trying, but it is also far easier to start trying again.

Anderson points to Michael Jordan, who says he is always trying to succeed:

> Jordan lists his failures: how many games in which he should have made the clutch shot and missed; how many games he's messed up that nobody knows about. He keeps those statistics because it fine tunes him. Why should we hold a child accountable for one shot? Are we going to fire Michael Jordan because he missed the final shot—bench him? No, we're going to bring him back in and see if he can do it better the next day. When I do seminars with teachers, the secondary teachers are tougher to convince because they're so subject area oriented. I keep saying, "You teach children. The curriculum happens to be the medium." They say, "No, I teach math." "No," I say, "you teach children." There's a big difference. And so if you can get them convinced that if a kid makes a 35 on the first major test—who wants to walk around with a 35, thinking they're a 35 person?—give them the test again. If he makes 100, he's still going to get a C minus. You're not going to hurt these A/B superstars, but now he's walking around on that borderline between C and D with an incentive to keep his grades in the C range. No children should ever perceive themselves as below average, and yet that's what we do. Consider athletics. You run the play wrong—you run it ten more times until you get it. The worst thing you could do to a team is run a play for the first time, then bust it up and say, "Well that's the one we're using Friday night. I hope you all can do it."

Our more expansive meaning of collaboration, then, is principals working with their staffs, teams working together, the whole school working together with a huge community that extends well beyond the boundaries of the school's locality. Perhaps, most important, we have to learn to recognize that our culture of collaboration is helping children in the classrooms to learn with and from one another.

At any level, the culture of collaboration can take more time to establish than people anticipate. In the final section of this chapter, Donna Morrison, principal of McLeansville Middle School, offers us the wisdom in the seeming contradiction that taking more time to achieve a long-hoped-for and urgently needed goal can be a good thing. In 1998, Donna Morrison was honored as a recipient of a Patrick Daly Memorial Award for Excellence in Educational Leadership.

Collaboration Slowed Us Down (and I Am Glad!)
by Donna Morrison

When I became principal of McLeansville Middle School three and a half years ago, I was eager, full of ideas, fired up. I wanted to increase the students' test scores. More important, I wanted to create a climate that was child-centered. I wanted the teachers to have high expectations for themselves and for our students. I don't know what the people here thought of me when I came. They probably thought, "This lady is absolutely crazy!" I think that for a while I ran around just trying to find people that would work with me. I felt like there was a cloud over us. We busted through, but it took a long time.

Initially, I guess I was thinking that the staff would readily help make changes. Yet the school had tried so many school reforms in the past. In the back of their minds the staff thought, "This new principal won't be here long anyway. Soon this new principal and her notions will be gone." Then the school district central office introduced the School Development Program. It sounded like it just fit me like a glove. I thought, "This process will help me bring people together."

I call the day that I introduced the Comer Process to the staff, "The Fateful Day." I introduced the Comer Process, and I said that we had to decide whether we were going to use the Process or not. The staff expressed great faith. On that fateful day, I didn't realize how difficult it would be. After we decided to implement the Comer Process, I felt like celebrating. However, days and months and years later, I was thinking, "My goodness, what have we done?" It just took so much time to change the mindset, to work through issues as a team, to involve everybody. I came to realize that this process delayed us in making changes because I could no longer simply tell people what to do. And I am glad!

To implement the Comer Process and make changes in our school took staff buy-in. It took a lot of convincing and leading by example. I couldn't say to the staff and parents that we were going to make decisions in the best interest of children without encouraging them to become part of the decision-making process. On my desk, I have a basket containing cards that read "collaboration," "consensus," and "no-fault." We put these cards on the table before every meeting to remind ourselves of the importance of adhering to the three guiding principles.

Collaboration slowed us down, but it is the best thing that ever happened. Collaborating built trust. Through collaborating, we made better decisions. It made me be less impatient. During the first year, I secretly regretted implementing the Comer Process. "This is killing me," I said to myself. "I can't wait. There's too much that needs to be changed, there's too much that needs to be done, and this is taking forever." But then, we accomplished one goal and then another and yet another. People were making decisions on behalf of the children. At first, the accomplishments and the improvements happened so gradually, but they happened, and then there was no stopping them! What helped us was our decision to stick with the Process. We did not say, "We'll try it for a year or two, and if everything isn't better by then, we'll switch to something else." We took the time to truly change our mindset and way of interacting with one another.

The students have improved tremendously in their performance on the state tests. I am really proud of the students' achievement in writing. In the period 1994–1996, the percent of students scoring at or above the proficiency level of 2.5 went up significantly, putting McLeansville sixth and eighth grade students at the top of district improvement rankings among middle schools in this subject. Last year was the first time that seventh-graders were mandated to take the writing test. Our students' scores were the highest of all the schools in the system. As our superintendent said, "Who would have thought three years ago that McLeansville would rank number one!"

References

Bleakley, F.R. (Tuesday, November 26, 1996). To bolster economies some states rely more on two-year colleges. *The Wall Street Journal*, p. 1.

Greensboro Area Chamber of Commerce Economic Development Department. (1997). *Competitive advantage.* Greensboro, North Carolina.

Weast, J. (October 1997). When bigger can be better. *The School Administrator*, pp. 38–43.

EPILOGUE

To Ask the Best of Children, We Must Ask the Best of Ourselves

Edward T. Joyner

Edward T. Joyner with his son Edward, Jr. Photograph by Laura Brooks.

Modeling matters.

School would look totally different if students were evaluated not just on the basis of how well they score on standardized tests, but also on whether they help out in the community, are peaceful, pursue justice and fairness, and help each other. Dr. Lester Young, Jr., superintendent of Community School District 13 in Brooklyn, New York, often says, "Who you are is just as important as what you know, because who you are determines what you will do with what you know." And who our students become and what they do is our responsibility. It takes the collective effort of parents, teachers, and every other adult in the school community to promote children's development. When I look back over the course of my own life, I realize that there were adults standing at every major crossroads, setting good examples, and pointing me in the right direction whenever my own compass failed me.

When I first became an educator in the 1970s, the deficit perspective was widespread, and many teachers labeled many children as being incapable. The deficit perspective assumes that a person's potential is fixed at birth, whereas the developmental perspective assumes that, with enough support, each person can get better in almost any area.

Within School Development Program (SDP) school communities, we train and support all our participating educators, parents, and community members to have patience with development. An acorn does not become an oak tree overnight. Some children are born in very hard places, and that temporarily disrupts their development. It is the responsibility of the schools to engage in coalitions with parents and community people to help these children. After all, they do not have genetic deficits; they have *experience* deficits.

The SDP's attitude is this: Individual programs are negotiable, but individual children are not. And in order to help children, we have to have personal relationships with them. Those of us who have taught know that you can know the subject matter well and not be able to deliver it if you don't know the children well. Like the good bedside manner of doctors who show their patients and their families incredible kindness and compassion in their time of need, such teachers exhibit a good deskside manner. They patiently and firmly exhort, inspire, and encourage their students to persist, maintaining a faith in their potential even when the students themselves have nearly given up. They are bridge builders, way makers, healers, and guides. For such teachers, their students do not have to look like them. They do not have to come from the same socioeconomic or religious background. Their parents do not have to be rich and famous. They simply have to be children that need to be taught. Teachers who are way makers help students think through five questions:

- What are the challenges in my life?
- How can I be who I want to be without hurting myself and others?
- How can becoming who I want to be help myself and others?
- What resources do I already have to meet these challenges?
- How can I develop additional resources?

The traditional school relies on the individual teacher to organize those experiences and maybe even to deal with questions one and two; the Comer Process involves the entire community.

The World Has Changed, but Children's Needs Remain the Same

I grew up in the small rural community of Farmville, North Carolina, during the 1950s and 1960s. I was very fortunate to have had loving parents, grandparents, and a host of uncles, aunts, cousins, friends, and a supportive community. I also had caring teachers. They believed in my potential as a human being and contributed to my growth and development. I was taught by a series of teachers who worked in concert with our parents and the larger community to insure that we were firmly planted in a rich value system and presented with the "right examples." I am absolutely convinced that although I lived in a poor, segregated community, it contained a rich culture of faith, hope, and spirituality that helped compensate for the lack of material advantages that are present in many communities today.

My father, John Elijah Joyner, played a central role in shaping my world view. He was born only 35 years after the end of the Civil War. His own father passed away when he was in third grade, and he quit school in 1909 when he was nine years old to help his mother work the little piece of land that was assigned to the family as sharecroppers. As the oldest male child he inherited the responsibility to help his mother provide for his two sisters.

From as far back as I can remember, he would take me, when possible, on the various jobs he worked throughout his life to help support the family. He never, to my recollection, made more than minimum wages and in many instances made far less since farm workers were exempt from federally regulated workers' compensation. Despite his low social and economic status, he modeled a quiet dignity. He made it clear to me that he wanted me to do better—that education and hard work were the way out. He cautioned me never to forget the various bridges that you had to cross to be successful and always to remember the people who helped you cross those bridges. He had a great sense of humor and used laughter as one of his weapons against the repressive conditions that often overwhelmed many of his peers. He was my first hero.

Parenting under such circumstances could have been difficult, but I was given a coat of armor that prepared me to weather the predictable assaults against my developing humanity. I was hugged, told stories, read to, tucked in, and disciplined. I was taught that I was as good as any mother's child, yet not better. It was also made clear to me that I would have to work twice as hard to go half as far. My parents never used poverty and caste status as an excuse for putting forth less than one's best efforts.

My school did not have a cafeteria or gym when I entered it in 1953. Salaries for Negro (the term in use at that time) teachers were less than their White counterparts. My English teacher was given a stipend by the state of North Carolina and bused to New York University to earn an advanced degree. She was not allowed to attend the segregated state schools that offered such degrees in her own home state. This was the social and political backdrop for communities and schools during my childhood and adolescence. Despite these clear and unjust disadvantages, we learned to cope, to struggle with courage and dignity—to make a way out of no way—as we prepared for a time when the barriers to our full participation in American life would come tumbling down.

I learned valuable lessons during this time, in and out of school, that are still with me. My great-grandmother told me, "You will be knocked down many times in life; don't lay there and wallow." My uncle taught me that the only time that you should be forced to your knees is in prayer. It was my third grade teacher, however, who convinced me that I should go to college, even if no one else in my immediate family had ever finished high school. She said that I was "college material" and that nothing would stop me once I made up my mind to earn a degree. She planted a seed of faith in my head that grew enough for me to dream of a time when I would be a teacher just like her.

Many of my former classmates overcame tremendous material disadvantages and achieved at high levels in American society because of the love, kindness, and high standards of personal responsibility set for us by our families, teachers, and a caring community. They have become teachers, bus drivers, factory workers, principals, college professors, physicians, engineers, lawyers, ministers, bankers, professional entertainers, and—above all—people of good character. This happened because we were our community's highest priority. The adults knew that they all had to assume collective responsibility for our well-being. They were unshakable in their conviction that we all would grow up to become self-respecting, fully contributing members of society.

In Some Measure, All Children Today Are at Risk

Contemporary parents and teachers face different challenges. My own children live in a world far more turbulent than the little town that shaped my development. We live in a society where even children who live in affluent families can suffer from spiritual and emotional deprivation that is masked and often very hard to address. We can also count children who perform well in the classroom but fail miserably in life. In some measure, all children are at risk in a society such as ours. Test score achievement is the number one goal of many school reforms at a time when the social fabric of America is unraveling. As a society, we have built an obstacle course for our children that is a direct threat to their immediate and future well-being. It is our responsibility as adults to dismantle it and build relationships that support rather than thwart the development of children.

If the Load Were Too Heavy, I Wouldn't Ask You to Carry It

In the Chicago Public School System, the implementation of the Comer Process is directed by a social service agency, Chicago Youth Guidance. They have created the Collegial Instructors Group (CIG), in which teachers work with other teachers to improve instruction. We helped them to conceptualize and plan their work, which includes brainstorming, study groups, mentoring, and observation. After one year they took more responsibility for their curriculum, and in the third year they were completely responsible for it. Among CIG's guiding precepts are these:

- All children can learn.
- Teachers make a difference.
- Growth as a teacher requires inquiry and reflection.
- Teachers are models of educated citizens.
- Learning is a life-long responsibility.
- There is power in collaboration.

Many of the teachers came to CIG knowing only how to stand in front of the classroom and lecture, and they couldn't name what they were doing. In addition, many of them had been doing what they were doing for years, and felt pretty set in their ways. Now, one of our ideas at CIG was that each teacher would learn two new, powerful teaching methods each year. When we announced this goal, one teacher said that she didn't believe she could do that, that it seemed like too much to accomplish. I thought that was ironic because she surely would say that we have to have high expectations for students. Well, what about high expectations for teachers? Not only do I believe that children can get better, I believe that teachers can get better. So I modeled the whole notion of high expectations: I told her, "If the load were too heavy, I wouldn't have asked you to carry it. You can lift this." And she did.

Let's Agree to Sustain Each Other So That We Can Remain Steadfast in Helping Children

It is critically important for us to be steadfast in improving the lifepaths of children. In the civil rights movement we used to sing the song, "I Ain't Gon' Let Nobody Turn Me Around. . . . Just like a tree planted by the water, we shall not be moved." We have to be steadfast.

Teddy Roosevelt (1913) said something that I believe helps us to move forward:

> It is not the critic who counts; not the man who points out how the strong man stumbles, or where the doer of deeds could have done them better. The credit belongs to the man who is actually in the arena; whose face is marred by dust and sweat and blood; who strives valiantly; who errs, and comes short again and again, because there is no effort without error and shortcoming; but who does actually strive to do the deeds; who knows the great enthusiasms, the great devotions; who spends himself in a worthy cause; who at the best knows in the end the triumph of high achievement, and who at the worst, if he fails, at least fails while daring greatly, so that his place shall never be with those cold and timid souls who know neither victory nor defeat. (pp. 143–144)

You cannot be a timid soul in this business of helping children. Faith is my favorite word, and it's a word that I think about every day. Whatever happens to you, be faithful because you are pursuing justice when you help children. There will be times when you will question whether you are doing the right thing, whether or not you are taking the right position. Be steadfast in your faith and draw on the support of your team members to sustain you when you may falter. Dr. James Fuller, director for Community Intervention in Guilford County, North Carolina, captures the essence of being a team member: "If you got to give, you can also take."

When I see a just and kind school community in which expectations are high, when I see it filled with people who are continually excited by the idea of becoming even better, when I see students who know that they can rely on the adults around them, on each other, and on themselves, then I know that we are making a tremendous difference in the way our society works. And our long experience here at the School Development Program is that we make this difference child by child, adult by adult, school by school.

Reference

Roosevelt, T. (1913). *History as literature and other essays*. New York: Charles Scribner's Sons.

ABOUT THE EDITORS AND AUTHORS

Editors

James P. Comer, M.D., is the founder and chairman of the Yale School Development Program, Maurice Falk Professor of Child Psychiatry at the Yale Child Study Center, and associate dean of the Yale University School of Medicine. He has published six books, more than thirty-five chapters, more than four hundred articles in popular journals, and more than one hundred articles in professional journals. He has served as a consultant, committee member, advisory board member, and trustee to numerous local, national, and international organizations serving children.

Dr. Comer has been the recipient of the John & Mary Markle Scholar in Academic Medicine Award, the Rockefeller Public Service Award, the Harold W. McGraw, Jr. Prize in Education, the Charles A. Dana Award for Pioneering Achievement in Education, the Heinz Award for Service to Humanity, and many other awards and honors, including thirty-eight honorary degrees.

Michael Ben-Avie, Ph.D., is an associate research scientist at the Yale Child Study Center. His research interests include psychology, education, psycholinguistics, and anthropology. As director of research of the Independent Evaluation Team, he conducts studies of educational intervention programs. He has co-edited books and published book chapters, articles, and reports on educational change initiatives, high schools, youth development, parent involvement, and the relationship between child development and student learning.

Norris M. Haynes, Ph.D., is professor in the Counseling and School Psychology Department and director of the Center for School Action Research at Southern Connecticut State University. He is also associate clinical professor of Child and Adolescent Psychiatry at the Yale University Child Study Center. His research interests include a focus on school climate factors and mental health interventions in promoting students' social and emotional development, motivation, self-concept, learning, and achievement.

Edward T. Joyner, Ed.D., is the executive director of the Yale School Development Program. He served as the SDP's first director of Training, designed the Leadership Development Academies, wrote training manuals that helped school districts address changing student and community needs, and initiated university-public school partnerships. He currently oversees all of the operations of the SDP and serves as the lead implementation coordinator for Chicago and Dayton.

Authors

Juan I. Alegría is the Comer facilitator for three of Chicago's public schools. Juan has had previous experience working with organizations that provide pastoral care. Juan is very actively involved in issues that affect Chicago's communities including AIDS and other health issues as well as educational concerns in the Hispanic community.

Della A. Alfred is one of Chicago's Comer facilitators. Della is the Chicago Program's Parent Specialist, which requires her to work closely with parents, including training them in the Comer Model and assisting them with the implementation of the Parent Programs at their schools.

Larry Allred is a member of the Comer Action Team of Guilford County, North Carolina.

Angelique Arrington is an SDP implementation coordinator at the SDP national office.

Thomas A. Barclay is the assistant director of Chicago's School Development Program and is the pastor of his own church in Chicago. Thomas' interests include church and youth ministry.

William Bellamy is PTO president, a security guard, and an active parent at the Isadore Wexler Elementary School in New Haven, Connecticut.

Terrence Biggs is a student at the Isadore Wexler Elementary School in New Haven, Connecticut.

Teasie Blassingame is a third grade teacher at the Isadore Wexler Elementary School in New Haven, Connecticut.

Sheila Brantley is a special education teacher at the Isadore Wexler Elementary School in New Haven, Connecticut, and was SPMT chairperson for the first three years of their renewal process.

Mike Booher is a member of the Comer Action Team of Guilford County, North Carolina.

Elizabeth Bridges is a member of the Comer Action Team of Guilford County, North Carolina.

Fay E. Brown, Ph.D., currently works as an implementation coordinator and director of literacy initiatives for the School Development Program. She is responsible for the design and delivery of a number of professional development activities in schools and at the National Academies. Her major focus is that of helping schools create and maintain developmentally appropriate conditions to ensure that every child is a fluent reader by third grade.

Pauline Brown is a member of the Comer Action Team of Guilford County, North Carolina.

Rodney L. Brown is a Comer facilitator for three Chicago schools. Rodney's past professional experience includes working as a pastor of a Methodist Church. Rodney is the talented vocalist of the Comer Team and often uses his gift at Comer functions. He is interested in sports, especially the Bulls.

Belinda Carberry, principal of Isadore Wexler Elementary School from 1992 through 1998, is currently the principal of Jackie Robinson Middle School and a doctoral candidate at Teachers College, Columbia University.

Liznell Carter is a student at Benjamin Banneker High School in Brooklyn, New York.

Jerrett Claitt is a student at Benjamin Banneker High School in Brooklyn, New York.

Joanne Corbin, Ph.D., is an epidemiologist and social worker. Her areas of interest include child and adolescent development and the effects of parent involvement.

Patrina Covington is a parent assistant at the Isadore Wexler Elementary School in New Haven, Connecticut.

Joan Dameron Crisler is principal of the Arthur Dixon Elementary School in Chicago. In 1998, she received a Patrick Daly Memorial Award for Excellence in Educational Leadership.

Phyllis Shalewa Crowe has been involved in education for years as a teacher and in administrative roles including executive director of the Institute of Positive Education New Concept Development Center. Phyllis is currently the Comer facilitator for three Chicago schools.

Deborah Davis is a family advocate in the Family Resource Center of the Isadore Wexler Elementary School in New Haven, Connecticut.

Doris T. Davis is principal of Washington Elementary School in Guilford County, North Carolina. In 1997, she received a Patrick Daly Memorial Award for Excellence in Educational Leadsership.

Carol Edwards is principal of the Lillian R. Nicholson School (K-8) in Chicago.

Christine Emmons, Ph.D., is an associate research scientist with the Yale Child Study Center, School Development Program. Her work focuses on program evaluation and the impact of environment on the development of children.

Ralph Esposito is a staff developer at the Isadore Wexler Elementary School in New Haven, Connecticut.

Shelia Evans-Tranumn is associate commissioner, New York City Office of School and Community Services. As associate commissioner, Ms. Evans-Tranumn has major responsibility for the direction and coordination of State Education Department services and technical assistance to New York City schools and the New York City public school system. She is the recipient of numerous awards, including the Reliance Award for Excellence in Education, the Administrative Women in Education Trailblazer Award, and the NAACP Richard Green Educational Award.

Matia Finn-Stevenson, Ph.D., is associate director of the Yale Bush Center in Child Development and Social Policy, and co-director of the School of the 21st Century and CoZi. Matia received her Masters degree in educational administration and a Ph.D. in child development from Ohio State University. Her research focuses on the development and evaluation of school reform initiatives and work/family life issues. She is the author of numerous publications, including a forthcoming book about changes in the traditional mission of the American public school.

Jeffie Frazier, principal of Helene Grant Elementary School, was honored with the 1997 National Educator Award from the Milken Family Foundation.

James Fuller is a member of the Comer Action Team of Guilford County, North Carolina.

Richard K. Gahr, M.A., a consultant in education and human development has been with the School Development Program for the last four years. He is interested in helping educators to think developmentally with their heads and their hearts, and in the process, to develop the inner self from which good teaching comes. In recent years, he has researched and designed several in-depth education programs that promote professional and organizational renewal.

Jeanette Gann is a member of the Comer Action Team of Guilford County, North Carolina.

Jonathon H. Gillette, Ph.D., is director of Professional Development and Consultation for the School Development Program. His responsibilities include overseeing the Yale and national professional development events, the activities of Yale implementation coordinators and the on-going development of the SDP concepts of school and district change. His special interests include organizational and group dynamics, school and district restructuring, structural change in complex organizations, and race relations.

Cassandra Grant, associate in education, is currently working for the New York State Education Department in the New York City Office of School and Community Services. Ms. Grant feels that her greatest accomplishments continue to be her passion and love for children and families through education.

Ida Greene is a parent assistant at the Isadore Wexler Elementary School in New Haven, Connecticut.

Louise Gugliotti is a kindergarten teacher at the Isadore Wexler Elementary School in New Haven, Connecticut.

Cheryl Hargrave is a student at the Isadore Wexler Elementary School in New Haven, Connecticut.

Alison J. Harmon, Ed.D., is an associate professor, Department of Leadership & Counseling, Eastern Michigan University. She is the university coordinator for the Detroit Comer Schools and Families Initiative. She has extensive experience in urban public schools as an elementary and middle school principal and director of state and federal programs.

Floyd Haywood is a student at the Isadore Wexler Elementary School in New Haven, Connecticut.

Fred Hernández, Ed.D., first principal of the Eugenio María de Hostos Micro-Society School, is currently the principal of the Foxfire School in Yonkers, New York. He was honored with a 1998 Patrick Daly Memorial Award for Excellence in Educational Leadership. In 1996 he was named Administrator of the Year by the Yonkers Public Schools and the Rotary Club. In 1995 he received the Cinco de Mayo Award from the Guadalupano Mexican Society and the Dr. Betances Award from the New York Puerto Rican Parade, Inc. In 1991 the Education Committee of Yonkers branch of the NAACP honored him for his "distinguished service and dedication to educating all children."

Christine Hides is a member of the Chicago Comer Team.

J. Patrick Howley, C.A.G.S., is an implementation coordinator who specializes in human relations work such as team building, communication, and conflict resolution. He has been with the SDP for seven years.

Mary Hoyle is a member of the Comer Action Team of Guilford County, North Carolina.

Marcia Herring is a special education teacher at the Isadore Wexler Elementary School in New Haven, Connecticut.

Sheila Jackson, head of the Prince George's County Comer Office in Maryland, has been with the program for nine years. She began her work in schools as a volunteer parent actively involved in the education of her four children and was soon hired by the Comer Office full time in 1994. Today, she supervises fifteen people in the Comer Office.

Iman Jameelah is a student at Benjamin Banneker High School in Brooklyn, New York.

Erwin John is a student at Benjamin Banneker High School in Brooklyn, New York.

Hazel Johnson is a community volunteer at the Isadore Wexler Elementary School in New Haven, Connecticut.

Sharon A. Johnson is a member of the Comer Action Team of Guilford County, North Carolina.

Tina Johnson is a member of the Comer Action Team of Guilford County, North Carolina.

Geoffrey Jones is a student at Benjamin Banneker High School in Brooklyn, New York.

Lillie Madison Jones, Ed.D., is the deputy superintendent of the Guilford County Schools. She has received numerous awards including: 1995–96 Phi Delta Kappa Outstanding Administrator of the Year; 1995–96 Guilford County Association of Educational Office Professionals Administrator of the Year; 1996–97 North Carolina Association of Educational Office Professionals District 6 Administrator of the Year; 1996 Human Relations Commission High Pointer of the Year Award; and 1996 NAACP Woman of the Year Award.

Basil Jordan was the principal of the Queen's Royal College in the Republic of Trinidad and Tobago during its implementation of the Comer Process.

Sherrie Berrien Joseph, M.S.W., an implementation coordinator for the Yale School Development Program, has worked for more than twenty-eight years in social services program planning and implementation. For more than twenty-five years she has been a social services and parent involvement specialist with Head Start, the public schools and other human service organizations and churches in Atlanta, New York, New Jersey, and the Virgin Islands.

John Lauritzen is a former vice-president of AT&T at the Greensboro, North Carolina, facility.

SuAnn Lawrence is a member of the Chicago Comer Team.

Debra Liburd is a fifth grade teacher at the Isadore Wexler Elementary School in New Haven, Connecticut.

Troy Long is a parent assistant and substitute teacher at the Isadore Wexler Elementary School in New Haven, Connecticut.

Vivian V. Loseth is assistant director of Youth Guidance, a non-profit social service agency in Chicago, and director of the Chicago Comer Team. For over twenty years, she has worked as a change agent to develop and advance improvements in the quality of education and enhance student learning in Chicago Public Schools.

Valerie Maholmes, Ph.D., has worked at the School Development Program for seven years and is currently director of the Learning, Teaching and Development Unit. Her areas of interest include examining the impact of school and classroom contexts on teachers' and students' sense of efficacy. She is currently a member of the Board of Education for New Haven Public Schools and chair of its Curriculum Committee.

Sherman Malone is a clinician with Project HOPE at the Isadore Wexler Elementary School in New Haven, Connecticut.

Lisa A. Marth is a team administrator for the Northwest Chicago Team at Youth Guidance, the agency that supports Chicago's Comer Program. Lisa has been involved with integrating the Comer model into the direct services that other teams at Youth Guidance provide.

Jim Maturo is a special education coordinator at the Isadore Wexler Elementary School in New Haven, Connecticut.

Cheryl McKenzie-Cook is an English teacher at Queen's Royal College. She has served as a Comer SDP facilitator at Queen's Royal College and one of the national Comer SDP facilitators in Trinidad and Tobago.

Lany Miller is chairperson of the Parent Connection Group at Chalmers Elementary School in Chicago.

Barbara Monsor earned her master's degree in sociology and has worked for Youth Guidance for 20 years. In this role, she was responsible for statistics and research which evaluate Youth Guidance's programs. Currently Barbara is a research consultant for the Chicago Comer Program. She is the mother of six and the grandmother of eight.

Charles Morris is a member of the Comer Action Team of Guilford County, North Carolina.

Omar Morris is a counselor at Benjamin Banneker High School in Brooklyn, New York.

Donna Morrison is principal of McLeansville Middle School in Guilford County, North Carolina. In 1998, she received a Patrick Daly Memorial Award for Excellence in Educational Leadership.

Michelle Adler Morrison is the project manager for Chicago's program concentrating on integrating the Comer model into the direct-service programs Youth Guidance provides. Michelle's interests include volunteering for service organizations, biking, and reading.

Judy Murphy is a school psychologist at the Isadore Wexler Elementary School in New Haven, Connecticut.

Gloria Nobles is a first grade teacher at the Isadore Wexler Elementary School in New Haven, Connecticut.

Makhosazana Ndlovu is a student at Benjamin Banneker High School in Brooklyn, New York.

Wendy Piggott is an active parent at Queen's Royal College. She has served as an advisor to the Comer SDP at Queen's Royal College.

Walter Matthew Pritchett, Jr., is a member of the Guilford County School Board in North Carolina.

Wilhelmina Quick-Hall, Ed.D., is the former district coordinator of the Comer Schools and Families Initiative. Prior to her retirement in 1997, she served in the Detroit Public Schools for 32 years as an elementary school principal, assistant principal, and teacher. She is currently deputy superintendent of the National Charter Schools Administrative Services.

Beckie Roberts first joined the Prince George's County Comer Staff in 1991 after 19 years teaching social studies in a middle school. She was a member of the pilot middle school involved with the middle school project in 1989. Parent of two adult children, Beckie facilitates the process in four schools and has also worked with the National Office.

Emma Rodriguez is an active parent and part-time paraprofessional at the Isadore Wexler Elementary School in New Haven, Connecticut.

Adelaide Sanford is on the Board of Regents of the University of the State of New York. In April of 1986, Regent Sanford was unanimously elected to a seven year term as a member-at-large of the Board of Regents. In April of 1993 she was re-elected to a second seven year term. As a member of the New York State Board of Regents, she chairs the Visiting Committee on Low Performing Schools and the Committee on Higher Education.

Kenan Smith is a student at Benjamin Banneker High School in Brooklyn, New York.

Savannah Browning Smith is a teacher at Brown Elementary School in Chicago.

George B. Spence is an active grandparent at the Bowling Park CoZi School in Norfolk, Virginia.

David A. Squires, Ph.D., is an implementation coordinator at the School Development Program. He specializes in curriculum, instruction, and assessment. His interests center on how school and district management interact with instructional improvement and human development.

Trudy Raschkind Steinfeld is an editorial consultant to the Yale School Development Program.

Barbara M. Stern was a CoZi project manager from 1992 to 1997. Today she is principal of a public elementary school in Connecticut.

Jan Stocklinski "retired" on March 1, 1998 after working 31 years in the Prince George's County Public School System in Maryland. Thirteen of those years were spent directing the County Comer Office. Presently she coordinates and teaches in the Western Maryland College Master's Degree Program (Prince George's County Campus) for teachers. She also assists with the SDP National Leadership Training sessions.

Vernice Thomas is a member of the Comer Action Team of Guilford County, North Carolina.

Richard Tuck is a member of the Comer Action Team of Guilford County, North Carolina.

Michelle Tyson is a student at Benjamin Banneker High School in Brooklyn, New York.

Leigh Tysor-Holt is a member of the Comer Action Team of Guilford County, North Carolina.

Edna Vega is the community superintendent of New York City Board of Education Community School District Seven.

Jerry D. Weast, Ed.D., is the superintendent of the Guilford County Schools. In 1997, he was named State Superintendent of the Year by the North Carolina Association of School Administrators. He has been recognized as one of the Outstanding Young Men in America and has twice received the prestigious honor of the Order of the Long Leaf Pine, North Carolina's highest civic award. He has served in consulting roles to the U.S. Department of Education and the U.S. State Department for Overseas Schools. He is published in a variety of education journals and often presents at professional meetings in the United States and abroad, including Tunisia, Morocco, Israel, Spain, Russia, and Japan.

Natrice Williams is a student at the Isadore Wexler Elementary School in New Haven, Connecticut.

Gwendolyn Willis is a member of the Comer Action Team of Guilford County, North Carolina.

Pamela Winstead is an active parent at the Bowling Park CoZi Community School in Norfolk, Virginia.

Darren W. Woodruff, Ph.D., was a member of the SDP's Research and Evaluation Unit for four years. He is currently a research analyst at the American Institutes for Research in Washington, DC. His interest is in the social and psychological relationships between children and school success.

Lester Young, Jr., is the community superintendent of New York City Board of Education Community School District Thirteen.

INDEX